CliffsAP®

Economics Micro & Macro

by

Ron Pirayoff

WILEY

Wiley Publishing, Inc.

About the Author

Ron Pirayoff teaches AP Economics at Burbank High School in Burbank, California. Ron received his Bachelor's Degree from the University of San Francisco, and his Master's Degree in social science with an emphasis on economics from Azusa Pacific University.

Publisher's Acknowledgments

Editorial

Project Editor: Tim Ryan

Acquisitions Editor: Greg Tubach

Copy Editor: Liz Welch

Technical Editor: Ted Lorenzen

Production

Proofreader: Arielle Mennelle

Indexer: Provided by Production

Wiley Publishing, Inc, Composition Services

CliffsAP® Economics Micro & Macro

Published by:
Wiley Publishing, Inc.
111 River Street
Hoboken, NJ 07030-5774
www.wiley.com

Copyright © 2004 Wiley Publishing, Inc. New York, New York

Published by Wiley Publishing, Inc., Hoboken, NJ
Published simultaneously in Canada

ISBN: 0-76455-399-x

Printed in the United States of America

10 9 8 7 6 5 4 3 2 1

1B/RQ/QS/QU/IN

Table of Contents

PART II: MACROECONOMICS

PART III: MICROECONOMICS

PART IV: AP MACROECONOMICS AND MICROECONOMICS TESTS

Introduction

AP Economics Exam Details

This book is designed to help you prepare for the AP Macroeconomics and Microeconomics exam. As a student, your task is to sum up all of the information that was given to you in your economics class. Taking the exam could earn you college credit and/or placement into advanced coursework at the college level.

About The Exams

There are two exams in economics: one in microeconomics and one in macroeconomics. You do not have to take both; however, you may choose to do so. Both exams are structured in the same way.

Section I
- 60 multiple choice questions   70 minutes

Section II
- 1 long free-response question and
- 2 short free-response questions   10 minutes for planning
                                           50 minutes for writing

Total Time: 2 Hours and 10 Minutes

Microeconomics Test Concepts

The microeconomics exam covers four major areas; the numbers in the parentheses indicate the approximate proportion of multiple-choice questions in each area. For example, 8-12% for basic economic concepts indicates that there are 5 to 7 questions on this topic.

Basic Economic Concepts (8-12%)
   Scarcity: The Nature of Economics Systems
   Opportunity Costs and Production Possibilities
   Specialization and Comparative Advantage; The Basis for International Trade
   The Functions of any Economic System
The Nature and Functions of Product Markets (60-70%)
   Supply and Demand
   Models of Consumer Choice
   Firm Production, Costs, Revenues
   Product Pricing and Outputs within Different Market Structures
   Efficiency and Government policy toward imperfect Competition
Factor Markets (10-15%)
   Derived Factor Demand
   Determination of Wages and Other Factor Prices
Efficiency, Equity and the Role of the Government (8-12%)
   Externalities
   Public Goods
   Distribution of Income

Macroeconomics Test Concepts

The Macroeconomics exam covers five major areas; the numbers in the parenthesis indicate the approximate proportion of the multiple-choice questions in each area. For example, 5-10% indicates there will be 3-6 questions on this topic.

> Basic Economic Concepts (5-10%)
> > Scarcity: the nature of Economic Systems
> > Opportunity Cost and Production Possibilities
> > Specialization and Comparative Advantage: the basis for international trade
> > The Functions of Economic Systems
> > Supply, Demand, Price Determination
> Measurement of Economic Performance (8-12%)
> > Gross National Product, Gross Domestic Product, National Income
> > Inflation and Price Indexes
> > Unemployment
> National Income and Price Determination (70-75%)
> > Aggregate Supply
> > Aggregate Demand
> > Money and Banking
> > Fiscal and Monetary Policy
> > Unemployment and Inflation Trade-Offs
> Economic Growth (4-6%)
> International Finance, Exchange Rates, and Balance of Payments (4-6%)

Exam Insight

Each exam consists of two sections. Section I consists of 60 multiple-choice questions. Most of these questions are not basic factual recall questions; rather, they demand an analytical processing of the material you already know. Section I accounts for two-thirds of your final grade.

Section II consists of three free-response questions (one long and two short). These analytical problem-solving questions involve several subject areas. Note that the essays do not require full paragraph explanations. Rather, each essay should have a brief explanation and a graph to support the explanation. The long-response essay is scored at twice the value of each of the shorter questions. Section II is one-third of your final grade.

Scoring the Exam

The raw score for Section I is tabulated by taking the correctly answered number of questions, subtracting one-quarter of a point for every incorrect response. If there is a question left blank, one-quarter point will not be deducted from your score.

If all 60 questions were answered and 50 were correct your raw score would be calculated as follows:

$$\text{Raw Score} = \# \text{ correct} - (.25)(\# \text{ incorrect})$$
$$= 50 - 1/4(10)$$
$$50 - 2.5 = 47.5$$
$$= 47.5$$

Section II accounts for one-third of the overall grade. This section holds one long essay question and two short essay questions each, with a different point value. Usually, the long question is worth 9-12 points, and each short question is worth 4-6 points. No matter how many points each question is worth, the long essay question is worth half the value of the whole section while the shorter questions account for one quarter of the section's value.

Evaluators are not only looking for a correct answer, they are also looking for the reasoning by which you arrived at the answer. Make sure to explain your steps thoroughly and coherently.

The scores from Sections I and II are combined to give a composite score. The composite score is finalized into an AP grade which is converted to a 5 point scale:

5 – Extremely well qualified

4 – Well qualified

3 – Qualified

2 – Possibly qualified

1 – No recommendation

Receiving Your Grade

AP grades are sent in July to your high school, your home, and any college you have designated. You can obtain your exam grade by phone in July for a $13 fee by calling toll-free (888) 308- 0013.

Test Day Materials

Be sure to get plenty of rest the night before your test, have a good breakfast that morning, and dress in multiple thin layers to maximize your comfort on the day of the exam. These practical tips will minimize the impacts of any distractions and help you focus on test taking strategies. Be sure to take the following items with you for the test:

- Several number 2 pencils
- Photo ID
- Your social security number
- Your student ID number
- A black or blue pen for the free-response section
- A watch to gauge your progress throughout the exam
- An eraser

Test Taking Strategies

Assuming that all distractions have been dealt with, it's now time to focus on some test taking strategies.

Simple regurgitation of material will not be of much help when taking this exam. You will not be required to recall historical data. Rather, this exam demands your ability to apply economic concepts. Memorizing the unemployment rate in 1976 will not be of use to you on this exam; however, being able to analyze the possible causes of unemployment or interest rate fluctuations is critical. Analyzing and interpreting graphs, applying economic concepts, and critically evaluating possible answers will all be required when taking this exam.

Multiple-Choice Questions

No matter how tempting it becomes, random guessing can very well hurt your score. With the one-quarter point deduction for a wrong answer, guessing can take a heavy toll on your final score. The best strategy is to first eliminate obviously wrong answer choices. This will improve your odds of making an intelligent guess. With each multiple-choice question having five choices, eliminating answer choices can only improve your odds of getting an answer correct.

Also, make sure you answer the easy multiple-choice questions first. The easy questions are worth just as much as the difficult ones. The best strategy to take is to answer as many of the easy questions first to maximize your ability to achieve a higher score. On your first pass through the section, answer all the easy questions and circle all the hard questions. Remember not to waste valuable time on the harder questions until you have answered all the easier questions.

Free-Response Section

Make sure to read the free-response question twice before attempting to organize your answer. Also, be sure to prepare an outline that includes all initial and detailed thoughts that come to mind when looking over the question. Both initial and "thought out" answers should be documented because sometimes these thoughts can give you a broader perspective of the answer. Describe, illustrate, graph, and list any thoughts that come to mind to ensure a stronger answer. When answering free-response questions, remember these five points:

- Answer this section directly and clearly. You will need to have a direct and precise answer with an illustration of how you got to this point. Graders of the exam are looking for appropriately labeled graphs, clear main points, and thorough explanations.
- Be sure to structure your response in the same fashion the test question is structured. If the essay question has roman numerals, then stick to the same format with your answers.
- Rank the difficulty of each question. With the difficulty assessed, you can focus on the easier questions to make sure you won't be cheated by time.
- Any graphs you use should be drawn in a clear and precise manner. The ability to draw graphs is usually learned in your AP economics test preparation class. While answering a question, although a graph might not be required, you may feel like adding one to further solidify your answer. This is a good idea as an accurate graph can only help the graders understand your answer.
- Use the test booklet as a thought pad. Feel free to mark up the booklet with any thoughts of price changes, shifts, or any other question-related thoughts. This is a great external way of thinking through the problem.

Check Your Numbering

Getting thrown off track is often a problem for test takers. Be sure to double-check the question number you're reading with the question number that was just completed on your answer document. Do this periodically, because if a problem isn't caught early, you may spend valuable time looking back to figure out where you lost your numbering.

Keep an Eye on the Clock

It's important to develop a sense of time as you are answering questions. Taking practice exams will help you develop this sense. The practice exams allow you to see how long you can afford to spend on a difficult question before having to move on.

In the multiple-choice section you'll have 70 minutes to answer 60 questions. In the free-response section you will have 10 minutes at the start to organize and outline your answers for all of the questions. You will then have 50 minutes to write your responses. Plan on spending about 25 minutes on the long free-response question while dedicating about 10 minutes each to the shorter questions.

Do Not Cheat

In economics terms, the short-run benefits are outweighed by the long-run costs. Cheating on AP exams is dealt with quite severely, so don't do it.

THE FUNDAMENTALS

The Basics

When thinking of economics, you should be aware of one simple synonym—choices. **Economics** is a social science involving the study of choices and what necessitates those choices. **Macroeconomics** is the branch of economics that examines the behavior of the whole economy at once. **Microeconomics** is the branch of economics that examines the choices and interactions of individuals producing and consuming one product, in one firm or industry.

When making a choice, you automatically have created a cost and a benefit. The **cost** is what has been relinquished, and the **benefit** is what has been gained. The term **opportunity cost** refers to the next best alternative. For example, if you have $500 and you go to the mall and see a stereo, a jacket, and a television each costing $500, which would you choose? If you rank the stereo as your first choice, the jacket as your second, and the TV as your third choice, which would be the opportunity cost? The jacket is the opportunity cost because it is your next best alternative. Note that the jacket and T.V. together are *not* the opportunity cost because there can only be one opportunity cost.

All participants in an economy must make choices. The basic economic problem that necessitates choices is **scarcity**, which occurs when limited resources are not sufficient to meet demand. Scarcity forces individuals, firms, and other members of society to decide how to use the three factors of production: land, labor, and capital. **Land** represents natural resources, such as oil and coal. **Labor** represents human resources, like manual work. And **capital** represents anything that can help produce these resources, such as education and machines. If a farmer has ten acres of land, she must decide how to use those ten acres. If a factory owner has three workers, then she must decide how to use her workers. If you have a hundred dollars in your pocket, you have to decide how to use these resources.

Some people confuse **capital** with **money**. In economics, **capital** is an economic resource, and **money** is a medium of exchange. What allows countries to produce more in the long run is an increase in their factors of production, not necessarily an increase in money. Increasing the factors of production allows a country to expand its production possibilities, which then allows that country's economy to grow for its population. It is important to note that a country can't afford to become satisfied with their goods and services—they must continually grow to meet the demands of the population. In economics there is no such thing as stagnant. Wants and needs are always growing; therefore, if an economy is not expanding then it is contracting.

Economic Systems

Every economic system has the following goals: efficiency, equity, security, freedom, and incentives. These goals are a present fixture in every economy; however, each economy may rank these goals differently. The ranking of these goals and the way in which each economy answers the three economic questions reveal what kind of economic system the country has.

Due to the concept of scarcity, every economy must address three main questions: What to make? How to make it? And for whom should it be made? Economic systems are categorized by how these questions are answered.

In a **command** economy, these questions are answered by a central government made up of an individual or individuals. **Traditional** economies rely on customs and rituals. **Market** economies rely on the forces of supply and demand to answer the three questions. The idea of allowing self-interest to guide prices and supply was introduced by Adam Smith in his book *The Wealth of Nations*, published in 1776.

Product and Factor Markets

Goods and services must be allocated between firms and households. When you go to the grocery store to buy your favorite cereal, you are part of a **product market.** In a product market, the monetary flow goes from households to firms, and the physical flow of goods and services goes from firms to households. In a **factor market**, the monetary flow goes from firms to households and, in exchange, the households give the firms the physical flow of goods and services. Labor is an example of a factor market because the physical flow (labor) is being given to the firms and the firms give the monetary flow (wages) to the households. This circular flow of goods, services, and money can be seen in Figure 1-1.

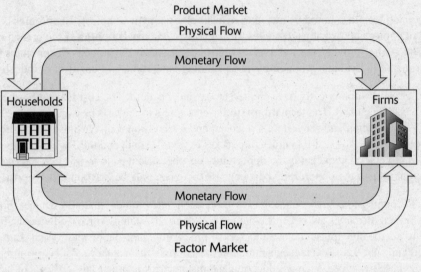

Figure 1-1

Opportunity Cost and Production Possibilities

By making the decision to take the AP exam in economics, you have decided to allocate time to studying. When you are studying for this exam, you are making a choice and thereby creating a benefit and an opportunity cost. The benefit is being better prepared for the exam, and the opportunity cost is your next best alternative (sleeping or eating, for example). Remember that the opportunity cost is the value of the next best alternative that is being given up.

In economics, countries, firms, and individuals have to make choices as to how to allocate (use) resources. Suppose a country has to make a decision on how to use steel. Its two choices are automobiles and chairs. When the country makes chairs, it cannot use the same resources to make autos. The choices an economy faces and the opportunity cost of making one good rather than another can be illustrated using a **production possibilities frontier (PPF)**. Figure 1-2 illustrates a PPF for a simplified economy that can use its resources to produce either autos or chairs.

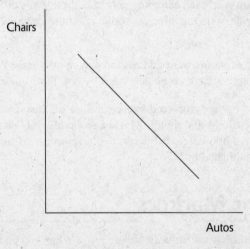

Figure 1-2

The curve, or frontier, symbolizes efficiency, and it represents all of the possible combinations of autos and chairs that could be produced using the country's available steel. For example, the economy could produce ten autos and 0 chairs, or ten chairs and 0 autos. Anything that appears outside the production possibilities curve is considered to be unattainable unless the economy has additional resources.

Specialization and Comparative Advantage

Because the goal of economies is centered on efficiency, specialization becomes an important focus for firms and countries. To **specialize** is to concentrate on what an entity is relatively good at to enhance productivity. This approach is more efficient than equally employing all resources. The basic idea is that instead of working on improving what you do poorly, dedicate all resources to improving something you already do well.

When looking at advantages, economists focus on two particular types of advantages. When a country or entity can produce a good or service using fewer resources per unit of output than any other country or entity, economists say this country has an **absolute advantage.** When a country or entity can produce a good or service at a lower opportunity cost than any other country or entity, that country has a **comparative advantage**.

Let's take Michael Jordan, for example. We already know that he is one of the best basketball players of all time; however, what if he were the second-fastest typist in the world? Should he split his time equally between typing and playing basketball? Or should he choose to specialize? We can assume safely for the purpose of this example that Michael Jordan has an absolute advantage over anyone in basketball. But does he have an absolute advantage over everyone in typing? The answer is no because he is only the second-fastest typist in the world; the fastest typist in the world has an absolute advantage over Jordan in typing. When you're looking at comparative advantage, the story gets a little more complex. If when Jordan plays basketball he is giving up virtually nothing to play the sport, we can say that he has a comparative advantage in playing basketball. But if Jordan chose to type instead of playing basketball he would almost certainly not have a comparative advantage in typing—chances are other typists would not have an opportunity cost as high as Jordan's.

Let's take a closer look at how comparative and absolute advantage can relate to trade. Consider Mexico and Colombia and the production of butter and coffee. Figure 1-3 illustrates the hypothetical PPFs for the two countries, simplified to form straight lines.

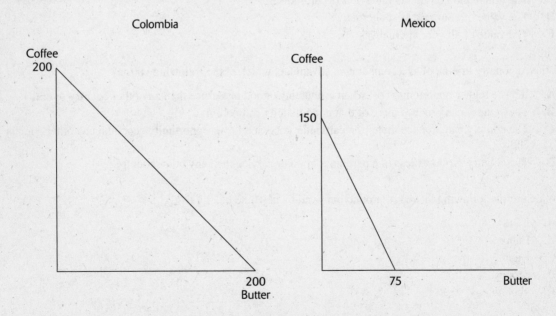

Figure 1-3

Assuming that the two countries have identical resources, the PPFs show that Colombia has an absolute advantage in both coffee and butter because it can produce more of each good with the same resources. When we look at comparative advantage, we must first examine the opportunity costs for each nation. When Colombia switches from producing 200 units of butter to 200 units of coffee, it is giving up one unit of butter for one unit of coffee. When Mexico decides to allocate all its resources to producing coffee, it is giving up 75 units of butter. In essence, Mexico is giving up one-half as much butter to produce coffee, so the opportunity cost of coffee in terms of butter is one half. So who has the comparative advantage in producing coffee? The answer is Mexico, because each unit of coffee costs Mexico one half as much as it does Colombia, which is giving up one whole unit of butter for one whole unit of coffee. On the other hand, Colombia has a comparative advantage in the production of butter, because each unit of butter costs Colombia one unit of coffee, which is less than the opportunity cost of two units of coffee per unit of butter in Mexico.

These two countries can certainly benefit from trade because production costs differ. Once a trade agreement can be reached, each country can specialize in the area in which it enjoys a comparative advantage. Mexico can allocate its resources to making coffee, thereby becoming Colombia's coffee supplier. On the other hand, Colombia can specialize in making butter, thereby becoming Mexico's butter supplier. In the end, each country enjoys more through trade.

Chapter Review Questions

1. Which one of the following is a factor of production?

   A. Money
   B. Government
   C. Land
   D. Checkable deposits
   E. None of the above

2. What is opportunity cost?

   A. The value of your choice
   B. The dollar value of all your choices combined
   C. The dollar and non-dollar value of all your choices
   D. The value of your next best alternative
   E. The value of all your alternatives

3. When a country or entity has a comparative advantage, which of the following is true?

   A. It has a higher opportunity cost when producing a good or service than any other country or entity.
   B. The country can produce more of that good than its competitor.
   C. The country can produce more of a particular good at a lower opportunity cost than any other country or entity.
   D. The country produces less of a particular good or service than any other country.

4. Which of the following factors of production would a machine belong to?

   A. Land
   B. Labor
   C. Capital
   D. Money
   E. Technology

5. If a country's production possibilities curve shifts outward, which one of the following is true?

    A. The country has underemployed its resources.
    B. The country has decreased its production.
    C. The country has increased its technology.
    D. The country is experiencing inflation.

6. What is the basic economic problem?

    A. Scarcity is a result of limited wants and unlimited resources.
    B. Scarcity results from the fact that prices are too high.
    C. Scarcity exists because there aren't enough people in the world.
    D. Scarcity results from the fact that if prices are too high people want less.
    E. Scarcity is caused by unlimited wants and limited resources.

7. Which of the following best describes the circular flow of economic activity?

    A. Firms earn money in exchange for goods and services in a factor market.
    B. Firms and households both lose money in a factor market.
    C. Households earn money in exchange for labor in a factor market.
    D. Households earn money in exchange for labor in a product market.
    E. None of the above.

8. What does every choice create?

    A. More choices
    B. An opportunity cost only
    C. An opportunity benefit only
    D. An opportunity cost and benefit
    E. A monetary cost

9. Suppose you can paint a room or walk backwards to the mall and back five times in two hours. Your friend Anup can paint a room in one hour. In order for him to have a comparative advantage in painting a room, how many times must he be able to walk to and from the mall backwards in two hours?

    A. More than five and fewer than ten
    B. More than five
    C. Fewer than ten
    D. Not enough information
    E. None of the above

10. Kelsey can eat 15 apples or peel 20 oranges in an hour. Ara can eat 30 apples or peel 25 oranges in an hour. Which of the following statements is true?

    A. Kelsey has a comparative advantage in eating apples.
    B. Ara has an absolute advantage in both activities.
    C. Kelsey has a comparative advantage in orange peeling.
    D. Kelsey has an absolute advantage in both activities.
    E. Ara isn't eating enough apples.

11. In which of the following economies does the government decide how to use the factors of production?

   A. Market economy
   B. Traditional economy
   C. Command economy
   D. Free-trade economy
   E. Trade-restrictive economy

12. Which one of the following is not an economic goal?

   A. Freedom
   B. Incentives
   C. Equity
   D. Efficiency
   E. Profit

13. Which one of the following is considered the regulating force of the market system?

   A. Government
   B. Government and firms
   C. Firms and taxes
   D. Suppliers and consumers
   E. All of the above

14. What do the plot points on the production possibilities graph represent?

   A. Taxes
   B. Unemployment
   C. Inflation
   D. Trade-offs
   E. Firms

15. Which one of the following is a factor of production?

   A. Money
   B. Revenue
   C. Profit
   D. Labor
   E. Taxes

Answers to Review Questions

1. **C.** Land is a factor of production. Money is a medium of exchange, not a resource. To produce a good or service, the government has to use one of the factors of production.

2. **D.** Opportunity cost is the value, both monetary and non-monetary, of your next best alternative. There can be only one opportunity cost.

3. **C.** When analyzing comparative advantage, you must remember to examine the opportunity cost of the country or entity. The country or entity with the lowest opportunity cost has the comparative advantage. Whoever is giving up the least to make something has the advantage.

4. **C.** Machines are used to produce other goods and services; therefore, they are considered capital. There are two forms of capital: human and physical. Education is human capital, whereas machines are considered physical capital.

5. C. A change in technology can make a country's allocation of resources more efficient. When it becomes easier or less costly, or if new resources are discovered, a country can produce more, thereby increasing its production possibilities. This is shown with an outward or rightward shift in the production possibilities curve (PPC).

6. E. Scarcity is caused by unlimited wants and limited resources.

7. C. In a factor market, firms pay households for goods and services. In a product market, households pay firms for goods and services.

8. D. Every choice automatically creates a cost and a benefit. Choices don't necessarily create monetary benefits or costs.

9. C. If Anup has a comparative advantage in painting rooms, he has to give up fewer trips to the mall than you do in the same amount of time it takes you each to paint a room. When you paint a room, you give up the chance to go (backwards) to the mall five times. Anup can paint one room in one hour, so in two hours he can paint two rooms. For his opportunity cost to be less than yours, he has to be able to make fewer than five trips to the mall in an hour. So in two hours he has to be able to make fewer than ten trips to the mall.

10. B. Ara has the absolute advantage because he can eat more apples and peel more oranges than Kelsey. Absolute advantage does not consider opportunity cost.

11. C. In a command economy, the government decides what to produce, how to produce it, and for whom to produce it.

12. E. Although profit may be a company's goal, it is not an *economic* goal. Efficiency, equity, security, incentives, and freedom are all economic goals.

13. D. Suppliers and consumers create the forces of supply and demand. These forces are responsible for setting prices and for answering the three economic questions of what to produce, how to produce it, and for whom to produce it.

14. D. Each plot point on the production possibilities graph represents a trade-off. As economies move from one point to another, they are giving up or trading off one good for another.

15. D. Labor is one of the factors of production. Workers, along with land and capital, help produce goods and services.

Supply and Demand

In a market system, the three economic questions what, how, and for whom to produce are answered by the forces of supply and demand. These forces depend on variables that shift consumer choices and set suppliers' prices. In a market, buyers and sellers exchange goods and services. Buyers demand products, and suppliers provide the product.

- **Quantity supplied** is the amount a supplier is willing and able to supply at a certain price.
- **Quantity demanded** is the amount a consumer is willing and able to buy at a certain price.

The **Law of Supply** states that the higher the price, the greater the quantity produced. When prices decrease, the quantity of that good is decreased. Think of the law of supply in terms of scales. In one hand you have prices and in the other you have quantity supplied. As one hand rises or falls (prices), the other hand follows (quantity supplied).

The **Law of Demand** states that as prices rise, quantity demanded decreases. As prices decrease, quantity demanded increases. There is an inverse relationship between prices and quantity demanded. You can think of the law of demand in terms of a seesaw. As one side rises (prices), the other side falls (quantity demanded).

A Closer Look at Demand

Does price change demand?

Polena (a nonsmoker) is walking by the cigarette section in the store and sees that cigarettes have dropped 50 percent in price. Chances are if she's thinking rationally, a price change in a product that she has no desire to consume will not affect her demand for the product. Now if she were a smoker and the price for cigarettes fell, then she would consume more, according to the law of demand. You can understand this scenario by looking at the difference between quantity demanded and demand. Quantity demanded is the amount consumers are willing and able to buy at a specific price. Figure 2-1 shows a demand schedule that illustrates this concept.

Individual Demand		Market Demand	
Price Of Baseballs	QD Per Day	Price Of Baseballs	QD
$1.00	10	$1.00	150
$2.00	7	$2.00	90
$3.00	5	$3.00	75
$4.00	2	$4.00	45
$5.00	1	$5.00	22
$6.00	0	$6.00	0

Figure 2-1

Figure 2-1 represents a demand schedule for both an individual firm's demand for baseballs and the whole market demand for baseballs. The firm's quantity demanded starts at ten baseballs per day at $1.00 each. As the price increases, the quantity demanded (the number of baseballs bought at each specific price) falls. The market demand is the sum of all firms' demand for baseballs. In the market demand, quantity also falls with each increase in price.

A common error for students is confusing demand with quantity demanded. Quantity demanded is the amount consumed at a specific price. A change in price will affect quantity demanded, whereas a change in one of the six determinants of demand will change demand (see the section "The Six Determinants of Demand" later in this chapter).

15

Constructing a Demand Curve

A demand curve is a graphic representation of a demand schedule. In economics, the vertical axis represents price and the horizontal axis represents the quantity, in this case the quantity demanded. Referring back to our demand schedule for baseballs, we can begin to graph the data provided in the table. Figure 2-2 demonstrates the downward slope of the demand curve where an inverse relationship exists between price and quantity demanded.

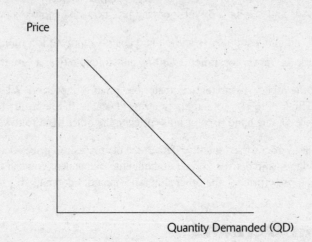

Figure 2-2

The demand curve is downwardly or inversely sloped because more people are willing to buy at a lower price or fewer people are willing to buy at a higher price.

The concept of **diminishing marginal utility** also contributes to the downward slope of the demand curve. If James goes to McDonald's and buys five cheeseburgers at $1.00 each, his satisfaction from each cheeseburger will slowly decrease with every cheeseburger eaten. The first burger always tastes the best, but with each additional cheeseburger consumed, James' satisfaction decreases because of diminishing marginal utility. You should take this concept into account when examining a demand curve.

The Six Determinants of Demand

The determinants of demand are factors that change demand. We already know that quantity demanded is changed or influenced by price. Demand, on the other hand, is changed by these six factors: tastes or preferences, income, the substitution effect, the price of complementary goods, population, and consumer expectations.

Taste or Preference

When Brenda decides to go to the mall and buy the smallest neon green t-shirt she can find, she is consuming a product according to her taste or preference. You or I may look at the t-shirt and think "You couldn't pay me to wear that thing," but the shirt happens to appeal to Brenda's taste or preference. In our earlier example, when Polena went to the store and discovered that cigarettes fell 50 percent in price, she did not feel compelled to start smoking because of the price change. Her taste or preference did not encourage her to take advantage of the decrease in price.

Income

When looking at the second determinant, income, we must consider the two types of goods:

- **Normal good**—Any good that consumers purchase more of as their incomes increase. Examples: luxury cars and gourmet meals.
- **Inferior good**—Any good that consumers purchase less of as their income increases. Examples: canned food and generic cereal.

The income effect changes demand by allowing consumers to purchase goods they wouldn't normally purchase due to a lack of affordability.

The Substitution Effect

When Lauren goes to the grocery store, she typically buys the name-brand cereal; however, this time Lauren is forced to buy the generic brand because the price of the name-brand cereal has climbed too high for her budget. This is an example of Lauren substituting the name brand for the generic brand. The **substitution effect** occurs because the price of the desired item is too expensive, so consumers find a close alternative to the initial item.

The Price of Complementary Goods

Complementary goods are goods that are used in tandem with other goods. You can't play a DVD movie without a DVD player, so these are complementary goods. Hot dogs and buns, peanut butter and jelly, and tires and cars are more examples of complementary goods. If the price of one good rises (the DVD player, for example), then the demand for the complementary good (DVD movies) will fall. If the price for hot dogs falls, then theoretically the demand for buns will rise. It is important to focus first on the price of the item and then on the demand of the complementary item.

Population

If an increase of immigration were to occur in a country, then the demand for any good or service would increase. If a decrease in population occurs (due to illness or people leaving the country), then the demand for any good or service would decrease.

Consumer Expectations

Expectations of future events affect the current demand for a good or service. If the price for hot dogs is expected to rise in the near future, then the demand for hot dogs will increase now. If the price for hot dogs is expected to drop in the near future, then the demand for hot dogs will decrease now.

Note: An increase in demand is demonstrated on a graph by a shift to the right, while a decrease in demand is indicated by a shift to the left.

Mini-Review

1. Which one of the following is not a determinant of demand?

    A. Taste or preference
    B. Income
    C. Expenditures
    D. Consumer expectations
    E. Population

2. When demand increases, what happens to a demand curve?

    A. It shifts left.
    B. It shifts right.
    C. No movement occurs.
    D. The quantity does not change.
    E. It becomes positively sloped.

3. What would happen to the demand curve for cars if the price of gasoline tripled?

    A. It would shift to the right because of income.

    B. It would shift to the right because of population.

    C. It would shift to the left because of price of the complementary good.

    D. It would shift to the left because of the price of the substitute.

    E. Both A and D are correct.

Mini-Review Answers

1. **C.** Expenditures is not a determinant of demand.

2. **B.** A graphical increase in demand is illustrated by a shift in all quantities and prices to the right.

3. **C.** A shift to the left in the demand curve would occur because the price of the complementary good would be increasing. Anytime the price of a complementary item increases, the demand curve for the complementary item will shift to the left.

A Closer Look at Supply

Students sometimes have a tough time with supply because they have never put themselves in the position of a business owner. All your life you've played the role of a consumer, buying products, looking for deals, and following the law of demand. Chances are you have never owned a business, so looking at economics through the eyes of a supplier may be a challenge at first. But with practice and patience, learning about supply can become an easy task. Remember the difference we discussed earlier between quantity demanded and demand? Well, supply has a similar distinction. The amount that producers are willing and able to sell at a specific price is called **quantity supplied**. Examine the data in Figure 2-3.

Individual Supply Schedule		Market Supply Schedule	
Price of Baseball Bats	Quantity Supplied	Price of Baseball Bats	Quantity Supplied
$10.00	50	$10.00	150
$20.00	65	$20.00	310
$35.00	82	$35.00	552
$42.00	97	$42.00	710
$60.00	140	$60.00	985

Figure 2-3

Figure 2-3 shows a supply schedule. Much like a demand schedule, a supply schedule has both the market supply and the individual firm's quantity supplied total. In our example, as the price of baseball bats rises, the quantity supplied also rises. The market supply is the sum of all individual suppliers. When suppliers lower the price for baseball bats, the quantity supplied also decreases because producers can't afford to make as many baseball bats. In supply, a positive relationship exists between price and quantity supplied.

The Supply Curve

The **supply curve** is a graphic representation of the data contained in our supply schedule. Different from the demand curve, the supply curve is positively sloped. The curve rises from left to right because of the positive relationship between price and quantity supplied. As firms increase output, they also have increasing costs. The only way that firms can increase production is if they increase price to offset their costs. Figure 2-4 shows our supply curve.

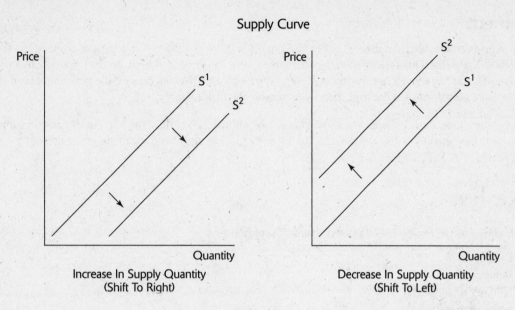

Figure 2-4

The Six Determinants of Supply

The following six factors shift the supply curve (in other words, change supply) either to the right (increase) or to the left (decrease): input prices, producers' expectations, technology, the change in the price of other goods, the number of suppliers, and government.

Input Prices

A firm's production costs dictate its supply curve. If a firm produces pencils and the price of lumber rises, then the firm has no choice but to either cut back on its production of pencils or raise the price for its pencils. Either option changes the firm's supply curve. If the cost of land, labor, or capital increases or decreases, a firm's supply curve will shift accordingly.

Producers' Expectations

Sometimes producers can anticipate a change in the price of raw materials. When this occurs, the producers' supply curve shifts accordingly. If an orange producer is expecting a bad winter, then it may try to harvest more oranges to compensate for a future shortage. The supply curve for the producer (all other things held constant) will shift to the right.

Technology

A change in technology makes production costs less expensive. If a new type of recyclable oil is invented, how do you think it would affect the supply for oil? The supply curve for oil would shift to the right, and oil would become cheaper because of a surplus. Technology improves efficiency, and efficiency allows producers to use their raw materials with lower opportunity costs.

A Change in the Price of Other Goods

If a supplier made hot dogs and buns and the price of hot dogs rose as a result of an increase in demand, the supplier could opt to make fewer buns and more hot dogs.

The Number of Suppliers

When more suppliers enter the market, the supply for that particular good increases (depending on how easy it is to enter the market). When the supply increases, the supply curve shifts to the right.

Government

Any change in taxes or subsidies can make it easier or more difficult for producers to make their product. If a firm is producing a product that yields a high social cost, then the government can choose to limit the firm's supply by increasing taxes. The opposite can happen if a firm is producing a product with a high social benefit: the government can either lower taxes or increase subsidies to the firm, thereby increasing the firm's supply.

Note: In economics, a decrease in supply or demand is always shown by a shift to the left. An increase in supply or demand is always indicated by a shift to the right. Do not refer to these shifts as movements up or down; they are left or right shifts.

Mini-Review

1. Which one of the following is not a determinant of supply?

    A. Income
    B. Input costs
    C. Number of suppliers
    D. Supplier expectations
    E. Government

2. The law of supply states that:

    A. As prices rise, so does demand.
    B. As prices rise, supply falls.
    C. Supply increases as demand increases.
    D. As prices rise, quantity supplied rises.
    E. Prices have nothing to do with supply.

3. On a supply curve, prices and quantity are:

    A. Inversely related
    B. Not related
    C. Not shown
    D. Positively related
    E. Independent variables

Mini-Review Answers

1. A. Income is not a factor that determines supply. Income is a term used for consumers, not producers.

2. D. The law of supply states that as prices rise, the quantity supplied rises. When producers raise their prices, they can afford to increase their supply by paying more for their input costs, thereby increasing their quantity of the product.

3. D. A positive relationship between price and quantity means that as one rises, the other follows. Producers increase supply by raising their price.

Supply and Demand

The point at which supply and demand curves intersect is called **market equilibrium**. The word *equilibrium* means balance, a point of harmony, where supply and demand meet. It is when the quantity demanded equals the quantity supplied. Equilibrium prices are all around us. When you visit a store, every price you see for a product is an equilibrium price. It is important to remember that equilibrium prices are not fixed; they fluctuate with the forces of supply and demand. When there is too much demand (shortage) or too much supply (surplus), we have what economists refer to as **disequilibrium**.

When a producer finds itself in disequilibrium, it has two choices: either adjust the price to meet demand, or adjust output to meet demand. If adjustments are not made in a timely manner, the firm will no longer be able to produce enough revenue to cover its costs.

When examining both supply and demand, we must construct both a supply and a demand curve on the same graph. Figure 2-5 shows a supply and demand graph.

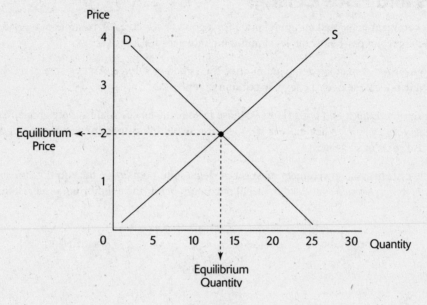

Figure 2-5

You can see that when the supply and demand curves intersect, we have both an equilibrium price and quantity. Each time the supply or demand curve shifts, a new equilibrium is created.

In Figure 2-6, the graph on the left shows the impact an increase in demand has on price and quantity. The graph on the right illustrates the impact an increase in supply has on price and quantity.

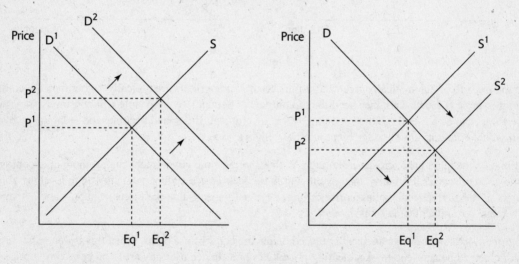

Figure 2-6

Let's look at some scenarios:

- When the supply curve shifts to the right and the demand curve is constant, we have a decrease in price and an increase in quantity.
- When the supply curve shifts to the left and the demand curve is constant, we have an increase in price and a decrease in quantity.

- When the demand curve shifts to the right and the supply curve stays constant, there is an increase in price and an increase in quantity.
- When the demand curve shifts to the left and the supply curve stays constant, there is a decrease in price and a decrease in quantity.

Price Floors and Price Ceilings

A **price floor** is a government-mandated minimum price for a good or service. An example of a price floor is the minimum wage. Producers may not pay below the legal minimum in wages for labor.

A **price ceiling** is a government-mandated maximum price for a good or service. An example of a price ceiling is rent control. A landlord may not charge over the legal maximum in rent.

The government uses price ceilings and price floors because in some instances when supply and demand intersect it is not beneficial to society as a whole. When this occurs, the government intervenes and sets a price floor or ceiling to purposefully create a surplus or shortage.

For a price floor to be effective, the government must set the legal minimum *above* the equilibrium price. For a price ceiling to be effective, the government must set the legal maximum *below* the equilibrium price. Both of these points are illustrated in Figure 2-7.

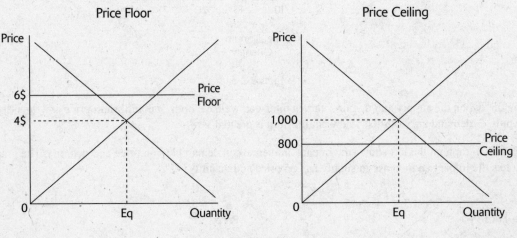

Figure 2-7

Notice that the price floor automatically creates a surplus because price floors are typically higher than the equilibrium price. If a higher price is established, then according to our law of demand, fewer people will consume and a surplus will result. Price floors can be a useful tool for rationing by the government. If demand becomes too great in any instance, a price floor would eliminate any shortage by promoting a higher price.

A price ceiling, on the other hand, creates a shortage. With a shortage, the government can promote or encourage demand for a specific good or service. Primarily, the government introduces a price ceiling in an attempt to level the playing field for consumers. If the government applies a price ceiling, it typically means that the forces of supply and demand are becoming a social *cost* rather than a social *benefit*.

Ineffective price floors and ceilings are usually placed below the equilibrium price. When this is done, the supply or demand isn't changed because the market clearing price takes precedence over any artificial price. For a price floor or ceiling to be truly effective, floors must be placed above the equilibrium price and ceilings must be placed below the equilibrium price.

Illustrations of Shifts in Supply and Demand

You'll notice that a properly illustrated shift in supply is shown with correctly labeled price and quantity changes. *P1* stands for the original price, and *P2* symbolizes the new or changed price. *Q1* is the original quantity; *Q2* is the new or adjusted quantity. In Figure 2-8, there is an increase in supply, illustrated by a shift of the supply curve to the right.

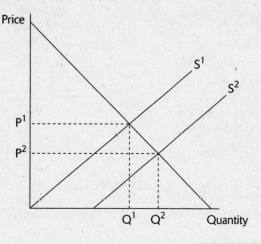

Figure 2-8

To become better at recognizing what changes demand and what does not, read the headlines for the next few graphs (Figure 2-9) and decide if there will be an increase, a decrease, or no change in demand. Be sure to draw a shift if there is an increase or decrease in demand, and explain which determinant was responsible for the shift.

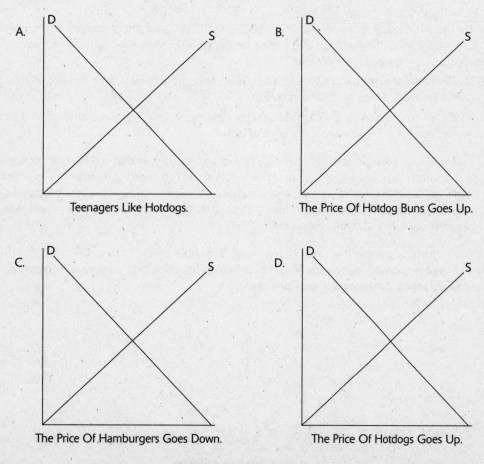

A. Teenagers Like Hotdogs.

B. The Price Of Hotdog Buns Goes Up.

C. The Price Of Hamburgers Goes Down.

D. The Price Of Hotdogs Goes Up.

Figure 2-9 (continues)

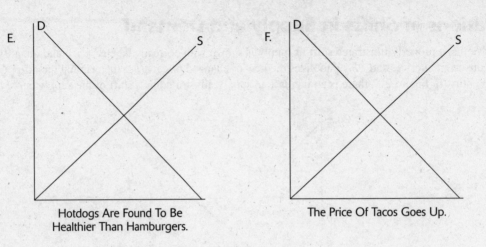

Figure 2-9 (continued)

Each graph represents a headline that has something to do with the market demand for hot dogs:

- **Graph A:** The demand curve shifts to the right because of taste or preference. The headline reads "Teenagers *like* hot dogs."

- **Graph B:** The demand curve shifts to the left because the complementary product (hot dog buns) went up in price; therefore, the demand for hot dogs will decrease. Anytime the complement's price rises (or falls), the demand for the actual product will decrease (or increase).

- **Graph C:** The demand curve shifts to the left because hamburgers become a substitution for hot dogs. Whenever a closely related product increases or decreases in price, it has a direct effect on the demand for the actual product, in this case, hot dogs. This is an example of the substitution effect.

- **Graph D:** There is no shift in the demand curve because price does not affect demand. Remember, we are talking about the market demand for hot dogs. If the price for the actual product goes up or down, the only aspect that changes is quantity demanded, not demand.

- **Graph E:** The demand curve for hot dogs shifts to the right because of taste or preference. People are going to prefer (generally) the hot dogs over the hamburgers.

- **Graph F:** The demand curve for hot dogs shifts to the right because of the substitution effect. More people will substitute hot dogs for tacos because of the price of tacos.

In economics, we tend to generalize rational behavior. There is no force saying that you have to like hot dogs more than hamburgers, or vice versa. This was a simple example of how demand can change because of the power of choice. Each determinant results for the core value of choices: tastes/preferences, substitutions, complements, income, population, and expectations are all rooted in your ability to choose. Regardless of your tendencies toward food, when you choose you are creating an increase or a decrease in demand.

To become better acquainted with shifts in supply, read the following headlines (Figure 2-10) and determine if there is a shift or just a change in quantity supply. The headlines are based on the market supply for hairspray. Illustrate a shift and be sure to explain which determinant caused that shift.

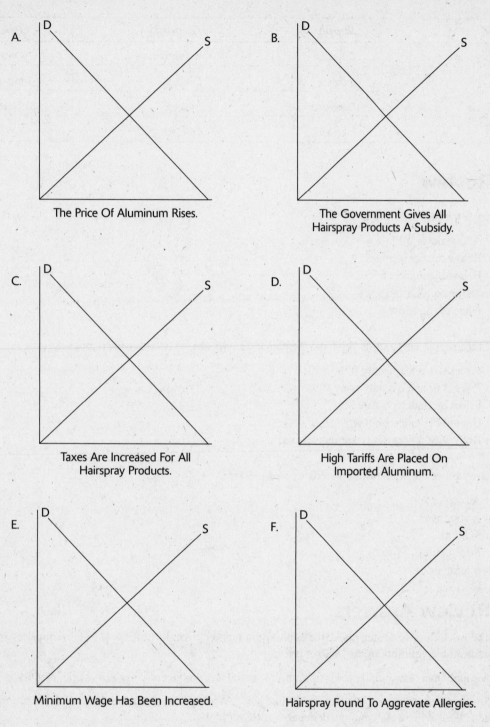

A. The Price Of Aluminum Rises.

B. The Government Gives All Hairspray Products A Subsidy.

C. Taxes Are Increased For All Hairspray Products.

D. High Tariffs Are Placed On Imported Aluminum.

E. Minimum Wage Has Been Increased.

F. Hairspray Found To Aggrevate Allergies.

Figure 2-10

We have just finished looking at supply and demand separately; next let's examine what happens to price and quantity when we have a simultaneous shift.

Demand	Supply	Quantity	Price
Decrease	Decrease	Indeterminate	Decrease
Decrease	Increase	Decrease	Indeterminate
Increase	Decrease	Increase	Indeterminate
Increase	Increase	Indeterminate	Increase

Mini-Review

1. Where is the price floor located?

   A. Above the equilibrium
   B. Below the equilibrium
   C. Below the market price
   D. At the equilibrium price
   E. None of the above

2. When the supply curve shifts right and the demand curve stays constant, what happens?

   A. Prices rise and quantity falls.
   B. Prices fall and quantity rises.
   C. Prices are indeterminate.
   D. Quantity is indeterminate.
   E. Both price and quantity are indeterminate.

3. The area above the equilibrium price is also known as:

   A. A surplus
   B. A shortage
   C. Scarcity
   D. Price ceilings
   E. Market price

Mini-Review Answers

1. **A.** The price floor is located above the equilibrium market price. Its purpose is to prevent prices from dropping to the undesirable equilibrium, or "market price."

2. **B.** A supply increase initially leads to a surplus; therefore, producers lower prices and quantity is increased.

3. **A.** Surpluses are located above the equilibrium price. When prices are above the market price, surpluses are created because there isn't enough demand.

Is It Elastic?

Elasticity is a measure of how a price responds to a change in either supply or demand. Economists use elasticity to gauge the effectiveness of a price change for a good or service. If the price of a good or service does not change as a result of supply or demand, it is said to be **inelastic**. (Elasticity is further discussed in Chapters 7 and 10.)

The law of demand tells us that consumers will buy more of a product at a lower price and less of a product at a higher price. Elasticity tells us just how much or more the consumer will buy at each price level. This amount varies from product to product because people take different variables into consideration when purchasing a good. Firms value elasticity because it tells them just how much of an impact their price change will actually have.

For products such as salt, price changes are less likely to attract attention. Substantial changes in the price for salt will cause only small changes in consumption. But for goods such as cars or vacations, substantial price increases are likely to produce an elastic reaction by consumers.

- **Price elasticity of demand** indicates the responsiveness of the quantity demanded to price changes. Economists use four measures of elasticity to determine the effects of price changes:

- **The number of close substitutes:** If 20 brands of skateboards are available and one of them increases in price, the quantity demanded for that skateboard company will likely decrease. However, if there are only 2 or 3 skateboard companies and one of them increases its price for a skateboard, the quantity demanded is less likely to fall, thereby making it less elastic and more inelastic.

- **How much of your income is spent on the good:** If the price of toilet paper were to increase by 50 percent and the price of airfare were to increase by the same amount, the airfare would be more elastic because of its impact on your income. The more expensive the good, the more likely it is to be elastic.

- **The personal value of the good:** The more important a good is to an individual, the more likely the good will be inelastic. If a diabetic's medication increases in price, chances are the good will be inelastic because of its importance to the diabetic.

- **Time:** When producers change their prices, one indicator of elasticity is time. The more time consumers have to adapt, the more likely they will find cheaper substitutes.

Here are the steps for calculating elasticity of demand:

1. Determine the percentage change in price and the percentage change in quantity demanded:
   a. Original number – new number
      Original number
   b. Multiply by 100
2. Calculate the elasticity:
   a. Percentage change in quantity demanded
      Percentage change in price
   b. Multiply by 100
3. If the answer is 1 or greater, the good is elastic. If the answer is lower than 1, the good is inelastic.

The Price Elasticity of Supply

Price elasticity also applies to supply. It measures the relative responsiveness to price changes by producers. The formula for price elasticity of supply is similar to that of demand, except you substitute the percentage change in demand for the percentage change in supply.

The steps for calculating price elasticity of supply are:

1. Find the percentage change in price and quantity supplied:
   a. Original number – New Number
      Original Number
   b. Multiply by 100
2. Calculate the elasticity:
   a. Percentage change in quantity supplied
      Percentage change in price
   b. Multiply by 100
3. If the answer is 1 or greater, the good is elastic in supply. If the answer is less than 1, the good is inelastic in supply.

The main determinant of the price elasticity of supply is the amount of time a producer has to respond to its price change. If a producer makes pencils and it raises its price, the amount of time it takes for the producer to translate that price change into a quantity supply increase determines the goods' elasticity.

Cross-Elasticity

While price elasticities measure the quantity demanded or supplied, **cross-elasticity** measures the consumer purchases in one product when there is a price change in another product. The impact one product's price makes on another product's demand is valuable information to a producer.

Cross-elasticity = Percentage change in

Quantity demanded for good 1
Percentage change in price
of product 2

Substitute goods: If Pepsi increases its price and it causes consumers to buy more Coke, this results in a positive cross-elasticity of demand, meaning that consumers have substituted Coke for Pepsi because of a price increase. If in the previous equation we get a positive number, it is safe to assume that the two goods are substitutes.

Complementary goods: If an increase in the price of a product leads to a decrease in demand for another product, then the two goods must be complements. For example, an increase in the price of DVD players leads to a decrease in consumption of DVD movies. If in the equation we get a negative number, it is safe to assume that the two goods are complements.

Independent goods: If the answer to the equation is a zero or near zero answer, the two goods are independent or unrelated.

You may be wondering why this cross-elasticity stuff is of any value to anyone. Let's take Gatorade, for example: suppose that Gatorade is considering whether it should lower the price of its flavored water product. Gatorade will want to know if the price decrease will affect total revenue, and it will also want to know if the price decrease will influence the sales of its energy fruit drinks (a related good). Will an increase in sales for Gatorade's water product come at the expense of its energy fruit drinks? How sensitive are the sales of one of its products to a change in the price of another product? Gatorade doesn't want to "chip away" at its success with energy drinks.

The government also uses this cross-elasticity to determine whether firms that propose a merger would be violating antitrust laws. If companies are close substitutes for each other, then the government would be inclined to decline a merger because it would lessen competition, thereby reducing efficiency.

The Income Elasticity of Demand

This type of elasticity measures how or if a change in income produces a change in consumption. When changes in income occur, consumers may or may not react with an increase in consumption. Typically, consumers spend more as they make more; however, how much more do they spend?

$$\text{Income elasticity of demand} = \frac{\text{Percentage change in quantity demanded}}{\text{Percentage change in income}}$$

Normal goods: When you have a positive relationship between an increase in income and consumption (as one rises, the other rises), you have what is called a **normal good**. A normal good is anything that increases in demand when income increases. Typical normal goods are gourmet meals and luxury cars.

Inferior goods: A negative or inverse relationship (as one rises, the other falls) between income and consumption designates an **inferior good**. Inferior goods are products you buy less of when your income increases. Canned soup and Spam are just two examples of inferior goods.

A Graphical Analysis of Elasticity

When a demand curve is perfectly vertical, the demand for that good is inelastic. If the demand curve is horizontal, then the product is elastic in demand. Figure 2-11 illustrates the inelastic and elastic demand curves.

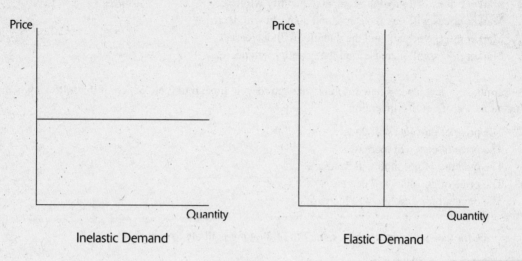

Inelastic Demand   Elastic Demand

Figure 2-11

Chapter Review Questions

1. If price increased by 5 percent and quantity supplied increased by 7 percent:

   A. Supply is elastic.
   B. Demand is elastic.
   C. Supply is inelastic.
   D. Demand is inelastic.
   E. Supply is unitary.

2. When income and consumption have a positive relationship, which of the following is true?

   A. The good is inferior.
   B. The good is normal.
   C. The good is complementary.
   D. The good is a substitute.
   E. None of the above.

3. When cross-elasticity of demand is positive, what are the goods in question?

   A. Substitutes
   B. Rivals
   C. Inferior
   D. Negative
   E. Complements

4. A tornado hits Kansas and wipes out Lauren's tomato crop. What effect will this have on the Kansas tomato market?

    A. Market prices will fall, and quantity will rise.
    B. Market prices will stay the same, and quantity will rise.
    C. Market prices will stay the same, and quantity will decrease.
    D. Market prices will fall, and the quantity will decrease.
    E. Market prices will increase, and the quantity will decrease.

5. Mr. Sarquiz has developed a new machine that can recycle trash into fuel. Which of the following is most likely to occur as a result of this invention?

    A. The price of gasoline will double.
    B. The price of cars will increase.
    C. The quantity of gasoline will decrease.
    D. The price of gasoline will decrease.
    E. The demand for gasoline will increase.

6. If the price for tacos increases, which one of the following is likely to occur?

    A. Fewer tacos will be made.
    B. More people will eat tacos.
    C. People will be less likely to substitute tacos for another product.
    D. Producers can make more tacos.
    E. None of the above.

7. A pharmaceutical company increases its prices for all of its medication and discovers that its total revenue increases. Which one of the following best explains how this could happen?

    A. The firm's supply has increased.
    B. The firm decreased production.
    C. The firm has elastic demand.
    D. The firm has inelastic demand.
    E. The firm has elastic supply.

8. In an effort to increase consumption, the government has increased the minimum wage. What has the government adjusted?

    A. Subsidy
    B. Grant
    C. Price ceiling
    D. Price floor
    E. Firms' demand

9. When the government establishes an effective price ceiling on rent, what will be the result?

    A. A surplus of vacancies
    B. A shortage of vacancies
    C. No effect on vacancies
    D. Higher prices
    E. Less demand

10. What impact will a future sale on computers have on the demand for computers today?

    A.   Shifts the supply curve to the left
    B.   Shifts the demand curve to the right
    C.   Shifts the supply curve to the right
    D.   No effect on demand
    E.   Shifts the demand curve to the left

11. What happens to a product's price if a close substitute is developed?

    A.   The price rises.
    B.   There is no change in price.
    C.   The price of the substitute product rises.
    D.   The price falls.
    E.   None of the above.

12. Which one of the following may have caused an increase in demand for oranges?

    A.   An increase in price
    B.   A decrease in price
    C.   A decrease in the price of grapes
    D.   An increase in the price of grapes
    E.   No change in the price of apple juice

13. Which one of the following may have caused an increase in supply for surfboards?

    A.   A fiberglass shortage
    B.   Cheaper surfboards
    C.   An increase in price for surfboards
    D.   A decrease in price for surfboards
    E.   An increase in minimum wage for workers

14. If supply and demand both increase, what will happen?

    A.   Prices will rise, and quantity will fall.
    B.   Prices will remain unchanged, and quantity will rise.
    C.   Prices will fall, and quantity will fall.
    D.   Prices and quantity will both rise.
    E.   Quantity will fall, and prices will remain unchanged.

15. Which one of the following best illustrates a determinant of supply?

    A.   A new machine has been developed to increase the production of oil.
    B.   Firms profits increase by 25 percent.
    C.   Consumer spending falls by 50 percent.
    D.   Consumers prefer apples over oranges.
    E.   Average consumer income rises by 10 percent.

Answers to Review Questions

1. **A.** After taking the percentage change in supply and dividing it by the percentage change in price, the answer 1.4 is elastic. Anything at or above 1.0 is elastic in demand.

2. **B.** Normal goods are consumed more when income rises. Inferior goods are goods that are consumed less as income rises. The good isn't a substitute because the demand for another product is not being affected.

3. **E.** Cross-elasticity refers to the impact one good's price has on another good's demand. If the cross-elasticity answer is a positive number, the goods are complements.

4. **E.** The supply curve for the tomato crop will shift to the left. When supply shifts to the left and the demand curve stays the same, the price will increase and the quantity will decrease.

5. **D.** When a cheaper alternative is discovered for a good, the good's price will drop because of the substitution effect.

6. **D.** The law of supply states that as prices rise, quantity supply rises. If the price of tacos increases, producers can afford to make more tacos.

7. **D.** If a firm increases its price and discovers that its total revenue (price times quantity sold) increases, the firm's demand is inelastic because consumers aren't buying less of the product.

8. **D.** Minimum wage is a price floor because it is set above the equilibrium price for labor. A price floor is designed to increase an inefficient market price.

9. **B.** If the government decided to "cap" rent on housing, a shortage might be created because lower rent prices will attract more demand.

10. **E.** Any future sales affect current demand by prompting consumers to wait for a cheaper price. This "waiting game" decreases current demand. A future sale on a product will affect a consumer's expectation of price; therefore, the consumer will wait to buy the computer until it is cheaper. The demand curve for the computer will shift to the left now and to the right later.

11. **D.** If a close substitute is developed for a product, the price of that product will fall because of an increase in competition. An increase in competition will force the two producers to become more efficient, and prices will fall.

12. **D.** An increase in the price of grapes will increase the demand for oranges because consumers are likely to substitute oranges for grapes. Substitution price is a determinant of demand.

13. **C.** The law of supply states that as prices rise, quantity supply increases as well. If the price of surfboards rises, the quantity of surfboards supplied will increase.

14. **B.** If supply and demand shifts to the right, the end result will be the return of the price to its original level and an increase in quantity. To understand this better, draw an increase in supply and demand and locate both price and quantity. You should be able to see that prices return to their original state while quantity increases.

15. **A.** Improvements in technology provide lower production costs for producers, thereby increasing their supply. Technology is a determinant of supply.

PART II

MACROECONOMICS

National Income Accounting

Macroeconomics is an overall view of the economy's performance. Areas such as unemployment, inflation, government expenditures, and banking are all a part of macroeconomics. We measure a nation's overall performance through national income accounting. Individual firms have private accounting to measure their performance, revenue, and costs, whereas the economy has national accounting to measure or assess this data. The accounting or measurement enables economists and policymakers to:

- Compare levels of production and efficiency at regular intervals
- Gauge the long-run status of an economy to see if it has grown, remained stagnant or declined
- Create policies that detour negative results and promote a positive outlook

Much like our circular flow chart we discussed in Chapter 1, the economy is divided into four sections:

- **Households**—This section represents consumers who pay for goods and services in the product market and get paid for goods or services in the factor market. The number of people in a household has no bearing on economic data; however, households as a whole represent 67 percent of consumption in the United States.
- **Firms**—This section represents the producers of goods and services in our economy. In a factor market, firms buy any of the three factors of production from the households. In a product market, firms sell any of the three factors of production to the households.
- **Government**—This section refers to any or all of the political entities of a country. Government purchases come in the form of defense spending, transfer payments, and subsidies that employ some of the factors of production.
- **Imports and exports**—This section refers to the participation of an economy in a global market. An **open economy** refers to the decision an economy makes to include trading imports and exports with the rest of the world. The more a country trades with the world, the more reliant that country becomes on the rest of the world's output.

In Figure 3-1, the government finances its expenditures through its ability to collect taxes. Firms and households continue to create factor and product markets; however, this time the government's expenditures help the flow move more smoothly.

The Circular Flow

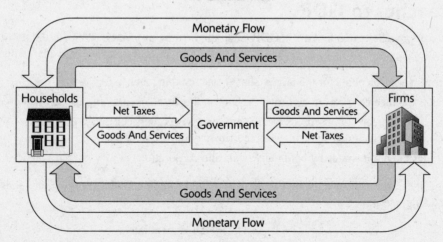

Figure 3-1

Gross Domestic Product

Gross Domestic Product (GDP) is the primary method used by the U.S. Bureau of Economic Analysis to measure the economy's performance. GDP consists of the total value of all final goods and services produced on a nation's soil in a year. For example, Ford Motor Company in Detroit is factored into the United States' GDP; Toyota Motor Corp. in Dallas is also considered a part of our GDP. However, a Ford factory in Japan would not be considered in our GDP because the goods are not produced on U.S. soil.

GDP is a monetary measure that allows us to compare relative values of goods and services. It enables us to gauge productivity based on the sheer value of a good or service. If an economy produces one car and two boats in year 1, and two cars and zero boats in year 2, GDP allows us to see which year was productive based on the monetary value of the boats and cars.

The key to understanding GDP is knowing the difference between **intermediate** and **final** goods. Intermediate goods are used to create final goods. Rubber, wood, and steel could all be used as intermediate goods used to manufacture a final good. The reason we have this distinction between intermediate and final goods is because economists want to avoid what's called **double-counting**. If we were to count steel as part of GDP and later counted the car that the steel went into as GDP, we would be double-counting, or overestimating the value of the steel. This is precisely the reason why we count all *final* goods rather than intermediate goods.

GDP Exclusions

Economists exclude some transactions in the economy because they have nothing to do with the creation of final goods. Purely financial transactions, such as buying or selling of stock and private and public transfer payments, are not counted in a nation's GDP.

Public transfer payments are payments that the government makes directly to households. Social security, welfare, and veterans payments are all public transfer payments. **Private transfer payments** are monetary gifts that produce no output.

Secondhand sales are excluded from GDP because they do not contribute to current production. If you sold your motorcycle that was made in 1976, it would not be included in this year's GDP because the sale would not monetarily contribute to this year's output.

Two Approaches to GDP

Economists use two approaches when looking at GDP. First, the **income approach** calculates GDP by examining all the money spent on final goods and services in the United States. The income approach considers four categories:

- **Wages to employees:** Accounts for the largest share of national income.
- **Rents:** Includes the income received by firms and households for the supply of property resources.
- **Interest:** Includes the interest households receive on savings accounts, certificate of deposit (CD) accounts, and corporate bonds. It also includes the money or fee firms pay for use of capital.
- **Profits:** Includes the profits made by both individuals and corporations.

The second strategy, the **expenditures approach,** calculates GDP by adding all the spending on goods and services that has taken place in a single year:

$$C + I + G + X = GDP \text{ expenditures}$$

The expenditure approach looks at four categories:

- **Personal consumption (C):** Consists of all expenditures by households on durable and nondurable goods.
- **Gross investment (I):** Includes the money spent on all purchases of machinery by businesses, construction of capital, and changes in inventories.

- **Government (G):** Includes all government expenditures from social capital to welfare and social security payments.
- **Net exports (X):** Includes the value of all money spent on exports minus imports.

Other National Accounting Systems

Other accounting systems that economists use include the following:

- **Net Domestic Product (NDP):** Economists derive NDP by taking GDP and subtracting the depreciation of capital equipment. In other words, NDP is GDP adjusted for depreciation.
- **National income:** This allows us to calculate how much Americans earned for their contributions of land, labor, and capital. To accomplish this, we must:
  - Subtract the income earned by foreigners in the United States.
  - Subtract indirect business taxes taken in by the government.
- **Personal income:** This consists of all income earned or unearned. It includes transfer payments (social security, welfare, and veterans payments) and wages earned.
- **Disposable income:** This consists of personal income minus taxes.

Nominal and Real GDP

We know that GDP is a measure of the monetary value of all final goods and services produced in a year on a nation's soil. This monetary value measurement presents a problem because dollar values change from year to year. **Inflation** and **deflation** are two fluctuations in the economy that sometimes distort the value of GDP. How can we accurately compare the value of GDP from year to year? We can minimize the effects of inflation or deflation by calculating nominal GDP and real GDP.

Nominal GDP calculates prices that prevailed when the output was produced; it is unadjusted for inflation. To adjust GDP for inflation or deflation, we use nominal GDP to calculate real GDP. **Real GDP** is adjusted (inflated or deflated) to reflect changes in the price level.

The **Price Index** is the measurement of a specific amount of goods contained in a "market basket" in a given year compared to an identical market basket in a reference year. A **reference year** is known as a base year, and it is used as a benchmark for prices of a certain time frame.

The formula for figuring real GDP is:

$$\text{Real GDP} = \frac{\text{Nominal GDP (current year prices)}}{\text{Price index (in hundredths)}}$$

GDP Shortcomings

Using GDP as a monetary measure has some drawbacks. For example, economists cannot measure the following:

- **Nonmarket transactions:** GDP cannot measure transactions that have no real paper trail, such as housework a homeowner does for his or her own home, air pollution, and the labor that business owners perform for their own businesses.
- **Mental or physical health:** GDP cannot measure stress-relieving activities, such as vacations, exercise, and laughter.
- **Underground economy:** GDP cannot measure illegal or unreported activities.

The Business Cycle

The business cycle is a four-phase normal fluctuation of a market economy. Whether we are examining a single firm, a particular industry, or the whole economy, market fluctuations are present at all levels:

1. **Expansion:** This phase of the business cycle denotes growth in the economy. In this phase, businesses, employment, and price level is growing.

2. **Peak:** The peak is the height of the expansion phase. This phase is usually not known until after it is over. Unemployment reaches its lowest point in the cycle and businesses reach their expansion limits.

3. **Contraction:** This is the downside of the expansion phase. In this phase, unemployment begins to grow while businesses are downsizing and making cuts. Two consecutive quarters of this phase denotes a recession.

4. **Trough:** The trough is the "bottoming out" of the contraction phase. Again, this phase is usually not known until after it has passed. Unemployment and firm contraction reach their lowest points in the cycle in this phase.

Figure 3-2 shows a typical business cycle. Notice how the severity of the fluctuations can vary depending on economic variables. One trough may not be as bad as another trough. The business cycle allows us to see the overall fluctuations of the economy over a sustained period of time.

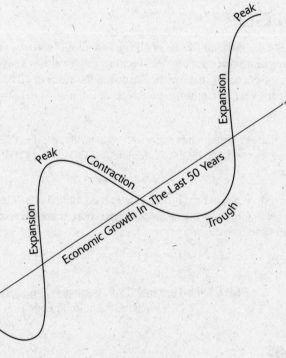

Figure 3-2

Injections and Leakages

Leakages and **injections** of the monetary flow cause fluctuations of the business cycle. Anytime a household decides not to use its income for consumption, we have a leakage. When a household decides to save rather than spend, it has created a leakage in GDP—that is, the monetary flow is not benefiting output or GDP. Taxes and imports are also leakages because the monetary flow for these categories is not directly benefiting GDP. An injection occurs when the government, businesses, or foreign firms spend money on U.S. goods or services. They are called injections because the money is being spent on U.S. goods and services, which in turn help GDP growth.

Mini-Review

1. Which of the following is a fact regarding the circular flow model?

    A. Both firms and suppliers are a part of a product market.

    B. Firms are consumers and households are suppliers in a product market.

    C. The government is a consumer in only the factor market.

    D. Firms and households never interact.

    E. None of the above.

2. Which one of the following is an example of a leakage?

    A. Consumption

    B. Investment

    C. Demand

    D. Imports

    E. Exports

3. Which one of the following is not part of the business cycle?

    A. Peak

    B. Consumption

    C. Expansion

    D. Trough

    E. Contraction

Mini-Review Answers

1. A. In a product market, firms supply and households consume; therefore, both firms and households are a part of a product market.

2. D. Imports are an example of a leakage because the money being spent on them is not injected into our economy; instead, it is leaked out of our economy and into another country's economy.

3. B. Consumption is the only option given that is not a part of the business cycle.

Unemployment and Inflation

Unemployment and inflation are the two main problems that arise from economic instability. They are two macroeconomic problems that garner the attention of the Federal Reserve and the government. As daunting as these problems may seem, weapons are available to control these macroeconomic hazards. Let's look at unemployment first.

The government defines an unemployed person as anyone who is willing and able to work but does not have a job. To measure the unemployment rate, we must determine who is eligible for employment and who is not. Two categories not included in the measurement of unemployment are people under the age of 16 and/or institutionalized and discouraged people (those who are not actively seeking employment). A person who works part-time employment is considered employed by the U.S. Bureau of Labor Statistics.

Types of Unemployment

There are three types of unemployment:

- **Frictional unemployment:** Some workers are between jobs, voluntarily moving from one job to another, or are fired from employment. Others have just graduated from college and are looking for employment or have just been laid off from employment. These people are all labeled *frictionally unemployed*. Essentially, frictional unemployment is when workers are either searching for jobs or waiting to take jobs.

- **Structural unemployment:** If Sally is working as a retail clerk and her store gets a new computerized register, Sally needs to become acquainted with the new technology or she will face being *structurally unemployed*. This category includes any worker who becomes unemployed due to a lack of skill with a new technology introduced by his or her employer.

- **Cyclical unemployment:** This results from the normal fluctuations of the business cycle. Cyclical unemployment is caused by a decline in total spending in the economy and is likely to occur in the contraction phase of the business cycle.

Full Employment

Because we have unemployment that is unavoidable (frictional and structural), between 4 percent and 5 percent of the labor force can be unemployed and we can still be considered at full employment. **Full employment** occurs when there is no cyclical unemployment and the economy is producing its potential output. When the economy is maximizing its efficiency, virtually all resources available are employed.

Full employment is illustrated in Figure 3-3. In the graph, full employment is present in range 2. In range 2, we have a slight increase in price level (to allow growth) and virtually all resources employed. At any point beyond range 2, we no longer have growth for the economy; rather, the price level begins to rapidly increase (inflation) because all resources have been employed.

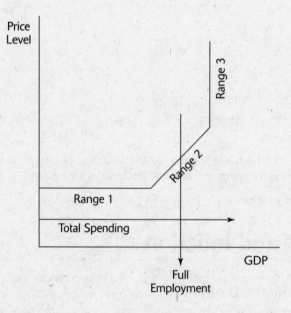

Figure 3-3

Inflation

If you walk into a coffee shop and the price of your usual cup of coffee has increased from $2.25 to $3.50, it's tempting to blame inflation; however, this may not be the case. Inflation is the biggest macroeconomic problem that economists face. Inflation is not an increase in price for one good, two goods, or even fifty goods. **Inflation** occurs when the U.S. Bureau of Economic Analysis examines the prices of its **market basket of goods** (which consists of approximately 300 goods), and discovers that the average price of this basket has risen. Indexes measure inflation by comparing general price levels in any year with prices in a base year. The most common index used to measure inflation is the **Consumer Price Index (CPI)**. Here is the formula for calculating CPI:

Price index =

$$\frac{\text{Price of market basket in specific year}}{\text{Price of market basket in base year}} \quad (100)$$

Price index, year 1 =   100

Price index, year 2 = $\frac{\$20}{\$10} \times 100 = 200$

Price index, year 3 = $\frac{\$25}{\$10} \times 100 = 250$

With our example you can see that for year 1, the price index has to be 100, since that is our base year. The index numbers tell us that the price rose from year 1 to year 2 by 100 percent and from year 1 to year 3 by 150 percent.

Another way to measure inflation is to use the GDP deflator. This formula measures the changes in prices of all goods and services produced in an economy:

$$\text{Real GDP} = \frac{\text{Nominal GDP}}{\text{Price Index}}$$

Types of Inflation

In this section, we'll take a look at the two types of inflation.

Demand-Pull Inflation

Typically, changes in the price level are caused by changes in total spending. As total spending increases, so does consumers' demand for products. When the economy reaches its capacity yet demand for products is still increasing, producers have no choice but to start raising their prices. A collective rise in the price level is a cause of inflation. This type of inflation, called **demand-pull inflation**, is illustrated in Figure 3-4.

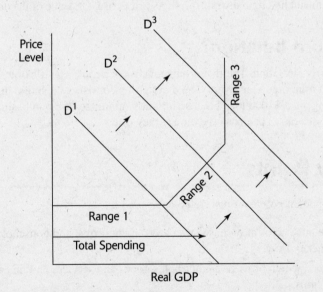

Figure 3-4

In Figure 3-4, we see that demand has increased from D1, to D2, to D3 as a result of an increase in total spending. In range 1, output is low in comparison to the economy's full employment abilities. This low output implies a low level of total spending, which causes high unemployment and stagnant production of resources. In range 2, demand continues to expand as a result of further increases in spending. Demand meets full employment output, which tells us that the economy is "running on all cylinders," or at productive capacity. The price level begins increasing, telling us that the economy is growing. In range 3, total spending is still increasing; however, the economy has virtually all of its resources employed. This means that as demand increases, it causes the price level to increase. Firms cannot respond to an increase in demand by increasing output, so they raise prices.

Cost-Push Inflation

Cost-push inflation occurs on the supply side of goods and services. This type of inflation is seen when producers' per-unit production costs rise. As goods become more expensive to produce, suppliers raise their prices in efforts to retain revenue. Raising prices freeze profits and decreases the supply of goods and services in the economy. A major source of cost-push inflation is supply shocks. **Supply shocks** are abrupt increases in the costs of production, such as raw materials and power inputs.

Who Does Inflation Hurt?

Unanticipated inflation hurts fixed-income recipients, savers, and creditors. **Fixed income** is income that remains the same over a long period of time. As inflation rates increase, the value or the purchasing power of the dollar drops. The most common example of people on a fixed income are the elderly. They receive pensions or other incomes that are fixed over a sustained period of time. Landlords with fixed leases are also hurt by inflation because their income may not be adjusted for a fixed period of time.

Unanticipated inflation hurts savers because accounts that don't offer interest payments equivalent or higher than inflation rates end up eating away a saver's purchasing power. If Nicole puts her money in a savings account that yields a 2 percent interest rate each year and the rate of inflation for this year is at 3 percent, Nicole ends up losing 1 percent of her purchasing power because of inflation. The old saying "Money can't buy today what it bought yesterday" is true because of inflation.

Finally, unanticipated inflation hurts creditors and lenders. Suppose Bulldog Bank lends Mr. Valencia $1000 to be repaid in two years. If during those two years the rate of inflation doubles, the $1000 that Mr. Valencia repays will have only half the purchasing power of the amount he originally borrowed. As prices rise, the value of the dollar falls.

Who Benefits from Inflation?

Two groups actually benefit from inflation. The first group consists of people on a flexible income who receive a cost-of-living adjustment (COLA) from their employers. The other group consists of debtors. In our earlier example, Mr. Valencia benefited from taking out a $1000 loan because inflation minimizes the purchasing power of the money owed. With inflation, it is easier for debtors to pay back the money they owe.

Review of Key Points

Here's an overview of the important points we just covered:

- Market economies have three areas of money flow. Government, firms, and households all exchange the factors of production for a monetary flow.
- A product market is one in which firms give households goods and services and, in exchange, households provide a monetary flow to the firms.
- A factor market is one in which firms purchase the factors of production from households.
- Economic growth, efficiency, and full employment are the goals of a market economy.
- Gross Domestic Product (GDP) is the value of total output in an economy. It can be measured with the income approach (adding up all incomes) or with the expenditures approach (adding up all expenditures in C, I, G, X). Only final goods and services count when you're calculating GDP.

- Inflation is the general rise of the price level over a sustained period of time. The Consumer Price Index and the GDP deflator measure inflation.

- There are two types of inflation: cost-push and demand-pull. Cost-push is when the production costs of a supplier increase, forcing the producer to raise its price. Demand-pull is when the overall demand in the economy surpasses the productive capacity of the economy, forcing producers to raise their prices.

- The Bureau of Economic Analysis calculates unemployment as all people 16 and over, not incarcerated, who are willing and able to work but do not have a job.

- There are three types of unemployment: frictional, structural, and cyclical. Between 4 percent and 5 percent of the labor force can be unemployed and the country can still be considered at full employment.

- Purchasing power is the value a consumer's money holds after the rate of inflation has affected it.

- The business cycle reflects the normal fluctuations of a market economy. The four phases of the business cycle are expansion, peak, contraction, and trough.

Chapter Review Questions

1. Which one of the following statements is true regarding GDP?

    A. It measures the total value of all goods and services inside and outside of the economy.
    B. It measures only the value of intermediate goods and services.
    C. It is calculated with two different approaches.
    D. It measures well-being and the underground economy.
    E. None of the above.

2. What does cyclical unemployment refer to?

    A. People who don't have jobs because of choice
    B. Students who just graduated from college
    C. Firms that hire workers and then fire them because of poor performance
    D. The part of the labor force that is unemployed due to the expansion phase of the business cycle
    E. None of the above

3. Which of the following best describes cost-push inflation?

    A. A rise in the price level as a result of too much demand
    B. A rise in the price level as a result of high production costs
    C. A rise in the price level as a result of too little demand
    D. A rise in the price level because producers want to make a bigger profit
    E. A fall in the price level as a result of production costs

4. The Consumer Price Index could most closely be associated with which of the following?

    A. A gauge of unemployment
    B. A measure of well-being
    C. A measure of GDP
    D. A measure of the price level
    E. A measure of taxation

5. How is the GDP deflator used?

    A. To calculate nominal GDP
    B. To deflate the Consumer Price Index
    C. To calculate real GDP
    D. To calculate inflation
    E. To calculate unemployment

6. Which of the following best describes what happens in range 2?

    A. The price level falls.

    B. Unemployment increases.

    C. Unemployment is irrelevant.

    D. The price level rises.

    E. Productive capacity declines.

7. What is the difference between cyclical unemployment and structural unemployment?

    A. Cyclical happens during the contraction phase, and structural occurs because of a lack of skills.

    B. Cyclical happens during the expansion phase, and structural pertains to those just graduating from college.

    C. Cyclical happens during the peak phase, and structural describes discouraged workers.

    D. Cyclical and structural occur in the contraction phase only.

    E. None of the above.

8. Which one of the following is the formula for the expenditures approach?

    A. $C + T + X + Y$

    B. $G + I + R + X$

    C. $C + I + G + X$

    D. $C + H + O + X$

    E. $I + X + T + Y$

9. What is the difference between real GDP and nominal GDP?

    A. Real GDP measures total value of goods and services with adjustment for inflation, and nominal GDP is not adjusted for inflation.

    B. Real GDP measures unadjusted values of final goods and services whereas nominal GDP is inflation adjusted.

    C. There is no difference between the two.

    D. Real GDP measures unemployment in current years, whereas nominal GDP measures unemployment in past years.

    E. Nominal GDP measures inflation, whereas real GDP does not measure unemployment.

10. What does the price index measure?

    A. Unemployment

    B. Taxes

    C. The underground economy

    D. Price levels

    E. GDP

11. What does Gross Domestic Product consist of?

    A. Taxes, military expenditures, and welfare

    B. Personal consumption, investment, and government purchases

    C. Savings, income, and taxes

    D. Goods, services, and taxes

    E. Savings appreciation and goods

12. What would be the effect of a large increase in labor productivity on the real GDP and the price level?

	Real GDP	Price Level
A.	Increase	Increase
B.	Increase	Decrease
C.	No effect	Increase
D.	Decrease	Increase
E.	Decrease	Decrease

13. The CPI measures which of the following?

A. The change over time in weighted prices of a particular group of goods and services

B. The change over time of the weighted wholesale price index

C. The change over time of the difference between GDP and the wholesale price index

D. Inflation in GDP

E. Inflation in the producer price index

14. What will be the result of an increase in the labor force participation rate?

A. Increased investment

B. Increased savings and decreased investment

C. No effect on unemployment

D. Decreased revenue for firms

E. Decreased purchasing power for consumers

15. What term is defined as two consecutive quarters of declining GDP?

A. Inflation

B. Stagflation

C. Recession

D. Expansion

E. A peak in the business cycle

Answers to Review Questions

1. C. GDP can be calculated using two different approaches: the expenditures approach and the income approach.

2. E. None is the correct answer because cyclical unemployment is when a worker is laid off or unemployed because of the contraction phase of the business cycle.

3. B. Cost-push inflation refers to a rise in the price level due to high production costs. When producers have to pay more for raw materials and/or energy outputs, they raise their prices in an effort to retain profits.

4. D. The CPI measures the price level by comparing a market basket of goods from the present year with a base year's prices of that identical market basket. The CPI cannot measure well-being, GDP, unemployment, or taxes.

5. C. The GDP deflator is used to adjust GDP for inflation. It does this by taking nominal GDP and comparing it to a base year.

6. D. In range 2 the price level rises as demand begins to increase. Productive capacity is approached and then passed, and unemployment decreases as more workers are employed and the economy is growing.

7. **A.** Cyclical unemployment occurs during the contraction phase of the business cycle, and structural unemployment takes place as a result of technology creating a lack of knowledge or skills.

8. **C.** Consumption + Investment + Government + Exports = GDP expenditures.

9. **A.** Real GDP is an inflation-adjusted measurement of all final goods and services produced; nominal GDP takes current-year prices that are not adjusted for inflation.

10. **D.** Price indexes measure the price level (inflation).

11. **B.** GDP components include consumption, investment, and government purchases. These are three of the four parts of GDP under the expenditures approach. Net exports make up the fourth part of the expenditures approach.

12. **A.** An increase in the price level and an increase in the real GDP would be the result of an increase in labor productivity. When more people have jobs, the economy is more productive and the price level rises.

13. **A.** The CPI measures price changes over time for a particular group (market basket) of goods and services. The CPI is calculated using a base year that examines relative prices.

14. **A.** When more people have jobs, consumption increases because purchasing power increases.

15. **C.** Two consecutive quarters with declining GDP usually indicates a recession. When the economy is experiencing a fall in output over an extended period of time, unemployment is growing and total spending is decreasing.

Aggregate Expenditures, Aggregate Supply and Aggregate Demand Models

An inverse relationship exists between aggregate expenditures and unemployment. The more people spend, the fewer people are unemployed; the less people spend, the more people are unemployed. In our economy, people tend to spend more than they save. This generalization is what helps our economy grow. When people spend money, they create jobs; when people "hold" money, the economy contracts. Although we may be able to generalize and say that people spend more money than they save, we need to analyze just how much people spend and save relative to their incomes.

The percentage of total income that consumers spend is called **average propensity to consume (APC)**. The percentage of total income that consumers save is called **average propensity to save (APS)**. The formulas for determining APC and APS are as follows:

$$APC = \frac{Consumption}{Income} \qquad APS = \frac{Saving}{Income}$$

When individuals earn more money, this change in income typically leads to a change in consumption and savings. The ratio or percentage of any change in income consumed is called the **marginal propensity to consume (MPC)**. The ratio or change in income saved is called the **marginal propensity to save (MPS)**. The formulas for determining MPC and MPS are as follows:

$$MPC = \frac{Change\ in\ consumption}{Change\ in\ income} \qquad MPS = \frac{Change\ in\ savings}{Change\ in\ income}$$

Since Gross Domestic Product (GDP) is an overall measurement of an economy's performance, we must now look at what forces create GDP. Aggregate supply and aggregate demand determine GDP; in this chapter we examine how GDP is determined in both a closed economy (without imports and exports) and an open economy (with imports and exports).

In a **private** (or **closed**) **economy**, equilibrium GDP changes in response to adjustments in either the investment schedule or the consumption schedule:

- **Investment schedule:** A curve or schedule that illustrates how much firms plan on investing at various values of real GDP.
- **Consumption schedule:** A curve or schedule that illustrates how much households plan on investing at various values of real GDP.

With an open economy GDP is slightly changed with the involvement of international trade. The example of a closed economy is used to simplify the concepts—closed economies allow us to see GDP working with the incomes and expenditures of domestic consumers and firms.

Consumers, suppliers, and the government are the main pieces in the aggregate puzzle (the whole economy). This chapter reviews how decisions to spend, save, or invest affect the real GDP of our economy. These decisions are the forces behind aggregate supply and aggregate demand, which in turn create equilibrium GDP.

Graphical Analysis of a Consumption Schedule

Figure 4-1 shows a graph that illustrates consumption and savings. The 45-degree line represents equality between the vertical axis and the horizontal axis. The value of what is being measured on the horizontal axis (GDP) is equal to whatever is being measured on the vertical axis (aggregate expenditures).

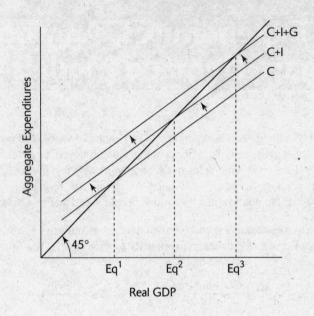

Figure 4-1

In Chapter 3, we examined the four parts of the GDP expenditures approach (C+I+G+X), which are personal consumption, gross investment, government, and net exports. On an aggregate expenditures graph, each curve represents the expenditures of these four factors.

In Figure 4-1, you'll notice that as each group is added to the expenditures graph, the expenditures curve shifts upward, denoting an increase in consumption for the economy. With each increase in consumption for the economy, our equilibrium GDP (EQ) shifts from EQ 1 to EQ 2, and eventually, with the addition of the government, to EQ 3. This, of course, is a simplified closed economy where the foreign sector is not considered.

Mini-Review

1. What happens to consumption when investment is added to it?

   A. It decreases as GDP increases.
   B. It increases and GDP increases.
   C. It remains constant.
   D. Investment decreases GDP.
   E. Consumption decreases GDP.

2. What does the 45-degree line on the aggregate expenditures graph represent?

   A. Consumption by firms.
   B. Consumption by households.
   C. A point of equality between expenditures and GDP.
   D. A point of equality between employment and taxes.

3. Why does the curve on the aggregate expenditures graph show different equilibrium points?

   A. As each level of consumption rises, a new equilibrium is created.
   B. As the government spends less money, the equilibrium rises.
   C. The equilibrium changes because of inflation.
   D. The equilibrium changes because of unemployment.
   E. None of the above.

Mini-Review Answers

1. B. When investment is added to the expenditures model, it increases the level of expenditures in the economy. Firms use investment to create capital, and this in turn creates employment.

2. C. The 45-degree line represents a point of equality between the vertical and horizontal axes. On the aggregate expenditures graph, the vertical axis shows consumption/expenditures, and the horizontal axis represents GDP.

3. A. When more expenditures are added to the graph, the result is a new equilibrium. No equilibrium is fixed because levels of expenditures may change.

Aggregate Demand

The forces of supply and demand are also used on a national and international level. Earlier in our review, we touched on supply and demand and the determinants that shift both curves. Let's now focus our attention on aggregate supply and aggregate demand, the forces that dictate GDP for our economy.

Aggregate demand represents the amount of real output that buyers collectively desire to consume at each price level. On the vertical axis of an aggregate demand curve, we have the price level, which represents the average of the total prices in a market basket. On the horizontal axis, we have the quantity of real GDP. GDP and price level are inversely related on this graph. When the price level rises, the quantity of real GDP demanded falls; when the price level falls, the quantity of real GDP demanded rises.

Figure 4-2 illustrates an aggregate demand curve. At first glance, it may seem identical to an individual firm's demand curve; however, this is not the case. The price level represents prices in the whole economy, whereas quantity represents the amount of real GDP demanded in the whole economy.

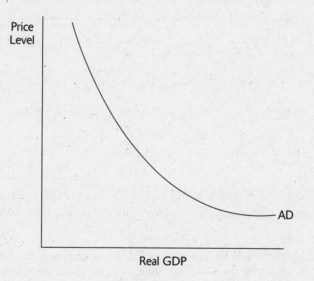

Figure 4-2

If this curve is different from an individual firm's demand curve, then what is the reason for the difference? The answer rests on three effects of a price-level change: the real-balance effect, the interest-rate effect, and the foreign-purchases effect.

- **The Real-Balance Effect:** A change in the price level diminishes the public's purchasing power. If a family is planning on buying a home, they will likely reconsider that purchase if inflation erodes the value of their purchasing power. A higher price level translates into less consumption spending.

- **The Interest-Rate Effect:** A higher price level increases the demand for money. This rise in demand for money increases interest rates, which can be thought of as the price of money. When interest rates rise, firms are less likely to buy capital, consumers are less likely to borrow or consume, and the economy as a whole has less consumption. Conversely, as prices fall, interest rates drop because the demand for money falls.

- **The Foreign-Purchases Effect:** When the U.S. price level rises in comparison to foreign price levels, foreigners buy fewer U.S. products and Americans buy more foreign goods. This causes U.S. exports to fall and imports to rise. When the price level rises, it reduces the quantity of U.S. goods demanded.

Determinants of Aggregate Demand

When aggregate demand increases, the curve shifts to the right. When aggregate demand decreases, the curve shifts to the left. Figure 4-3 illustrates an increase and decrease in aggregate demand.

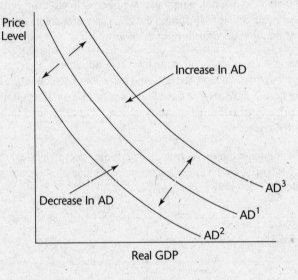

Figure 4-3

Let's take a look at the factors affecting aggregate demand: consumer spending, investment spending, government spending, and exports.

Consumer Spending

Even when the price level of goods and services is stable, U.S. consumers may choose to consume more. When consumers decide to purchase more, the aggregate demand curve shifts to the right. Some of the factors that alter consumer spending habits are:

- **Wealth:** Stocks, bonds, and physical assets are all considered consumer wealth. A sudden increase in any of these physical or financial assets allows producers to consume more, thereby increasing aggregate demand as a result of the wealth effect. Conversely, a major decrease in consumer wealth lowers aggregate demand.

- **Consumer expectations:** Changes in consumer expectations affect aggregate demand. For example, if Joe is expecting his annual Christmas bonus, in anticipation of receiving his bonus he will consume more goods. This effect increases the current consumption for goods and increases aggregate demand.

- **Household debt:** If households experience higher debt than normal, consumers may be forced to cut current spending to pay off the amassed debt. If this occurs, consumption declines and the aggregate demand curve shifts to the left.

- **Taxes:** When personal income taxes decrease, consumers have more disposable income to use for goods and services. This shifts the aggregate demand curve to the right. Tax hikes shift the curve to the left.

Investment Spending

Sometimes investment spending is confused with investing in stocks and bonds, or "financial assets." To an economist, **investment** is when firms purchase factors of production to facilitate their supply. When investment spending declines, it shifts the aggregate demand curve to the left; when investment spending increases, it shifts the curve to the right. Investment spending is determined by two factors:

- **Real interest rates:** Interest is the price of money. As interest rates rise, fewer firms will invest because it will become too costly to borrow money.

- **Expected returns:** If firms expect high returns from their purchases of capital, they will be more likely to consume more, thereby shifting the aggregate demand curve to the right.

Government Spending

When the government decides to spend more on the economy, the aggregate demand curve shifts to the right. This happens because the revenue that the government spends increases employment and expands businesses. With more jobs, people have more money, therefore increasing aggregate demand. However, if the government decreases spending, the aggregate demand curve shifts to the left.

Exports

When U.S. and foreign consumers increase spending on U.S. exports and decrease spending on imports, this translates into an increase in aggregate demand. The aggregate demand curve thus shifts to the right. On the other hand, the aggregate demand curve shifts to the left if U.S. and foreign consumers buy more imported products. The change in exports is caused by three factors: the price level, the level of income for foreigners, and the strength of the dollar relative to other currencies.

Aggregate Supply

Aggregate supply represents the combined domestic output that firms will produce at every price level. According to the law of supply, the higher the price level, the more output produced by firms; the lower the price level, the less output produced; thus a positive relationship exists between price level and output.

The aggregate supply curve has three ranges that illustrate the effect on production costs as GDP grows or contracts:

- **Range 1 (horizontal range):** Typically represents a low level of employment, implying that the economy is in either a depression or a recession. The productive capabilities of the economy (machines, labor, and raw materials) are unused. The economy is operating below its productive capacity; therefore, it can employ unused resources without creating an increase in the price level.

- **Range 2 (intermediate range):** In this stage, real output is expanding due to a rise in the price level. This rise in the price level is allowing the economy to expand production and increase employment. The economy is made up of many product and factor markets; some of these markets do not reach full employment when the economy reaches full employment. It is possible to have a market or an industry operating below full employment when the aggregate economy is considered to be operating at full employment. Once the full employment GDP has been reached, additional increases in the price level may yield increased output for a short time. This is possible because firms may extend work hours for labor, individuals may take on second jobs, and raw materials may be used more efficiently. In range 2, the economy reaches full employment, the price level rises, and output is increased.

- **Range 3 (vertical range):** At the beginning of this stage, the economy reaches its full capacity. Any change in the price level will no longer increase production. Resources are being fully employed; therefore, any increase in demand will yield a higher price level (inflation).

Figure 4-4 illustrates the three ranges in which aggregate supply can move. From point A to point B, there is high unemployment with no increase in the price level. Between these points, output can increase without changing the price level. From point B to C, the price level begins rising as output increases. It is between these points that full employment is reached and passed. Between points C and D, the economy cannot sustain any more growth, thereby causing the price level to rise without an increase in output.

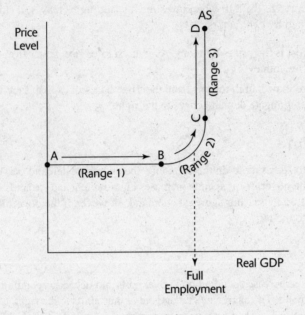

Figure 4-4

Determinants of Aggregate Supply

According to the shape of the aggregate supply curve, output rises as the economy moves from range 1 to range 3. Let's now shift our attention to what makes the aggregate supply curve shift: input prices, changes in productivity, and government and environmental changes.

Input Prices

Input prices are the costs that producers pay for resources. When producers have to pay a higher resource cost, aggregate supply shifts to the left. Lower resource costs allow producers to make more of their product, thereby shifting the aggregate supply curve to the right. The availability and efficiency of resources plays a key role in a firm's production. How a firm uses the factors of production dictates aggregate supply:

- **Land:** Raw materials (such as oil and wood) are subject to availability for firms, meaning that the materials must be available for purchase or in some way accessible. Land resources have the possibility of expanding if new deposits are discovered or if technology helps us use less of what we already have.

- **Labor:** The wages workers earn also play a key role in how much a firm produces. Changes in labor costs may change the aggregate supply curve. Depending on labor availability and skill level, firms may have to endure higher costs for labor, thereby increasing their production cost, which affects aggregate supply.

- **Capital:** If the amount of capital (anything that is used to create another good or service) increases in an economy, chances are aggregate supply will shift to the right. Machines and education (human and physical capital) are two typical forms of capital. For example, if the level of education in the economy increases, productivity increases.

- **Entrepreneurial ability:** Government incentives, market profits, and the amount of information about industries can all motivate entrepreneurs to launch businesses. When entrepreneurs enter the market, they are increasing the aggregate supply curve while creating competition and efficiency.

Changes in Productivity

Productivity is the relationship between a nation's resources and its output. An increase in productivity allows a country to obtain more output from its resources. If a coal mine boosts productivity by increasing the number of hours worked per week, the coal mine is contributing to an aggregate increase in output. Productivity is different than efficiency; **efficiency** is using productivity to allocate resources to meet demand. We will discuss efficiency in more detail later.

Government and Environmental Changes

Governments can influence aggregate supply by altering taxing or subsidy policies. A government may choose to increase or decrease taxes, thereby limiting or increasing a firm's output. The government may also choose to give industries a subsidy (a payment or tax break) and thus increase aggregate supply. For example, the government may choose to subsidize firms that use electricity as opposed to gasoline because electricity burns cleaner and is better for the environment. Further regulation means less output for firms because it is costly for them to comply with government requirements.

Changes in the environment also affect aggregate supply. For instance, natural disasters and unusual seasonal conditions can contribute to changes in aggregate supply. If an orange grower experiences an unusually cold winter, its supply of oranges will fall. If this happens to enough orange growers nationwide, aggregate supply could be affected.

Figure 4-5 shows an increase and a decrease in aggregate supply. The price level is located on the vertical axis; output or GDP is located on the horizontal axis.

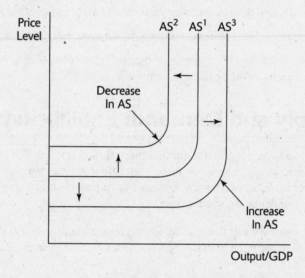

Figure 4-5

A change in one or more of the determinants of aggregate supply shifts the aggregate supply curve. In Figure 4-5, AS1 to AS2 represents a decrease in aggregate supply. AS1 to AS3 represents an increase in aggregate demand.

Review of Concepts

- AS curve has 3 ranges
- Alteration of production costs change aggregate supply
- An increase in aggregate supply is a shift to the right, while a decrease in aggregate supply is a shift to the left.

Mini-Review

1. Why does the aggregate demand curve slope downward?

    A. Production costs fall as GDP increases.
    B. As price level rises, so does aggregate demand.
    C. Real-balance, interest-rate, and foreign-purchases effects increase the amount of real GDP demanded.
    D. The Substitution effect provides alternatives
    E. None of the above.

2. The aggregate supply curve slopes upward as a result of which of the following?

    A. Increases in the price level lower demand.

    B. Decreases in the price level lower demand.

    C. Resource prices rise as real GDP expands toward and beyond full-employment.

    D. Inflation.

    E. Unemployment.

3. What effect can the government have on aggregate supply?

    A. It can change aggregate supply by making it illegal to sell certain products.

    B. It can change aggregate supply by increasing or decreasing subsidies.

    C. It has no effect on aggregate supply in a market economy.

    D. It can increase consumer spending.

    E. None of the above.

Mini-Review Answers

1. **C.** Real-balance, interest-rate, and foreign-purchases effects all have an impact on aggregate demand.

2. **C.** As demand for products rises, firms increase output until the economy has reached productive capacity.

3. **B.** The government can influence aggregate supply by increasing or decreasing subsidies. Subsidies can make production costs cheaper, thereby enabling firms to increase their supply.

Aggregate Supply and Demand: Equilibrium

When aggregate supply and demand come together, **equilibrium output** is formed. The aggregate demand curve can intersect the aggregate supply curve at any point in the three aggregate supply ranges. Depending on the point of intersection, the price level and output are influenced when aggregate supply and demand come together. Let's see what happens when aggregate supply and demand come together.

Figure 4-6 shows the aggregate demand curve intersecting the aggregate supply curve in range 1. The equilibrium formed here represents no change in the price level because resources are still underemployed.

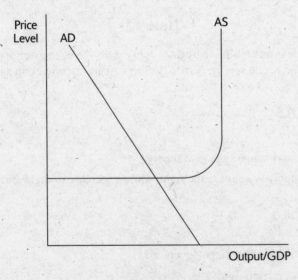

Figure 4-6

Figure 4-7 shows an increase in aggregate demand. This increase shifts the economy into range 2. In this range, we have a slight increase in the price level and growth. Full employment is reached and surpassed in this range. Equilibrium GDP is enhanced as a result of an increase in aggregate demand.

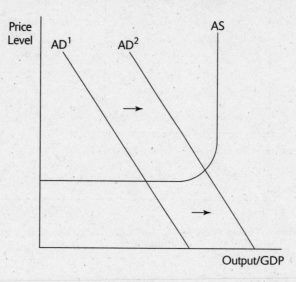

Figure 4-7

Figure 4-8 illustrates what happens to an economy that can no longer employ any additional resources. Aggregate demand has increased but the economy can no longer sustain growth. Firms begin raising their prices in an effort to contain demand.

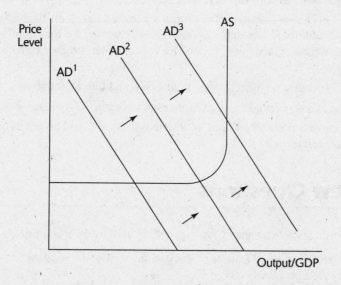

Figure 4-8

Figure 4-9 shows what happens to the economy when both aggregate supply and aggregate demand shift to the right. The initial shift to the right by the aggregate demand curve prompts the economy to move into stage 3. Initially, the economy cannot sustain this growth, so the price level rises. However, with an increase in aggregate supply, the economy has increased its productive capacity. This effect has stabilized the price level and allows firms to employ more resources.

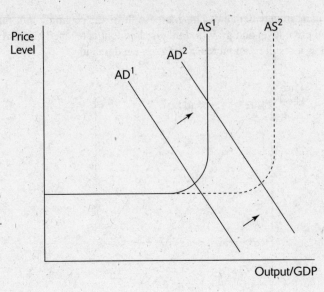

Figure 4-9

Review of Key Points

- Aggregate demand is the quantity of all goods and services in an economy that consumers are willing to purchase at various price levels.

- The aggregate demand curve is sloped because of the real-balance, interest-rate, and the foreign-purchases effect. Any change in these determinants will shift aggregate demand.

- Consumption increases as incomes increase. The propensity to consume is the likelihood that one will purchase more. The percentage of additional disposable income that will be used for consumption is called the marginal propensity to consume. Whatever income is not used for consumption is then used for savings (the marginal propensity to save).

- A firms' investment is dependent on interest rates, availability, and future profitability.

- Changes in imports and exports depend on relative prices of goods in the foreign sector.

- The aggregate supply curve is positively sloped. It describes the quantity of all goods in the economy that suppliers are willing to sell at each price level.

Chapter Review Questions

1. Which one of the following is an example of "investment" as used by an economist?

   A. A schoolteacher purchases 10,000 shares of stock in an automobile company.
   B. Newlyweds purchase a previously owned home.
   C. One large automobile firm purchases another large automobile firm.
   D. A firm purchases $10,000 worth of government securities.
   E. An apparel company purchases 15 new sewing machines.

2. Which one of the following will cause the aggregate demand curve to shift to the right?

   A. Expectations of surpluses of goods in the future
   B. An increase in income taxes
   C. An increase in government spending
   D. An increase in foreign income
   E. Unemployment

3. Technological improvements cause the aggregate supply curve to:

    A. Shift left

    B. Remain the same

    C. Shift right

    D. Become smaller

    E. None of the above

4. If consumer confidence is running high, what effect will this have on aggregate demand?

    A. The aggregate demand curve will shift to the right.

    B. There will be movement along the aggregate demand curve.

    C. Consumer confidence has nothing to do with demand.

    D. The aggregate demand curve will shift to the left.

    E. A decrease in the amount of inflation results.

5. What happens when the economy is in range 1?

    A. Unemployment is low; spending is high.

    B. Spending is low; unemployment is high.

    C. There is not enough aggregate supply.

    D. All resources are being employed.

    E. The economy is at full capacity.

6. What best describes full employment?

    A. Everyone in the economy has a job.

    B. The aggregate demand curve moves into range 3.

    C. There is only 4- to 5-percent unemployment.

    D. The aggregate supply curve decreases.

    E. No effect appears on the aggregate supply and aggregate demand curves.

7. What term describes when aggregate supply and aggregate demand come together?

    A. Full employment

    B. Inflation

    C. Equilibrium GDP

    D. Equilibrium government spending

    E. None of the above

8. Which one of the following is a reason that the aggregate demand curve is downward sloping?

    A. The substitution effect

    B. The income effect

    C. The price level

    D. The consumer-expectations effect

    E. None of the above

9. What happens to aggregate expenditures when investment rises?

    A. Real income falls.

    B. Real income does not change.

    C. Aggregate demand decreases.

    D. Real income rises.

    E. Aggregate supply increases.

10. What role does the government play in aggregate demand?

    A. The government has no role in aggregate demand.

    B. The government buys and sells stock.

    C. The government can increase or decrease spending, thereby affecting aggregate demand.

    D. The government can only influence aggregate supply.

    E. The government can manipulate inflation rates.

11. If the aggregate demand curve were in range 2 and total spending decreased, what would happen to the economy?

    A. Inflation would become a problem.

    B. Unemployment would rise.

    C. The economy would be at productive capacity.

    D. The economy would be experiencing lower levels of unemployment.

    E. The economy would shift into range 3.

12. Which one of the following would cause aggregate demand to shift?

    A. Substitution

    B. Complementary-good prices

    C. An increase in resources

    D. An increase in technology

    E. A change in consumer spending

13. How do subsidies affect aggregate supply?

    A. They can make it cheaper for firms to produce their products, thereby allowing them to increase supply.

    B. They can increase taxes.

    C. They can help decrease taxes.

    D. They allow firms to pay the government excess revenue.

    E. None of the above.

14. What type of employment is present in range 1?

    A. High employment

    B. Low employment

    C. Full employment

    D. Cyclical employment

    E. Range 1 has no impact on employment

15. Which one of the following is a determinant of aggregate supply?

    A. Input costs

    B. Consumer expectations

    C. Prices

    D. Substitute goods

    E. Tastes or preferences

Answers to Review Questions

  1. E. Remember that "investment" involves the purchase of capital for firms. When firms purchase capital, sewing machines in our example, they do so with the hopes of increasing efficiency.

  2. C. An increase in government spending is an increase in total spending. An increase in total spending will increase aggregate demand. A rise in the income tax rate will lower aggregate demand, and expectations of surpluses will lower aggregate demand now and increase it later.

3. C. An increase in technology lowers production costs for firms and allows firms to increase the production of their good or service. Aggregate supply increases because of an increase in technology.

4. A. Consumer confidence will lead to an increase in aggregate demand because buyers will demand more products. Increased demand shifts the aggregate demand curve to the right.

5. B. In range 1, total spending in the economy is low and unemployment is high. The economy is underemployed in its resources, and firms have idle machines and equipment.

6. C. Full employment is when all resources are employed. Realistically, full employment for our economy is when only 4–5 percent of the labor force is unemployed.

7. C. When aggregate supply and aggregate demand come together, it is called equilibrium GDP. Equilibrium GDP is when the economy's suppliers will provide goods and services at the same price level consumers in the economy will purchase.

8. E. The interest-rate effect, real-balance effect, and foreign-purchases effect are reasons the aggregate demand curve slopes downward.

9. D. When investment increases, real income increases. Real income is the total income (GDP) for the economy. As spending increases, income increases as well.

10. C. The government can increase aggregate demand by spending more. When the government increases spending, jobs are created and goods and services are demanded.

11. B. If the economy was performing at or near full employment in range 2 and total spending decreased, firms would experience less demand and would therefore have to decrease resources costs (employment). The economy would experience a decrease in aggregate demand, which would then translate into an increase in unemployment.

12. E. A change in consumer spending would cause aggregate demand to shift. Anytime spending decreases, the likelihood of aggregate demand being affected increases.

13. A. Subsidies allow firms to decrease their production costs. When production costs fall, firms can increase output, and this increases aggregate supply.

14. B. Low employment or high unemployment is present in range 1. Firms have idle machines and output in range 1. When resources are underemployed, so is labor, so unemployment is high in this range.

15. A. Input costs are a determinant of aggregate supply. Aggregate supply is influenced by firms' ability to create output. If creating output becomes expensive for firms, suppliers will cut back on production, thereby influencing aggregate supply.

Fiscal Policy

In the previous chapter, we examined concepts of aggregate supply and demand, consumption, and investment. We took a brief look at government expenditures and the influence they have on consumption as well as aggregate supply and demand. In this chapter, we examine more closely the role of the government in a market system, what it can and cannot do, and the incentives it provides for firms and households.

There are two basic types of fiscal policy: discretionary and nondiscretionary fiscal policies. **Discretionary** fiscal policy is "active" government involvement in the economy. Tax changes and changes in government spending are both considered discretionary fiscal policy. **Nondiscretionary** fiscal policy is when the government decides to take a "nonactive" role in the economy.

Classical Economics

Classical economics is based on the premise that supply creates its own demand. According to classicalists, the forces of supply and demand (self-interest) are the factors that aid the economy in times of market failures. French economist J. B. Say was a major force in creating this theory. Classicalists believe that the act of producing goods generates income equal to the value of the goods being produced. The production of any output automatically provides the income needed to buy that output. The only problem with this is that individuals do not spend all of their income on goods and services. Savings is one area Classicalists do not consider; prices and wages are sticky and do not quickly respond to short-run fluctuations.

Keynesian Economics

During the 1930s, British economist John Maynard Keynes developed a new theory on the role of government in a market system. He recommended active government involvement in times of economic turmoil. The Classical view that government should adopt a laissez faire attitude toward the economy was no longer working in the case of the Great Depression. The government could no longer afford to let the economy repair itself. Keynes developed the expenditures model, the multiplier, and the propensity to consume. Keynes' basic premise for governmental influence is that short-run instability is caused by a lack of spending. It is the government's responsibility to stimulate demand through spending.

Expansionary Fiscal Policy

As you'll recall, in chapter 3 we discussed the business cycle and its four phases. Each phase in the business cycle revealed the state of the economy. The federal government can implement what is called **expansionary fiscal policy,** decreasing taxes and or increasing government spending, during a period of contraction. The aim of expansionary fiscal policy is to stimulate the economy and steer it in the direction of growth.

Increased Government Spending

When the government increases its spending, it uses tax revenue to increase aggregate demand. If the government's budget is balanced at the outset of spending, an increase in spending creates a deficit (in this case, spending in excess of tax revenue). Figure 5-1 illustrates the effect of government spending on aggregate demand.

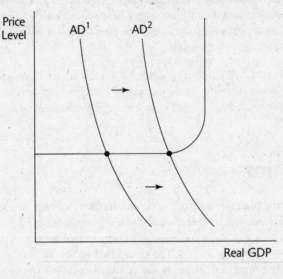

Figure 5-1

The government spends money on national defense, roads, education, and other parts of the economy. Transfer payments, or government payments to households (social security, welfare, Medicare, veterans payments, unemployment compensations), are not included in government purchases. Paying for expenditures becomes a daunting task in some cases for the government. Increased tax revenue and borrowing are two main ways the government can fill deficits.

When the government is operating on a deficit or deficit spending, it usually elects to borrow money from the loanable funds market. When the government borrows money, it is in fact increasing the demand for money in the economy. A byproduct of this increase in demand for money is higher interest rates. When the government has to borrow money, it "crowds out," or takes money away from, the private sector. This forces the private sector to compete for a lesser share of funds.

The other option the government has is taxation. Tax cuts are made when the economy is in a contraction, and tax increases are made when the economy is in a healthy state of expansion.

Contractionary Fiscal Policy

When demand-pull inflation occurs, the government implements **contractionary fiscal policy**, which means restrictive spending and/or increased taxes. These tools are used to offset the increasing demand in the economy. Sometimes too much demand is not good for the economy; it erodes purchasing power and creates a rise in the price level. The government attempts to strengthen purchasing power by limiting the ability of consumers to spend. Although this concept may sound confusing, when the government makes it more difficult for consumers to demand products, the price level and the value of the dollar stabilize.

Figure 5-2 illustrates what happens to aggregate demand when the government chooses to implement contractionary fiscal policy. Aggregate demand decreases and the price level is stabilized as a result of the government's restrictive spending and/or increased tax rate.

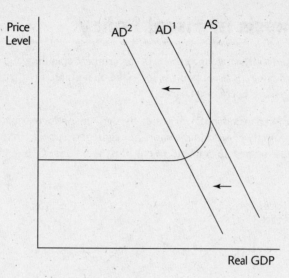

Figure 5-2

The Effects of Government Spending

The **spending multiplier** is used by the government to determine the impact of the government's dollar on the economy. If the government's goal is to reduce aggregate demand by $20 billion, then, depending on the marginal propensity to consume, the government may reduce its spending by only $5 billion. Let's assume that the economy's marginal propensity to consume (Chapter 3) is 0.75. That is, consumers spend 75 percent of any additional income they earn. To achieve a $20 billion decrease in aggregate demand, the government needs to decrease spending only by $5 billion. The basic idea behind the multiplier is to measure the impact on the economy that money spent by the government has. Figure 5-3 simplifies the economy's reaction to changes in government policies.

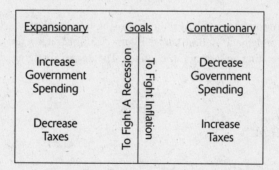

Figure 5-3

Built-In Stabilizers

Government tax revenues fluctuate automatically over the course of a business cycle to stabilize the economy. This type of taxation is considered nondiscretionary fiscal policy. A **built-in stabilizer** is anything that increases or reduces a government's budget deficit without requiring "action" by policymakers.

A Graphical Analysis of Fiscal Policy

For the AP exam, you will be asked to illustrate the effects of government spending and taxation. You will have to know what both expansionary and contractionary fiscal policies look like on a graph. First let's take a look at expansionary fiscal policy (increased spending and/or decreased taxes).

Figure 5-4 illustrates the effects of expansionary fiscal policy by showing an increase in aggregate demand designed to meet both the long-run aggregate supply curve and the short-run aggregate supply curve. Any increase of aggregate expenditures (C, I, G, X) will increase aggregate demand. In our illustration, real GDP and the price level both increase.

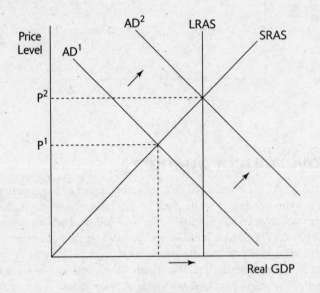

Figure 5-4

If the government implements a contractionary fiscal policy—raising taxes and/or restricting spending—its goal is to reduce aggregate demand to prevent demand-pull inflation. Figure 5-5 illustrates a decrease in aggregate demand as a result of decreased government spending and/or increased taxes. The aggregate demand curve shifts to the left; the price level and real GDP decrease.

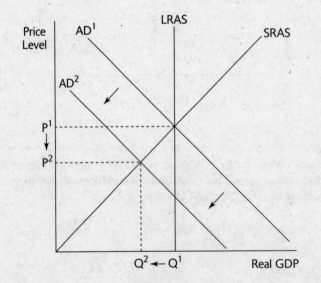

Figure 5-5

Contractionary fiscal policy is used to fight inflation. The government's goal is to contain the price level and reduce aggregate demand so that the economy does not lose its purchasing power.

Problems with Fiscal Policy

Although used to correct macroeconomic problems, fiscal policy may sometimes prove to do more harm to the economy than good. Two major issues are associated with fiscal policy: problems with timing and political bureaucracy. Three examples of timing issues are:

- **Realization lag:** This represents the time between the beginning of a macroeconomic problem and the time when the problem is discovered. This lag occurs because of the difficulty of predicting economic cycles. In reality, the economy may be into a recession or inflationary period for a few months before policymakers realize it.

- **Administrative lag:** This is the amount of lag time after policymakers realize the problem but before they elect to do anything about the problem. Administrative lags are usually bureaucratic tie-ups that have more to do with the political than the economic scene. In the past, the U.S. Congress took so much time to decide on a type of action that the economy reversed its situation by the time Congress came to a resolution.

- **Operation lag:** This type of lag occurs between the time policymakers have agreed on and implemented the action and the time it takes to actually affect the economy. Typically, government spending takes the longest to have an appreciable effect on the economy because of planning and creation of new capital.

Political bureaucracy is another factor influencing fiscal policy. Reelections and hidden agendas sometimes come into play when policymakers are deciding on actions for the economy. Policymakers are elected to do what is best for the economy and put political pressures and agendas on the backburner. Economists argue that this is difficult for politicians to do because they have to maintain an awareness of reelection.

Review Points

- The spending multiplier has a greater impact on the economy than a tax change.
- Government deficits occur during recessions because of expansionary fiscal policy.
- When the government increases spending, aggregate demand increases.
- Government finances spending through taxation and borrowing.
- Crowding out is a result of the government entering the loanable funds market. This increases the demand for money, which increases interest rates.
- Expansionary fiscal policy increases government spending and/or decreases taxes. It is financed by deficit spending.
- Contractionary fiscal policy is implemented to contain inflation. The government raises taxes and/or restricts spending to slow the economy down.
- Discretionary fiscal policy is when the government elects to take an "active" role in the economy. Discretionary fiscal policy involves changing spending and taxes.
- Nondiscretionary fiscal policy is when the government does not take an active role in influencing the economy. Automatic stabilizers (taxes) are relied on instead of policymaking.
- Fiscal policy is the government's policy on increasing/decreasing government spending and taxes.

Chapter Review Questions

1. According to Keynesians, which of the following would increase aggregate demand?

   A. An increase in investment
   B. An increase in the tax rate
   C. A decrease in unemployment benefits
   D. A decrease in government expenditures
   E. A decrease in government loans

2. If the economy is in a severe recession, which of the following measures is most appropriate?

    A. An increase in government spending
    B. A decrease in government spending
    C. An increase in personal income taxes
    D. A decrease in welfare payments
    E. A decrease in transfer payments

3. The long-run aggregate supply curve is likely to shift to the right when what occurs?

    A. An increase in the cost of productive resources
    B. An increase in productivity
    C. An increase in the federal budget deficit
    D. A decrease in the money supply
    E. A decrease in the labor force

4. Which of the following is a basic premise for Classical economists?

    A. Saving is greater than investment.
    B. The economy is self-correcting to full employment.
    C. The economy may be at equilibrium below full-employment.
    D. Inflation is not a serious economic problem.
    E. The prices of products tend to be too high.

5. Which of the following will most likely result from a decrease in government spending?

    A. An increase in output
    B. An increase in the price level
    C. An increase in employment
    D. A decrease in aggregate supply
    E. A decrease in aggregate demand

6. If a large increase in total spending has no effect on GDP, it must be true that:

    A. Only the price level is rising.
    B. The economy is experiencing high unemployment.
    C. The spending multiplier is equal to 1.
    D. The economy is in short-run equilibrium.
    E. Aggregate supply has increased.

7. Which of the following would increase the value of the multiplier?

    A. An increase in the government's expenditures
    B. An increase in exports
    C. A decrease in government employment benefits
    D. A decrease in the marginal propensity to consume
    E. A decrease in the marginal propensity to save

8. Which of the following policies is most likely to encourage long-run economic growth in a country?

    A. A restriction on high-technology products
    B. A decline in the number of immigrants to the country
    C. A decrease in government transfer payments
    D. An increase in the savings rate
    E. An increase in defense spending

9. Which is an example of discretionary fiscal policy?

    A. The government increases the stabilizers.
    B. The government decreases the stabilizers.
    C. The government increases taxes.
    D. The government does nothing.
    E. None of the above.

10. For deficit spending to occur, which of the following must be true?

    A. Government taxes exceed spending.
    B. Government spending is less than taxes.
    C. Government spending is more than tax revenue.
    D. Government spending is equal to tax revenue.
    E. None of the above.

11. Generally, the government finances a budget deficit by:

    A. Reducing the national debt
    B. Printing more money
    C. Issuing common stock
    D. Selling bonds
    E. Borrowing money

12. Which best describes fiscal policy?

    A. The buying and selling of stock
    B. The adjustment of stabilizers
    C. Government spending coupled with taxation changes
    D. Government noninvolvement
    E. All of the above

13. When a recession occurs, which of the following is appropriate fiscal policy?

    A. Increased taxes
    B. Decreased spending
    C. Decreased taxes
    D. Both A and B
    E. None of the above

14. When inflation is too high, which of the following is appropriate fiscal policy:

    A. Decreased unemployment
    B. Increased spending
    C. Increased price level
    D. Increased taxes
    E. Decreased taxes

15. An increase in the price level will result in:

    A. Increased employment
    B. Decreased employment
    C. Increased demand
    D. Increased taxes
    E. None of the above

Free Response Section

1. The economy is underachieving at an unemployment level of 9 percent and the government has a balanced budget.

a. Draw a correctly labeled aggregate supply and aggregate demand graph to illustrate how government spending will affect the following:

   i. Price level

   ii. Aggregate demand

   iii. Real output

b. Draw a correctly labeled aggregate supply and aggregate demand graph to illustrate and explain how a decrease in business taxes will influence each of the following:

   i. Aggregate supply

   ii. Price level

Answers to Review Questions

1. **A.** An increase in investment according to the Keynesian model will increase aggregate demand. Keynesians believe that spending increases demand and that demand creates supply.

2. **A.** An increase in government spending increases aggregate demand and pulls an economy out of a recession (in theory).

3. **B.** An increase in productivity shifts the long-run aggregate supply curve to the right because firms are increasing output.

4. **B.** A basic premise of Classical economics is that the economy is self-correcting. Classicalists believe that the natural forces of supply and demand will correct the economy in a time of macroeconomic disequilibrium.

5. **E.** A decrease in government spending will result in a decrease in aggregate demand. Government spending helps consumers increase purchasing power.

6. **A.** If a large increase in total spending has no effect on GDP, the economy must be in range 3, and only the price level is rising. The economy is at productive capacity and any increase in spending at this point would have no effect of GDP; rather, it would only increase the price level.

7. **E.** A decrease in the marginal propensity to save results in an increase in the marginal propensity to consume. When the marginal propensity to consume increases, the multiplier increases.

8. **E.** An increase in defense spending creates more jobs and increases purchasing power for consumers. This increase in purchasing power benefits the economy in the long run by providing employment and growth.

9. **C.** Discretionary fiscal policy means that the government has chosen to take an "active" role in policymaking for the economy. Raising taxes is an active role in policymaking.

10. **C.** Deficit spending is when the government is spending more money than it is taking in with tax revenue. When tax revenues do not cover government spending, the government has to deficit-spend.

11. **E.** Since the government can't really finance a budget deficit by increasing taxes, the government borrows money from the loanable funds market to finance an increase in spending.

12. **C.** Fiscal policy involves government spending and altering taxation to increase or decrease aggregate demand. Inflation and lack of growth are the two problems the government attempts to alter with fiscal policy.

13. **C.** To fight a recession, the government enacts expansionary fiscal policy, which means decreasing taxes and/or increasing government spending.

14. **D.** Increasing taxes would take away disposable income from consumers and decrease aggregate demand. Once aggregate demand falls, the price level is contained.

15. **A.** All things constant, an increase in the price level will allow firms to employ more workers and increase supply. Typically, an increase in productivity decreases unemployment.

Free Response Answers

A.

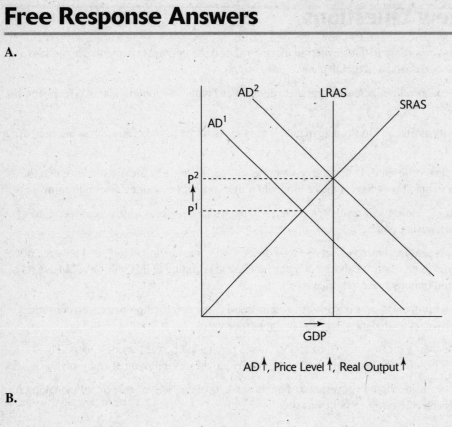

AD↑, Price Level↑, Real Output↑

B.

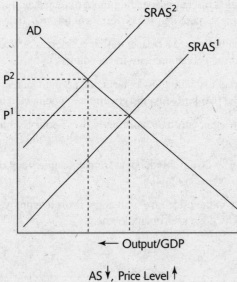

AS↓, Price Level↑

Monetary Policy

Once upon a time, settlers moved westward from the eastern United States. Before the move out West, the settlers had to choose which belongings to take and which to leave behind. Some converted their possessions into gold. This strategy not only allowed them to travel "light," it also ensured that they didn't advertise their belongings. Nevertheless, as the settlers headed West, they sometimes encountered individuals who were after the gold they were carrying. Over time, this became a problem for settlers because they were easy targets for robbery and theft. To prevent theft and minimize the likelihood of losing their fortune, settlers began leaving their gold with blacksmiths along the route. Blacksmiths would give the settlers a receipt for the gold and, for a nominal fee, guard the gold until the settlers had some use for it. When the settlers reached their destinations, instead of backtracking for their gold they would exchange their receipts for purchases. In time, the receipts acted as currency for the settlers because their gold was inaccessible. Meanwhile, the blacksmiths had all of this idle gold. They began making loans to other settlers for a mutually agreed-upon interest rate and time period. In this way, the blacksmiths and the settlers became pioneers of the U.S. banking system.

Money is anything that is generally acceptable to sellers in exchange for goods and services. You can use the cash you have on hand to go to a Dodgers game or to purchase a movie ticket. All you have to do is present your money to the cashier, who readily accepts it. If you wanted to use your Dodgers ticket to buy a movie ticket, the exchange would be a little more complicated. You would probably have to sell the ticket before you could use it to buy other goods and services. Because goods aren't generally acceptable means of paying for other goods and services, we don't consider them money. Money is the most liquid asset, an asset that can be easily exchanged for goods and services.

While the validity of the old saying "money is everything" is debatable, in this chapter money *is* everything. So far in this book we've reviewed concepts of supply and demand, unemployment, inflation, and government spending with an understanding that each one involves money. Money, in essence, is a medium of exchange. People use money to satisfy their needs and wants. Earlier in the book, we talked about choices and how everything revolves around choices. Now we shift our attention to what happens *after* you've made a choice. How will you pay for this choice, and does it have a monetary value? To establish order, routine, and value, societies have accepted money as a medium of exchange. In this chapter, we focus on how money travels, who controls it, and what role it plays in a market economy.

The Three Functions of Money

Some people might think that money's function is limited to one use (to buy things), however, money actually has three functions that make it a practical form of payment. These three functions allow money to be durable, exchangeable and valuable.

- **A medium of exchange:** Money is used as a medium of exchange because it is an efficient way to allocate resources. Economies have goods and services that need to be allocated to people. The best way to do this is to establish a currency because it establishes structure. If we didn't have currencies, people would likely be bartering (or stealing!) their way through life. Economics as we know it would take on a different role, one that involved a survival of the physical fittest.

- **A unit of account:** Money helps us understand relative values of goods and services. We can gauge how much a day of work is worth in terms of goods and services. The value of a diamond ring can be distinguished from the value of shoes. Money allows us to determine how valuable labor and wages are relative to goods and services.

- **A store of value:** We can exchange money for a good or service at any time without worrying about our money expiring. Our currency doesn't rot, wither, or melt away. It can be kept for long periods of time without a loss of exterior value. However, the value money holds in terms of what goods and services it can purchase varies as a result of the fluctuating forces of supply and demand.

You should be aware of two types of money for the AP exam:

- **Fiat money:** Money that is decreed by the government as an acceptable means of exchange for goods and services.
- **Commodity money:** Money that has intrinsic value (in other words, it's worth its weight in a precious metal). Gold, silver, and any other precious metal is considered commodity money.

The Money Supply

The quantity of money available for the public is a key determinant in many economic variables because changes in the money supply affect interest rates, inflation, consumption, and savings. Not all money is considered a part of the money supply. When economists measure the money supply, they measure **spendable** assets.

Distinguishing between spendable assets has become a problem for economists. To remedy this problem, economists have come up with several definitions of the money supply:

- M1 (the most liquid form of the money supply)
- All currency in the hands of the public (paper money and coins)
- All checkable deposits in commercial banks
- Travelers checks

M1 is the most common form of the money supply. Consumers can use M1 for direct transactions and instant exchange for goods and services.

M2 encompasses M1 along with the following types of money:

- Savings deposits
- Certificates of deposit ($100,000 or less)
- Money market mutual funds

While the components of M1 are the most liquid assets, M2 includes M1 and less liquid assets. In other words:

$$M2 = M1 + \text{saving deposits, CDs (\$100,000 or less), and money market mutual funds}$$

Finally, M3 consists of M1, M2, and large-time deposits (certificates of deposits) of over $100,000:

$$M3 = M2 + \text{large-time deposits}$$

Businesses usually own large-time deposits, which are used for future investments.

You may be wondering what backs the money supply. Long ago, the U.S. Federal Reserve backed the money supply with gold. Today, because of impracticalities (such as the size of the population and the amount of money in circulation), the U.S. money supply is no longer backed by gold. You may be surprised to learn that the only thing that backs the money supply is the federal government's promise to keep its value stable.

For the AP exam, it is important to remember that paper money issued by the Federal Reserve banks is debt belonging to the Federal Reserve. The paper money acts as a promissory note of the Fed to be exchanged for goods and services. **Checkable deposits** are the debt of commercial banks, which are responsible for upholding the value of checkable deposits.

Three factors give money its value:

- **Acceptability:** Money is money because people accept it as value. When you present money in exchange for a good or service, you can feel confident that it will be accepted.

- **Government:** The government has given currency value by granting its ability to be exchanged for goods and services. People feel confident exchanging currency for goods and services because the government has made it legal tender.

- **Scarcity:** The supply and demand of money dictates its value. The more money in the economy, the less value it holds. Purchasing power declines if there is too much money in the economy. On the other hand, the less money in the economy, the greater consumers' purchasing power becomes.

Mini-Review

1. Which of the following is not a function of money?

    A. Store of value
    B. Medium of exchange
    C. Interest rates
    D. Unit of account
    E. None of the above

2. Which one of the following is not a part of M1?

    A. Checkable deposits
    B. Coins
    C. Paper money
    D. Savings accounts
    E. Travelers checks

3. Which one of the following is an example of commodity money?

    A. Paper currency
    B. Coins
    C. Travelers checks
    D. Silver
    E. Checkable deposits

Mini-Review Answers

1. **C.** Interest rates are not an example of a function of money. Interest is the cost, or price, of money. The three functions of money are a unit of account, a medium of exchange, and a store of value.

2. **D.** Savings accounts are not a part of M1 because of their lack of liquidity relative to checkable deposits, paper currency, coins, and travelers checks.

3. **D.** Silver is a form of commodity money. Silver has intrinsic value; paper money and coins do not have the same intrinsic and extrinsic value.

The Federal Reserve and Member Banks

The United States' central bank is the Federal Reserve. The Federal Reserve is made up of the Board of Governors, who are the monetary policymakers in the United States. The Board of Governors consists of seven appointed individuals who are nominated by the president of the United States and approved by the U.S. Senate. Terms are 14 years and are staggered so that a new member will be appointed every 2 years. The president selects the chairperson and vice chairperson of the Board from among the members. The chairperson and vice chairperson serve four-year terms and can be reappointed to new four-year terms by the U.S. president.

The **Federal Open Market Committee (FOMC)** is made up of the seven members of the Board of Governors and five of the presidents of the Federal Reserve Banks. This committee is responsible for setting the nation's monetary policies to stabilize our economy. The FOMC sets the Fed's monetary policy by directing the sale and purchases of government securities in the open market.

The 12 District Banks

The 12 district banks collectively form the nation's central bank. The central bank was established to accommodate the economic and geographic diversity of the nation. The 12 banks are located all over the country, from New York to California. While the locations of these member banks are not important for the AP exam, their functions are.

The Functions of the Federal Reserve

The Federal Reserve is responsible for being the central monetary authority in the United States. With this responsibility the Federal Reserve performs its duties with the intention of creating macroeconomic harmony. Following are the responsibilities of the Federal Reserve:

- **Issuing currency:** The Federal Reserve does not print money. Rather, the Fed issues the money that is printed. It decides just how much of the printed money should be released into the economy. This includes paper money and coins.

- **Setting the reserve requirements:** The Fed sets the reserve requirement for banks in the nation. The *reserve requirement* is the fraction or percentage of a checking account balance that must be maintained in banks' reserves.

- **Lending money:** The Federal Reserve occasionally lends money to other banks and charges them an interest rate on this money called the **discount rate**. When banks' reserves are running low, the Fed lends them money to replenish their vaults.

- **Supervising banks:** The Fed examines other banks to make sure that they are adhering to the standards and regulations that the Fed has set for appropriate monetary policy. The Fed is ultimately responsible for developing a course of action for economic policies; therefore, it is in the Fed's best interest to see that banks carry out these policies.

- **Securities intermediary:** The Fed acts as the government's bank. The government's collection of taxes, spending of revenue, and the buying and selling of open market securities is done through the Federal Reserve.

- **Controlling the money supply:** The Federal Reserve controls the money supply. It regulates how much money is made available to the general public. The careful regulation of the money supply is a task the Fed is most associated with because of its economic impact.

Mini-Review

1. What is the FOMC?

   A. The committee that regulates taxation
   B. The government's revenue collectors
   C. The committee that sets monetary policies
   D. The committee that is made up of four banks
   E. Both A and B

2. The Board of Governors contains how many members?

   A. 5
   B. 6
   C. 4
   D. 7
   E. 9

3. Which one of the following is a function of the Federal Reserve?

   A. Printing money
   B. Collecting taxes
   C. Controlling the election process
   D. Electing the members of the board
   E. Examining banks

Mini-Review Answers

1. C.

2. D.

3. E.

The Demand for Money

Individuals want money for various reasons. While we can accept that everyone wants money, let's now examine, in a general sense, what people want money *for*. People need to pay bills, as well as purchase goods and services like movies, food, concerts—the list goes on and on. When people want money for these types of expenses, they have a **transaction demand for money**. A transaction demand for money is essentially wanting money to spend it. Spending money is not demanding it; it is exchanging money for a good or service.

The **precautionary demand for money** exists because of the potential of unexpected events. People never know when an unexpected expense will arise or when actual expenditures will exceed planned expenditures.

The **speculative demand for money** is the demand created by uncertainty of value of other assets. If an individual wants to buy stock but he believes that the value of the stock will fall in the near future, he will hold his money until the price falls. The speculative demand for money is the practice of holding money while waiting for a price to become more conducive to your liking.

The Money Creation Process

As you know, the Fed does not print currency; rather, it controls the money supply. We refer to this process as **money creation**. Using the fractional reserve banking system creates money. The Fed controls the money supply by regulating how much member banks can lend out and how much they are mandated to keep in their vaults. Member banks must keep a percentage of each deposit in their vaults to cover withdrawals customers may want to make. The money that is not kept in the vault is lent out to people in the form of home loans, car loans, or any other type of loan the bank may be offering. The ability to lend out excess reserves allows member banks to create revenue based on customer deposits by charging consumers interest on loans.

The amount of money created by an initial deposit is called the **money multiplier**. The formula for the money multiplier is:

$$\frac{1}{\text{Reserve Requirement}}$$

If our reserve requirement is 20 percent (0.20), then an initial deposit of $20,000 will lead to a total of $200,000 in money supply.

On the AP exam, you will be asked what portion of this scenario is an increase in the money supply. To answer this question, you must understand that the original deposit of $20,000 was already a part of the money supply, so when you calculate the money multiplier, you must subtract the $20,000 from the total amount to determine what part of the deposit was created by the banking system. In our example, $180,000 was created by the banking system, not $200,000, because you must subtract the amount that already existed when the deposit was made.

The power of the multiplier depends on two factors. First, when a bank holds onto excess reserves, it is not fully maximizing its ability to create new money. Second, for the multiplier to be fully effective, consumers must deposit all of the money borrowed into another account. If consumers do not elect to deposit all of the borrowed money into another account, there will be less money for banks to lend.

Tools of Monetary Policy

The following tools are used by the Federal Reserve to aid the economy in times of macroeconomic instability. It is important to remember that these tools do not fix problems; rather, they provide a blueprint for supply and demand to follow.

Reserve Requirement

The Fed requires banks to hold a fraction of their transaction deposits in their vaults. **Transaction deposits** are checking accounts and other deposits that can be used for consumption.

Discount Rate

When a bank needs more reserves (money to keep on hand or lend out), it typically borrows from other banks in what is called the **federal funds market**, so named because money is being lent from one bank's account with the Fed to another bank's account with the Fed. For example, if Bulldog National Bank has $1 million in excess reserves, it can lend money to another bank. When a bank borrows money in the federal funds market, it pays an interest rate called the **federal funds rate**.

There are times when banks borrow directly from the Federal Reserve. When they do, the Fed charges what is called the **discount rate**. The discount rate is changed periodically by the Fed to control the money supply. When the Fed raises the discount rate, it is trying to discourage other banks from borrowing money and thereby restricts the money supply. When the Fed lowers the discount rate, the expansion of the money supply is made easier for banks because the Fed is encouraging banks to borrow.

It is important to remember that the discount rate is relatively stable, and it remains this way for months at a time.

Open Market Operations

Open market operations are the buying and selling of U.S. government bonds. This tool is the most effective way in which the Federal Reserve controls the money supply. The FOMC is in charge of open market operations, and it can regulate the money supply through buying and selling government bonds. Suppose the FOMC wants to stimulate growth in the economy and increase bank reserves. The committee can elect to buy government bonds, which will increase the money supply. By buying bonds, the Fed is giving money to the economy in exchange for a bond. In actuality, the Fed is paying banks for bonds, and this increases the banks' reserves. With more reserves, banks can lend out more money to consumers.

If the Fed wants to decrease the money supply, it sells bonds. With this strategy, the Fed takes money away from banks in exchange for bonds. This reduces the amount of money that banks can loan out, thereby making it more difficult for consumers to obtain loans.

A simple way to remember the effects on the money supply this process has is to remember the following acronym:

> **B**uying
> **G**ives
> **S**elling
> **T**akes

When the Fed decides to buy, it gives money to banks (or the economy), and this expands the supply of money. When the Fed decides to sell, it takes money from banks (or the economy) and contracts the supply of money.

Mini-Review

1. Which one of the following is not a tool used by the Fed?

   A. Open market operations
   B. Discount rate
   C. Reserve requirements
   D. Taxes
   E. None of the above

2. Which tool does the Fed most commonly use to remedy economic instability?

   A. Reserve requirements
   B. Discount rate
   C. Open market operations
   D. Taxes
   E. Both the reserve requirement and the discount rate

3. If the Fed were trying to fight a recession, it would:

   A. Sell bonds
   B. Raise the reserve requirement
   C. Increase the discount rate
   D. Buy bonds
   E. Decrease taxes

Mini-Review Answers

1. **D.** Taxes is not a tool used by the Federal Reserve. The Fed does not hold the power to tax. Taxation is fiscal policy.
2. **C.** The Fed uses the buying and selling of securities as its most common tool for remedying instability. Reserve requirements and discount rate changes offer a less subtle effect on the economy, increasing the likelihood of adverse effects.
3. **D.** To fight a recession, the Fed buys bonds to increase the money supply. This is called "loose," or expansionary, monetary policy.

Monetary Policy in Action

It is the Federal Reserve's responsibility to monitor the fluctuations of the business cycle. With its "tools," the Fed can influence the business cycle in one way or another. During a contractionary period, the Fed may want to implement **expansionary monetary policy**. The main purpose of expansionary monetary policy is to increase the money supply and help the economy climb out of a contractionary period.

During an expansionary phase of the business cycle, the Fed may want to slow down growth to avoid inflation. To achieve this, the Fed can decrease the money supply (contractionary monetary policy) by raising the reserve requirement, raising the discount rate, or selling government bonds.

The Effects of Monetary Policy

The following tables illustrate the effects of monetary policy on various portions of the economy.

Discount Rate	Effect	Reason
Raise	Less money	Banks borrow less money because of higher interest.
Lower	More money	Banks have more money in reserves.

Reserve Requirement	Effect	Reason
Raise	Less money	Banks are required to keep more and lend less to borrowers.
Lower	More money	Banks keep less in vaults and lend more to borrowers.

Open Market Operations	Effect	Reason
Buying	More money	The Fed gives money to banks in exchange for bonds.
Selling	Less money	The Fed takes money from banks in exchange for bonds.

Monetary Perspectives

Macroeconomic theories have been formed to shed light on situations that deal with instability and imbalance. These theories range from supply-side remedies to demand-side remedies. For the AP exam, it is important for you to understand different macroeconomic perspectives.

Classical Theory

Classicalists believe that there is a true correlation between supply and prices. If there is a change in the money supply, this change will have a direct effect on aggregate demand. A change in aggregate demand in turn affects GDP and employment. If there is an increase in the money supply that is greater than the growth rate of the economy, the result will be an increase in the price level. Classicalists also believe that the economy is self-correcting, so if any unbalance exists in the price level, aggregate demand, or aggregate supply, the economy will eventually return to an equilibrium state.

Monetarist Theory

The monetarist view is a branch of the classical theory. Monetarists argue that the Fed inadvertently contributes to economic instability on occasion by changing interest rates. According to monetarists, the Fed should shift its focus from interest rates to focusing on balancing the money supply with the growth rate of GDP (the economy). This change in focus will lessen the likelihood of the Fed contributing to macroeconomic instability. Essentially, monetarists insist that the Fed mimics the money supply with the growth rate of real GDP.

Keynesian Theory

Keynesians believe that any change in the money supply will initially affect interest rates. Once interest rates have been affected, aggregate demand responds to the change in interest rates. Any change in monetary policy influences the money supply. This change in money supply directly affects interest rates, which then either encourages or discourages borrowers and consumers. Keynesians essentially believe that the Fed can use discretionary monetary policy to remedy economic problems through interest rates and aggregate demand.

Mini-Review

1. Which of the following is a main principle held by monetarists?

    A. Aggregate demand depends on government involvement.
    B. The Fed should use GDP as a guide to policymaking .
    C. The Fed should act independently of GDP.
    D. The government should be more involved in the economy.
    E. None of the above.

2. Which one of the following is true regarding Keynesians?

    A. Keynesians believe in no government involvement.
    B. The Fed must act in accordance to inflation rates.
    C. The government should be involved in the economy at all times.
    D. The Fed can treat economic problems through interest rates and aggregate demand.
    E. The government must control all interest rates.

3. Which one of the following is true regarding the classical theory?

    A. The economy is healthy only when the government contributes spending.
    B. The economy is self-correcting and all inequalities will find equalities in the long run.
    C. Aggregate supply is influenced by aggregate demand.
    D. It is the government's duty to control inflation.
    E. None of the above.

Mini-Review Answers

1. B. Monetarists believe that the Fed should use GDP as a gauge for policy decisions. Essentially, the Fed should mimic its actions after the progress of GDP.

2. D. The Fed can treat economic problems through interest rates and aggregate demand. When the Fed changes the money supply, this affects interest rates, which then influence aggregate demand. According to Keynesians, this is an affective way to affect aggregate demand.

3. B. Classicalists believe that the economy is self-correcting. The main premise behind this theory is that supply affects demand. When firms choose to produce more, consumers will buy more.

The Money Demand Function

If you understand why people hold money, then you can understand what changes the amount of money they hold. People hold money for two reasons: (1) to carry out transactions (**transactions demand**), (2) to be prepared for emergencies (**precautionary demand**), and (3) to speculate on purchases of various assets (*speculative demand*). The interest rate and income measured in current dollars (adjusted for inflation) influence how much money people hold in order to carry out these three activities.

The Interest Rate

An inverse relationship exists between interest rates and the quantity of money demanded. The interest rate becomes the **opportunity cost** of holding money. If you recall, opportunity cost is the next best alternative given up. If you have a thousand dollars hidden under your mattress, you are earning no interest on that money. You are relinquishing, or trading off, the interest for some other reason. The higher the interest rate, the higher your opportunity cost because you are choosing to give up more value added to your money. Typically, people react to higher interest rates by holding money (sometimes in mattresses!). Instead of physically holding money, individuals may decide to take advantage of the higher interest rates and put their money in various interest-earning accounts. To sum it all up, the higher the interest rate, the less money held. The lower the interest rate, the more money held.

Figure 6-1 illustrates the relationship between the demand for dollars and interest rates. Notice the downward slope of the demand curve? This slope is attributed to the inverse relationship between quantity demanded and interest rates.

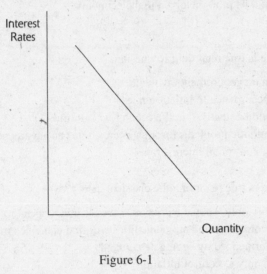

Figure 6-1

Nominal Income

The demand for money also depends on **nominal income**. Money demand varies directly with nominal income because as income increases, more transactions are carried out and more money is required for those transactions.

The greater the nominal income, the greater the demand for money. Whether it is an increase in the price level or an increase in real income, nominal income increases the demand for money. A rise in the price level or an increase in real income can generate a greater volume of dollars for transactions. People are using more money due to an increase in either the price level or real income. As real income increases, purchasing power increases as well. Individuals are buying and selling more goods and services. Aggregate supply and aggregate demand both increase because of a rise in real income.

The Money Supply Function

The Fed is responsible for promoting macroeconomic stability, which it accomplishes by controlling the money supply. It is important to realize that by controlling the money supply, the Fed changes interest rates. When the money supply is changed, interest rates follow. However, the Fed's decision to change the money supply is not the final determining factor of interest rates. The *combination* of the Fed's control of money and how consumers react to this change makes up equilibrium in the money market. To find the equilibrium interest rate, you must combine both the demand for money and the supply of money. Once you combine these two factors, you can determine at what interest rate borrowers are willing to borrow and at what point the Fed is controlling the supply of money.

At times, the interest rate can change without a change in money supply. If people attempt to increase their money holdings by converting assets into money, interest rates will rise. Conversely, if people decide to increase their assets by converting money into bonds or other non-monetary holdings, the interest rates will decrease.

Note that the Fed can only *assume* how the public will react to a change in the money supply. If consumers for some reason decide to react differently to a policy change, the Fed must then reexamine the situation and try to introduce a policy that will best remedy the problem. Ultimately, it is the consumers and borrowers who change interest rates. The Fed can provide incentives to motivate the public; they cannot ultimately control these variables.

Problems the Fed Encounters

Part of the responsibility of being the central monetary authority of the United States is creating aid for macroeconomic instability. From inflation to consumer expectations, the Federal Reserve deals with a variety of problems. The following sections describe how the Fed deals with them.

Demand-Pull Inflation

To remedy demand-pull inflation, the Fed calls for a policy that discourages aggregate demand. Policymakers can implement contractionary, or tight, monetary policy. The Fed can decrease the money supply and cause interest rates to rise, which in turn discourages investment and reduces aggregate demand. Once aggregate demand is reduced, GDP/output will stabilize, and so will the price level. Figure 6-2 depicts the economy's reaction to a tight monetary policy.

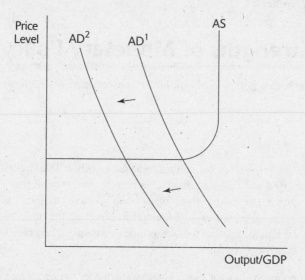

Figure 6-2

On the other hand, if policymakers decide to stimulate aggregate demand, they elect to increase the money supply, which in turn decreases interest rates. This then provides incentives for consumers to spend money. Figure 6-3 illustrates an economy after the Fed has implemented expansionary, or loose, monetary policy.

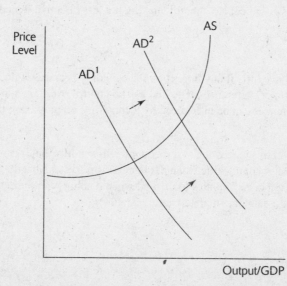

Figure 6-3

Stagflation

Stagflation is when the economy is experiencing negative growth in GDP with a simultaneous rise in the price level. Monetary policymakers fight stagflation with changes in rates, reserves, and the supply of money. It is necessary to have policies that influence aggregate demand or aggregate supply because it ensures a long-term healthy economy. To remedy stagflation, the Fed must increase aggregate supply through proper monetary policy. The result of an increase in aggregate supply is an increase in employment and a decrease in the price level. The effects of the Fed's policy toward stagflation are illustrated below.

To increase aggregate supply, the government needs to play an active role in policymaking. When the Fed implements a monetary policy that increases aggregate supply, the government needs to follow the Fed's lead by implementing a fiscal policy that will do the same. The government can increase aggregate supply by making it easier and cheaper for businesses to make their products. Tax cuts, government grants, and subsidies can all increase aggregate supply by decreasing production costs for businesses.

Problems and Strengths of Monetary Policy

Although it is tempting to see monetary policy as a solution for most economic situations, it has both its strengths and its weaknesses.

Strengths

Monetary policy is the primary stabilizing force for macroeconomic stability. The Federal Reserve is responsible for monitoring instabilities in a nonbiased and coherent manner. When the government introduces action for economic stability, it can sometimes be mixed up in the "bureaucratic black hole." Policies that the government introduces can be influenced by hidden agendas and political pressures. The Federal Reserve, on the other hand, can perform independently of the government. This allows the Fed to function without political pressures. Fed officials are relatively isolated from the lobbying that government officials may encounter.

The successful use of monetary policy speaks for itself when you consider the economic instability in the 1980s and 1990s. Tight monetary policy in the early 1980s reduced the inflation rate, whereas an easy money policy helped us climb out of the recession of the early 1990s.

Monetary policy is usually more flexible and less likely to get caught up in legislation. Policymakers can create a remedy for economic instability and almost immediately have it introduced to the economy. Fiscal policy, on the other hand, can get caught up in legislation and debate, thereby making it a less effective remedy.

Problems

Sometimes the actions of the Fed have little if any impact on the economy because of uncontrollable variables, such as the velocity of money and consumer preferences. The Fed has no control over how quickly consumers spend or save their money. Consumer preferences can be influenced by technology, employment, the price level, and many other variables.

Monetary policy may be highly effective in slowing macroeconomic instability, but it cannot be relied on to cure a recession. Recessions often have greater complexities than the Federal Reserve can handle. The old phrase "you can lead a horse to water but you can't make it drink" applies to the Fed when dealing with the economy. The Fed can point the economy in the right direction, but it cannot completely cure instability.

A Closer Look at Unemployment and Inflation

Low unemployment and low inflation are both goals of economic policymakers. Both monetary and fiscal policy officials seek these goals with the intention of stabilizing the economy. In the short run, there is a trade-off between the rate of inflation and unemployment. The **Phillips Curve** illustrates the relationship between unemployment and inflation. As fiscal policies are designed to eliminate unemployment, there comes a point where a decrease in unemployment will cause an increase in inflation.

A Short-Run Phillips Curve

In the short run, there is a trade-off between unemployment and inflation because an increase in spending increases output and stimulates employment. As the unemployment rate falls due to higher spending, the inflation rate rises. This trade-off between unemployment and inflation is temporary.

Figure 6-4 below is an example of a Phillips Curve in the short run.

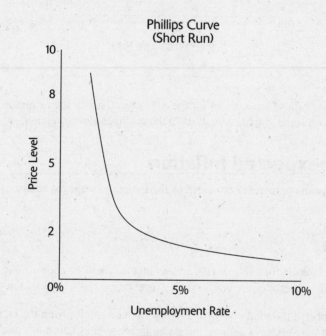

Figure 6-4

In the graph in Figure 6-4, we can move from an unemployment rate of 10 percent to 5 percent with little or no impact on the price level. However, when we move past 5 percent unemployment, you can see that the price level begins to rise significantly. In the short run, a trade-off exists between unemployment and inflation. In the long run, there is no trade-off because the economy is at full employment.

A Long-Run Phillips Curve

The long run produces no trade-off between unemployment and inflation because aggregate supply shifts to stabilize the price level. The shift in aggregate supply lowers real GDP. As income falls, the unemployment rate goes up. In the long run, as the economy adjusts to an increase in aggregate demand and expectations adjust to the new inflation rate, there is a period in which real GDP falls and the price level rises.

Over time, there is no relationship between the price level and the level of real GDP. The long-run Phillips Curve in Figure 6-5 shows that there is no relationship between real GDP and the price level.

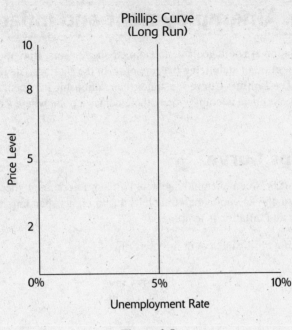

Figure 6-5

You will need to understand the Philips Curve model for the AP exam. Usually, the exam includes several questions related to the Phillips Curve, with some graphical analysis in the multiple-choice section.

Expected and Unexpected Inflation

Unexpected inflation affects the unemployment rate through three factors: wage expectations, inventory changes, and wage contracts.

Wage Expectations

Unemployed workers who are looking for a job specify a wage that they will be comfortable accepting as monetary compensation. Workers continue to search for work until they meet or exceed this particular wage.

The correlation between unexpected inflation and the unemployment rate stems from the fact that wage offers are unexpectedly high when inflation is unexpectedly high. A surprising increase in inflation means that prices are higher than anticipated, as are nominal income and wages. If aggregate demand increases unexpectedly, it has a positive influence on prices, output, employment, and wages. If a worker has a set wage in his mind that he is willing to work for, then any unexpected rise in wages will employ the worker. In essence, more unemployed workers find jobs, and they find those jobs quicker than they do in a period where inflation is expected. The unemployment rate falls during a period of unexpected inflation.

Suppose a teacher named Michelle decides that she must find a job that pays at least $100 a day. Michelle's minimum wage expectation is $100, and she expects prices and wages to be pretty stable while she is looking for a job (she expects no inflation). As Michelle is looking for a job, she finds that the ones she qualifies for are only offering her $90 a day. Because her offers are all paying less than her minimum wage, Michelle keeps looking for a job. Now let's say that aggregate demand increases unexpectedly. This translates into firms increasing production and raising prices. Firms now need to hire more workers to meet the demands of their customers. Now that firms need more workers, they must create incentives for workers to come work for them, so they raise wages. If wages increase 5 percent, now the jobs Michelle qualifies for are paying 5 percent more than they were. These wages now meet Michelle's minimum wage, and Michelle is no longer unemployed.

Inventory Fluctuations and Unemployment

Businesses hold inventories based on what they expect their sales to be. When aggregate demand becomes greater than what was expected, shortages are created and inventories fall below targeted levels. To compensate for this sudden increase in aggregate demand, firms increase production to restore inventory levels to optimum numbers. This increase in production leads to an increase in employment. The opposite can happen when inventories are higher than expected; firms lay off workers (thus reducing their labor force) or cut back on employment (hire fewer new workers) when inventories are too high.

Inventory, production, and employment are all key parts of the Phillips Curve. When firms form expectations on sales and inventory, they look at expected levels of aggregate demand. If aggregate demand is greater than expected, inventories fall, prices increase, and employment rises. If aggregate demand is less than expected, inventories rise, and prices and employment fall. With an unexpected rise in inflation, the unemployment rate falls as businesses hire more workers to increase output to offset falling inventories.

Mini-Review

1. Which one of the following is true regarding the Phillips Curve?

    A. It measures profits and revenue.
    B. It can only be used with nominal GDP.
    C. The relationship between taxes and inflation is measured by this curve.
    D. It measures the relationship between price level and unemployment.
    E. Economists really have no use for it.

2. Which statement best describes the short-run relationship between unemployment and the price level?

    A. Unemployment and the price level are positively related.
    B. Unemployment and the price level are inversely related.
    C. There is no relationship.
    D. The relationship depends on the level of GDP.
    E. None of the above.

3. What is the main difference between the long-run Phillips Curve and the short-run Phillips Curve?

    A. In the long run, everything relates to inflation; in the short run, everything relates to unemployment.
    B. The short-run unemployment is influenced by inflation; in the long run, inflation does not affect unemployment.
    C. The short run and the long run are the same.
    D. There is no short-run Phillips Curve.
    E. In the short run, both curves affect inflation, and in the long run, both curves affect unemployment.

Mini-Review Answers

1. D. The Phillips Curve measures the relationship between unemployment and the price level.

2. B. Unemployment and inflation are inversely related in the short run.

3. B. In the short run, unemployment is affected by inflation; in the long run, inflation does not affect unemployment.

Chapter Review Questions

1. Which of the following are considered open-market activities?

   A. Raising taxes
   B. Increasing spending
   C. Increasing the reserve requirement
   D. Selling government bonds
   E. Decreasing interest rates

2. If policymakers wanted to fight a recession using monetary policy, which of the following would be appropriate?

   A. Decreasing taxes
   B. Increasing spending
   C. Increasing interest rates
   D. Lowering the discount rate
   E. Increasing transfer payments

3. Which of the following would be the most appropriate monetary policy to achieve equilibrium output?

   A. Increase the money supply.
   B. Increase the reserve requirements.
   C. Increase taxes.
   D. Increase the discount rate.
   E. Decrease inflation.

4. Which of the following would weaken the value of the multiplier?

   A. High interest rates
   B. High velocity of money
   C. People holding their money in the form of currency
   D. A low unemployment rate
   E. An increase in government spending

5. If the Fed wanted to fight a recession, which monetary policy tool would it employ first?

   A. Increasing interest rates
   B. Lowering interest rates
   C. Buying government bonds
   D. Selling government bonds
   E. Raising the discount rate

6. Which of the following explains the role of the Federal Reserve?

   A. To control interest rates
   B. To control the printing of money
   C. To control the demand for money
   D. To control the money creation process
   E. To work closely with the government to reduce deficits

7. When does the value of the spending multiplier decrease?

    A.   When taxes are reduced
    B.   When imports decline
    C.   When exports decline
    D.   When the marginal propensity to save increases
    E.   When government spending increases

8. When would the Fed implement a restrictive monetary policy?

    A.   During low inflation
    B.   During high unemployment
    C.   During high inflation
    D.   When aggregate demand is low
    E.   During a budget deficit

9. Which one of the following is a part of M1?

    A.   Gold
    B.   Silver
    C.   Savings accounts
    D.   Checkable deposits
    E.   Certificates of deposits

10. An increase in the money supply would lead to which of the following?

    A.   Lower interest rates
    B.   A recession
    C.   Higher government spending
    D.   Higher interest rates
    E.   An increased reserve requirement

Answers to Review Questions

1. D. Selling government bonds is an example of an open-market activity. Open-market operations are designed to control the money supply through the banking system. When the Fed decides to sell open-market securities, it is decreasing the money supply; when it buys securities, it is increasing the money supply.

2. D. Lowering the discount rate encourages banks to offer a more consumer-friendly interest rate on loans. When interest rates decrease, consumers increase their demand for money. The Fed hopes that the decrease in interest rates leads to an increase in consumption.

3. A. Increasing the money supply helps the economy achieve full employment by encouraging consumers to increase spending.

4. A. High interest rates would weaken the value of the spending multiplier because it would give consumers a negative incentive to spend money. When interest rates are high, consumers are discouraged from spending money, thereby reducing the value of the spending multiplier.

5. C. To fight a recession, the Fed would buy government bonds. The purchase of government bonds increases the money supply, lowers interest rates, and stimulates consumption.

6. D. The Fed's role is to control the money creation process. The money supply is an area that can help the economy pull out of a recession or slow down an increasing price level.

7. **D.** Whenever the propensity to save increases, the value of the spending multiplier decreases because as people are saving more, they are spending less. Saving and consumption are inversely related.

8. **C.** When the economy is experiencing a rising price level, the Fed is likely to implement a restrictive monetary policy to help slow down the rate at which the price level is rising. The Fed cannot directly influence the employment level.

9. **D.** Checkable deposits are a part of M1.

10. **A.** An increase in the money supply will lead to a decrease in interest rates. Banks will lower their rates to create incentives for consumers to borrow.

PART III

MICROECONOMICS

Elasticities

We are now going to shift our attention to taking a closer look at our economy. With macroeconomics, we reviewed concepts that affected our economy as a whole. Microeconomics enable us to examine revenue, costs, profits, and economic costs generated by individual business.

It is wise on the part of individuals and firms to evaluate both the costs and benefits of a decision. Individuals base their decisions on the availability of incentives that appeal to their self-interests. Firms also base their decisions on incentives, and one main incentive firms consider before making a decision is profit. The expected profit helps firms evaluate the costs and benefits of a decision. As you learned in Chapter 1, costs and benefits do not necessarily have to carry a price tag. There are both monetary and nonmonetary values to both costs and benefits. Opportunity cost and rational behavior play a large role in decision making and sorting through the monetary and nonmonetary costs. Rational behavior involves recognizing that people make decisions based on self-interest and what will make them the happiest. People compare the additional or marginal benefits or costs that each choice will bring them. It is the next glass of water, the next minute, the next day, or the next dollar that influences people's decisions.

People compare the marginal benefits and marginal costs of every decision. If marginal benefits outweigh the marginal cost of some choice, then people make that choice. If marginal benefits are less important than the marginal costs of a particular decision, then people do not make that choice. Individuals make the decision to trade and exchange. When people choose to trade or exchange, they do this only if they feel that they are going to benefit from it.

Microeconomics is the branch of economics that examines choices and interaction of individuals in which the unit of analysis is *one* person, *one* product, *one* firm, or *one* industry. This branch is concerned primarily with individual decision making. An example of a microeconomic choice is how individual beef farmers respond to higher beef prices in the market. Each farmer must decide whether to supply more or less or the same amount of beef to the market. Individual consumers must decide whether to buy more, less, or the same amount of beef.

In Part II, we examine choices made by individuals and the incentives that help them make choices. Individuals are motivated by incentives all the time. Incentives drive people into making decisions, whether it's going to the grocery store or deciding how much to charge for a shirt. Incentives are based on an individual's self-interest. One common incentive producers have is profit. Profit drives producers to compete, be efficient, and provide some good in a market economy. If Jerry opens a lemonade stand, he was probably motivated by the possibility of making a profit on his lemonade. Profit, however, is not to be confused with revenue. **Revenue** consists of all the monies generated as a result of a sale of a product. You determine profit by taking that revenue and subtracting the costs from it.

At this point in our discussion, you need to be familiar with two types of costs: implicit and explicit costs. **Explicit costs** are what you see on the surface when operating a business. Monetary values of labor, power, raw materials, and machines are all explicit costs. **Implicit costs** pertain to opportunity costs, trade-offs, and time. These are all things producers consider when making decisions for their business. Economists argue that all costs are not considered until the implicit costs are weighed. You may ask, "How do I determine the value of the implicit costs?" You do this by determining the value of the assets that are given up. If Jerry, our lemonade entrepreneur, chooses to sell lemonade on a cold winter day, what could he be giving up? It's likely that selling hot chocolate would have been a wiser decision on a cold day. Jerry's opportunity cost becomes the additional sales he lost by not selling hot chocolate. Jerry's explicit costs may include lemons, water, cups, and sugar. Depending on whether Jerry has anyone working for him, labor could be another cost. To determine a profit for accounting purposes, Jerry must take the price for a glass of lemonade, multiply it by the number of glasses sold, and then subtract from that number all the explicit costs. Here's the formula for figuring profit:

$$\text{Profit} = \text{Total Revenue} - \text{Cost}$$

Elasticity of Demand

Suppose you are in charge of setting the price for a single slice of pizza. Your business has not been doing very well as of late, and competing firms have been snatching up market power. You are left with very few options at this point;

however, you elect to lower your price for pizza to increase sales. The problem is that you don't know just how much you should lower it. Should you go from $1.50 to $1.25, or should you just make it an even $1.00? The answer depends on how consumers are responding to a price change. Economists have devised measures that reveal how much consumers alter their purchases in response to price changes. These measures are called **elasticities**.

The **price elasticity of demand** is a measure of the responsiveness by which consumers alter their quantity demanded due to a change in price. The more price elastic demand is, the more responsive consumers are to a price change. On the other hand, the less price elastic demand is, the less responsive consumers are to a price change. The price elasticity of demand is the percentage change in quantity demanded divided by the percentage change in price:

$$\text{Price elasticity} = \frac{\%\,\text{Quantity demanded}}{\%\,\text{Change in price}}$$

For instance, if the quantity demanded for pizza falls 3 percent, every time the price of pizza goes up 1 percent, then we know that the elasticity of demand is 3. Based on this answer, we can state that the demand for this pizza is elastic. When trying to determine this answer, we sometimes have to deal with negative numbers. Whenever you're faced with a negative number, you should drop the negative sign and take the absolute value of the number. Absolute values help us clear out some of the confusion when dealing with elasticities.

Demand can be elastic, unitary elastic, or inelastic. When the answer to the elasticity formula is greater than 1, a product is elastic in demand. This means that when the price of the good is increased, there will be a significant response in the quantity demanded for that product. When demand for a good is inelastic, the elasticity formula reveals an answer that is below 1. This means that a change in price will not have a significant impact on the quantity demanded for that product. When the formula reveals an answer of 1, it means that demand is unitary elastic; a change in price is equivalent to the change in quantity demanded.

Demand Curves and Elasticity

A perfectly elastic demand curve is illustrated by a horizontal line stretching from the price axis outward. This means that consumers will buy any quantity desired at one price. This is illustrated in Figure 7-1.

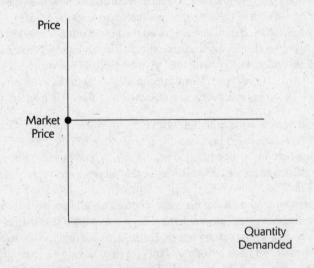

Figure 7-1

An example is the demand for wheat. A wheat farmer is only one producer who makes a product identical to that of his competition. Because he is just one among many and sells an identical product, the wheat farmer cannot charge anything but the market price for his product. If he sets his price too low, competitors will follow and revenue will be lost. If he chooses to increase his price, his customers will go to competitors. A perfectly elastic demand means that even the smallest change in price will have a significant impact on the quantity demanded.

In a perfectly inelastic demand curve, a vertical line illustrates that consumers are unwilling or unable to change quantity demanded regardless of the price. Prescription medication is a good example of this. Quantity demanded, over a certain price range, will not fluctuate because of a change in price. People on prescription medication are going to continue to purchase the amount needed because it is a necessity. Figure 7-2 shows that a perfectly inelastic demand curve is completely vertical, with one quantity at every price level.

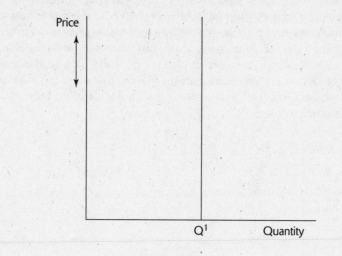

Figure 7-2

In between these two extremes of elasticity we have the demand curves for most products. As you know, the demand curve for most products is a downward sloping line that illustrates the relationship between prices and quantity demanded.

The price elasticity of demand varies along the demand curve, declining as we move downward. The reason for this is that elasticity is calculated using percentages. Along a straight-line demand curve, equal changes in price mean equal changes in quantity. However, these same changes in quantity and price do not translate into the same changes in percentages. A $1.00 change at the top of the demand curve is a significantly different percentage change from a $1.00 change at the bottom of the demand curve. Therefore, as we move down the demand curve from higher prices to lower prices, from lower quantities to higher quantities, a given price change becomes a larger percentage change in price. The opposite is true of quantity changes. As we move downward along the demand curve, the same change in quantity becomes a smaller percentage change.

The demand curve is divided into three regions of elasticities. The top portion is the elastic part of the good. All price changes will have a significant impact on quantity demanded. The middle portion of the demand curve is the unitary elastic point. This is where price and quantity rival each other. From the unitary point to the base of the demand curve, we have the inelastic region. Here, any price changes will have little or no impact on the quantity demanded.

Applying Price Elasticity of Demand

Price elasticity of demand is an extremely useful tool. It informs firms just how much they can increase their prices without affecting their total revenue or quantity demanded. Questions like what price to charge, whether to advertise, whether to charge different prices at different times of the day, all can be answered by looking at the price elasticity of demand.

Any firm concerned with increasing revenue must know what the current price elasticity of demand is for its product. A close relationship exists between total revenue and elasticity. Total revenue is the price of the product times the number of times it is sold. This is not to be confused with profit because profit is revenue minus costs. If the price rises by 10 percent and quantity falls by more than 10 percent, then total revenue declines as a result of a price increase. If price rises by 10 percent and quantity falls by less than 10 percent, then total revenue increases as a result of a price increase. Total revenue increases as a result of a price increase if the product is inelastic. Total revenue decreases as prices increase when the product is elastic in demand.

Whenever the price elasticity of demand for a product is in the elastic region, the firm must lower the price to increase total revenue. Think about it: if people are sensitive to your prices changing, are you going to raise your prices to gain more money? The answer is no because not enough people will buy your product to increase your revenue. The price of your product is too sensitive to a change in quantity demanded. For instance, if Marty's marbles were found to be elastic at 2.4 percent because he increased his prices by 1 percent, we can say that every time Marty raises his price by 1 percent his quantity demanded will decline by 2.4 percent.

We know that as long as demand is elastic, a firm must lower its price to increase total revenue, but by how much does the firm lower its price? Well, we can find the answer on the demand curve. As the firm lowers its price, it leaves the elastic region of the demand curve and enters the unitary elastic region. At this point, any further decreases in price will lead to an inelastic result and revenue will fall. Firms must realize that when they are in the elastic range of the demand curve, they must lower prices; when they are in the inelastic range of the demand curve, they can raise prices. Figure 7-3 illustrates the relationship between total revenue and demand. The demand curve has a downward slope where the three regions of elasticity are illustrated. The total revenue curve has a point called the maximum point. This is the area where firms' revenues decline if surpassed.

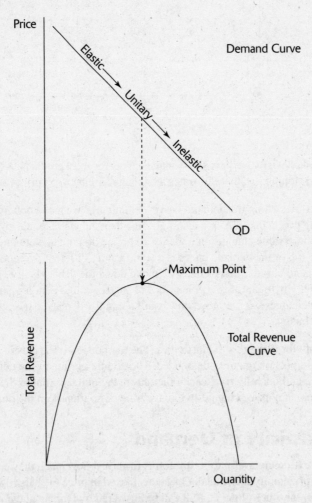

Figure 7-3

Determinants of Price Elasticity of Demand

Different groups of consumers have different price elasticities for the same product. The degree to which the price elasticity of demand is inelastic or elastic depends on these factors:

- The existence of substitutes
- The importance of the product relative to a consumer's budget
- The time period

The Existence of Substitutes

If consumers can substitute easily, switching from one product to another without losing any value or quality, the product will be elastic. Consumers will purchase a substitute rather than the original product because of the lower price.

For example, some movie theaters offer price discounts to teenagers. More substitutes may be available to teenagers than to other consumers, so movie theaters offer these discounts as an incentive to lure them to the movies.

In contrast, people who are on prescription medication have no substitutes. No substitutes means inelasticity. The fewer options there are, the higher the degree of price control and inelasticity for producers.

When few close substitutes for a product are available, the price elasticity of demand for that product is low. It is for this reason that firms attempt to create brand names and customer loyalties. A lower price elasticity of demand enables a firm to increase its prices without a decrease in sales.

Product Importance Relative to Budget

Consider the monetary values of a vacation in Europe and a new car. Any small percentage change will require a significant portion of income. As a result, a one-percent change in the price of the vacation or the car may delay the purchase of either one. Toilet paper, on the other hand, accounts for such a small portion of an income that a 1 percent change in its price will have no impact on consumption. Although the demand for the vacation or the car is a lot more elastic than the demand for toilet paper, consumption of anything is relative to the budget of the consumer.

The Time Period

The time allowed for a consumer to respond to a price change is crucial when determining elasticity. If we consider an hour or two, chances are the product will be closer to inelastic than elastic because of the lack of time consumers have to respond to a price change. If we are talking about a year or longer, then the demand for products will tend to be more elastic in comparison. Consumers for one reason or another may take a while to react to a price change. Additional time allows consumers to alter their behavior based on economic cycles, recent purchases, and even the ability of finding close substitutes. If you go to the mall and see a pair of shoes you really like but realize they may be out of your price range, chances are you will continue to search for the same shoe at a lower price or find a pair that are very similar.

Price Cross-Elasticity of Demand

Price cross-elasticity of demand measures the correlation between goods and their substitutes or complements. To derive the price cross-elasticity of demand, you take the percentage change in the quantity demanded for one good and divide it by the percentage change in the price of a related good:

$$\text{Price cross-elasticity} = \frac{\text{Percentage change in quantity for X}}{\text{Percentage change in Y}}$$

When price cross-elasticity is positive, the goods are deemed substitutes, and when the price cross-elasticity is negative, the goods are complements. If a one-percent increase in the price of cereal leads to a five-percent increase in quantity demanded of oatmeal, then oatmeal and cereal are substitutes. If a one-percent rise in the price of cereal leads to a 5 percent decrease in oatmeal, then the two goods are complements.

Knowing competitors' pricing and marketing strategies is crucial for a firm. Firms can estimate the impact of their price changes in relation to their substituted or complemented good. This allows firms to set more effective prices using a formula that can tell just how closely related the two goods are.

Income Elasticity of Demand

Income elasticity of demand measures the level of responsiveness consumers have to income changes. It is derived using this formula:

$$\text{Income elasticity of demand} = \frac{\text{Percentage change in quantity demanded for a good}}{\text{Percentage change in income}}$$

Goods whose income elasticity of demand is greater than zero are normal goods. Goods that have an income elasticity of less than zero (negative number) are inferior goods. In other words:

- **Normal goods:** As income increases, quantity demanded of this good also increases.
- **Inferior goods:** As income increases, quantity demanded of this good decreases.

Normal and inferior goods can be examined to see the effects of increases in income. When individuals increase consumption as a result of an increase in income, normal goods are often consumed. An example of a normal good would be a luxury car, a house, or even a gourmet meal. When individuals decrease their consumption of certain goods because of an income increase, they are decreasing quantity demanded for inferior goods. An example of an inferior good would be canned soup or generic brand sneakers.

The income elasticity of demand provides useful information to a firm. If the firm knows the income elasticity of its product to be low, the firm may want to upgrade or improve its product to improve the level of income it commands.

Price Elasticity of Supply

Let's not forget that elasticity is a measure of *responsiveness* to price changes. The response of buyers to price changes is measured by the price elasticity of demand. The measure of responsiveness suppliers have to price changes is called the **price elasticity of supply**. Remember that the law of supply states that as prices rise, producers can increase their quantity supplied. The price elasticity of supply is usually a positive number because of the positive relationship between price and quantity supplied. Supply is elastic over a price range if the price elasticity of supply is greater than one percent over that price range. It is inelastic over a price range if the price elasticity of supply is less than one percent over that price range.

$$\text{Price elasticity of supply} = \frac{\text{Percentage change in quantity supplied}}{\text{Percentage change in price}}$$

There are certain goods for which the price elasticity of supply is zero; land surfaces, the ocean, new Elvis Presley songs. These are all goods that cannot be increased in supply no matter what the price. There are some goods for which the quantity supplied at the current price can be whatever anyone wants given sufficient time. Food is an example that, with advancements in technology, farmers have been able to make more of due to increases in prices.

Price elasticity can be illustrated in both the short run and the long run. Following are some examples that demonstrate the impact of price elasticity in different time frames:

- **The short run:** In the short run, everything is fixed; therefore, producers have a limited time to increase production. Even so, firms can still increase production by increasing labor force, land use, and efficiency. However, relative to the long run, supply has a less elastic effect.
- **The long run:** In the long run, firms have enough time to change quantities of all their resources and for new firms to begin producing the same product. Typically, the greater the time period allowed, the more likely firms will increase quantity supplied in response to a price change. Supply curves applicable to shorter periods of time tend to be more inelastic than curves that apply to longer periods of time. If firms have to change more of their production techniques to meet supply needs, they have a longer response time. Essentially, firms need time to switch resources such as raw material amounts, location of production, and the amount of labor. A restaurant can switch from making burritos to tacos in a relatively short period of time because of the similarities in resources. So, we can safely say that the restaurant has a large elasticity of supply. If the restaurant has to switch from burritos to donuts, it will take a longer period of time because of a lack of similarity in product.

Chapter Review Questions

1. Which one of the following is true regarding price elasticity of demand?

   A. It determines the relationship between price and taxes.
   B. It determines the relationship between supply and demand.
   C. It can be calculated by dividing price by supply.
   D. It is a relationship between price changes and the responsiveness of consumers to those changes.
   E. It determines the value of supply for firms.

2. If the price of a movie ticket increased by three percent and the quantity demanded decreased by one percent, we could say that:

   A. The tickets are elastic.
   B. The tickets are inelastic.
   C. The tickets are unitary elastic.
   D. The quantity demanded is not affected.
   E. None of the above.

3. Which one of the following is true regarding price elasticity of demand?

   A. It does not measure the relationship between complementary products.
   B. It measures the value of inflation.
   C. It does not measure the relationship between substitutes.
   D. It measures the relationship between price changes and quantity demanded.
   E. None of the above.

4. Which one of the following could typically be inelastic in demand?

   A. Automobiles
   B. Houses
   C. Vacations
   D. Prescription medication
   E. Gourmet meals

5. Which one of the following is true regarding price elasticity of supply?

   A. It measures the responsiveness demand has to supply.
   B. It measures the responsiveness supply has to inflation.
   C. It measures the responsiveness quantity demanded has to prices.
   D. It measures the responsiveness quantity supplied has to prices.
   E. It measures the responsiveness prices have to quantity demanded.

6. Which one of the following is a determinant of price elasticity of demand?

   A. Tastes and preferences of consumers
   B. The time period
   C. Technology
   D. Unemployment
   E. Inflation

7. What does price cross-elasticity of demand represent?

    A. The relationship of substitutes and complements
    B. The relationship between prices and quantity demanded
    C. The relationship between prices and quantity supplied
    D. The level of income an individual spends on goods and services
    E. The level of income an individual saves on goods and services

8. How many elasticity ranges are on a demand curve?

    A. 1
    B. 4
    C. 2
    D. 5
    E. 3

9. Which of the following is not a range of elasticity?

    A. Elastic
    B. Inelastic
    C. Unitary elastic
    D. Secondary elastic
    E. None of the above

10. What does a total revenue curve represent?

    A. The relationship between prices and quantity supplied
    B. The relationship between prices and units made
    C. The relationship between revenue and quantity sold
    D. An illustration of quantity demanded
    E. An illustration of quantity supplied

Answers to Review Questions

  1. D. Price elasticity of demand determines the responsiveness of consumers' demand to a price change.

  2. B. A one-percent change in quantity demanded because of a three-percent change in price does not yield an elastic demand. The answer to the equation (change in quantity demanded divided by the change in price) is .33 (inelastic).

  3. D. Price elasticity of demand measures the change in quantity demanded due to a price change.

  4. D. Prescription medication is typically an inelastic product. People need their medication; therefore, in a particular price range, quantity demanded will be inelastic.

  5. D. Price elasticity of supply measures the responsiveness quantity supplied has to a price change.

  6. B. The time period taken into account is a determinant of price elasticity of demand because time allows consumers to change and shift their behaviors, thereby creating a more accurate reaction to a change in price.

  7. A. Cross-elasticity of demand represents the relationship between substitutes and complements.

  8. E. There are three ranges of elasticities on the demand curve: unitary elastic, inelastic, and elastic.

  9. D. Secondary elastic is not a range of elasticity.

  10. C. Total revenue curves represent the relationship between revenue (prices) and quantity sold. Total revenue is equal to the number of products sold times the price.

Choices and Utility

Decisions are being made every day, every hour, every second. We look around us and see people making decisions: Should I go to college? Should I get married? Should I buy this car? The choices never end. We always have to make choices because of scarcity, and scarcity will always be with us. In this chapter, we take a close look at *how* we make choices. Some decisions seem to be based on feelings or come from personal experiences. Other decisions take a more calculated approach, a cut-and-dried evaluation of our choices. Some decisions are quick and impulsive, while others are based on time-consuming research. Think about what factors you look at when making a choice. For example, what made you want to take the AP exam in economics? What benefits and costs did you consider? Ultimately, how will your benefits exceed your costs in this decision? Were you influenced by your peers? Or were you more influenced by your parents?

Answers to all of these questions depend on your self-interest. The lessons you have experienced all play a role in your decision-making process. Although the details of decisions vary from person to person, everyone makes a decision in pretty much the same way. Individuals (rational-thinking individuals, that is) evaluate the costs and benefits of a choice. How will it affect them directly? Will they feel good about the decision? After this comparison of costs and benefits, people tend to react differently; some act on impulse whereas others take the time to figure out what suits them best.

Common sense says that as the price of a product rises, consumers will be discouraged from buying that product. On the other hand, people will buy more of a product if the price is lowered. To understand which factors influences consumers' decisions, we must take a closer look at what is called **utility**. Utility describes the satisfaction one gets from making a choice. If Erin has to choose between going to school or going to the beach, she must weigh the utility both choices give her. While on the surface the beach would give her plenty of satisfaction, would going to school ultimately give her more utility?

Consumers make choices that give them the greatest satisfaction, thereby maximizing their utility. Each individual's utility varies depending on the taste or preference of that person.

Diminishing Marginal Utility

Utility is also used to demonstrate the law of demand. To better understand this concept, let's look at an example. Suppose Doug has just come back from a long run. When Doug walks into the house, the first thing that pops to mind is that he is thirsty. So Doug walks over to the refrigerator and pours some cold water for himself. He quickly gulps down the first glass of water and thinks that another glass of water would be a great idea. So Doug drinks the second glass of water, thinks for a minute, and then decides to pour a third glass of water. Doug then slowly drinks half of the third glass of water and can't finish it. What has happened here is what occurs all over the world—diminishing marginal utility. Doug has suffered from a bad case of diminishing marginal utility. His first glass of water was by far the best glass. He was tired and thirsty, and his mind was set on getting water into his body. The first glass is always the best because of your need for it. The second glass of water dropped a little in utility. Doug didn't need the second glass of water as badly as the first; nevertheless, he drank it with some satisfaction. By the time Doug got to the third glass of water, his utility had dropped so low that he couldn't finish the whole glass. This was because he received most of his satisfaction from drinking the first two glasses.

Diminishing marginal utility describes the lessening of utility or satisfaction as each additional unit is consumed. Marginal utility is the change in total utility that occurs because one more unit of a good is consumed:

$$\text{Marginal utility} = \frac{\text{Change in total utility}}{\text{Change in quantity}}$$

According to the law of diminishing marginal utility, the more units consumed, the less satisfaction additional units provide.

Total Utility and Marginal Utility

Total utility is the total amount of satisfaction an individual derives from consuming a specific quantity. The total utility for Doug when he drank all that water was enough to satisfy his wants. The marginal utility in that scenario decreased with every unit consumed. The difference between the two is that total utility measures all of the units consumed and the overall satisfaction it gave that person. When eating food, we may consider total utility; however, subconsciously we may be thinking marginal utility. When marginal utility becomes negative, total utility begins to decline. This occurred when Doug began to drink his second glass of water. Not only did the second glass of water provide a diminishing marginal utility, it also caused total utility to decrease.

Mini-Review

1. What is marginal utility?

    A. The extra unit of production that results from added units of labor
    B. The relationship between quantity supplied and prices
    C. The concept that satisfaction rises as more goods are consumed
    D. A term that explains the extra satisfaction gained by consuming one more unit
    E. Both A and B

2. What is total utility?

    A. The difference between each unit consumed
    B. The overall satisfaction consumption gives
    C. The usefulness of a product
    D. The total number of labor hours worked to produce a product
    E. None of the above

3. What is utility?

    A. The usefulness of a product
    B. The satisfaction a product brings to an individual
    C. The time it takes to consume a product
    D. The durability of a product
    E. The price of a product

Mini-Review Answers

1. **D.** Marginal utility explains the extra satisfaction one derives from consuming an extra unit.

2. **B.** Total utility is the overall satisfaction consumption gives. It is not to be confused with the overall usefulness of a product.

3. **B.** Utility is the satisfaction the unit brings to an individual. Again, it is not to be confused with usefulness. A picture on the wall is not useful; however, it may bring plenty of satisfaction to someone.

Consumer Choices

Rational behavior, preferences, budget considerations, and prices all factor into the choices that consumers make. Let's take a closer look:

- **Rational behavior:** If the consumer is a rational person who considers costs and benefits before making certain choices, she will try to use her income to produce the greatest amount of satisfaction. Getting the best "bang for your buck" is the goal of all consumers. People do not want to feel cheated, and they want to get the most out of their choices.

- **Tastes and preferences:** Self-interest and what appeals to consumers create preferences. Each consumer has his or her own preferences when it comes to consumption. Some tastes and preferences can be swayed by marketing; however, individuals ultimately make their decisions based on what appeals to them. Marginal utility plays a large role in preferences because it allows consumers to gauge the satisfaction a product brings to them.

- **Budget considerations:** Consumers sometimes have fixed amounts of income that limit their ability to consume goods and services. This limitation makes people choose between products. Although budget limitations are less severe for millionaires than they are for an average household, individuals, no matter what the income, are limited by a budget.

- **Prices:** Setting prices creates an allocative method for goods and services in our economy. Prices force consumers to choose between products, creating substitutes and complements along the way. If a product is scarce, consumers will typically have to pay more to obtain it. The opposite is true for a product that consumers can find in abundance.

Utility Maximization

Consumers must decide what specific combination of goods will yield the greatest utility. To maximize utility, consumers must spend their money in such a way as to ensure that every dollar spent equals the same amount of marginal utility the product yields. In essence, the dollar you spend should equal the additional satisfaction each unit gives you. If the dollar is not equal to the value of marginal utility, then total utility declines.

The Demand Curve

As prices rise, the quantity demanded of a product declines. An inverse relationship between quantity demanded and price exists on the demand curve. This inverse relationship between price and quantity arises from diminishing marginal utility and consumer equilibrium.

Consumers allocate their income among goods and services to maximize utility. Consumers are in equilibrium when their total budgets are expended and the marginal utilities per dollar of expenditure on the last unit of each good are the same. A change in the price of a good will disturb consumers' equilibrium because it will cause the perceived values of the utility and price to change. Once prices change, consumers alter their quantity demanded, and this alters consumers' equilibrium.

Consumer Surplus

Consumers value each good differently at each price. The demand curve is proof of this because quantity demanded changes with each price change. For example, if Ernie buys five CDs for $10, he will get a CD for $2 a piece. If the price of CDs increased to $3 a piece, Ernie will more than likely lower his quantity demanded in CDs. At each point on Ernie's demand curve, his values of quantity change because of prices. The value that Ernie places on the first CD is the price he is willing and able to pay for it. **Consumer surplus** is the difference between what a consumer is willing and able to pay for a good or service and the market price for that good or service.

The overall theme for this chapter is costs and benefits. You must be able to distinguish between utility, marginal utility, and total utility. Remember that costs and benefits affect every decision and that rational behavior allows us to evaluate those costs and benefits. Consumer choice involves evaluating what appeals to self-interest and satisfaction. Producers are forced to appeal to various self-interests and that in turn creates variety and selection for products. When consumers choose products, they are taking into account the costs and benefits of choosing that product. Consumers should also weigh the value of total utility.

Chapter Review Questions

1. What is the difference between total utility and marginal utility?

    A. Total utility is the average of both variable and marginal utility

    B. Total utility describes the total satisfaction of a product while marginal utility describes the additional satisfaction gained from a product

    C. Marginal utility describes the total satisfaction while total utility describes the additional satisfaction gained from a product

    D. Marginal and total utility have the same meaning

    E. Total utility is not used when gauging overall satisfaction or use of a product

2. What is created by making a choice?

    A. Choices create costs and opportunity costs only

    B. Choices create costs and benefits

    C. Choices create monetary costs only

    D. Choices create monetary benefits only

    E. None of the above

3. What type of relationship exists between price and quantity demanded on a demand curve?

    A. Positive relationship

    B. No relationship

    C. Inverse relationship

    D. Variable relationship

    E. Fixed relationship

4. Which of the following is NOT a factor that helps consumers make choices

    A. External preferences

    B. Prices

    C. Tastes and preferences

    D. Rational behavior

    E. Consumers' budget

5. What impact will a surplus have on the quantity and price of goods?

    A. Quantity will rise and price will rise

    B. Quantity will fall and price will fall

    C. Quantity will rise and price will fall

    D. A surplus has no impact on quantity and price of a good

    E. Surpluses will cause quantity and prices to act independent of each other

Answers to Review Questions

1. B. Total utility is a term that accounts for overall use or satisfaction of a product. It measures the sum of all uses. Marginal utility only accounts for the additional satisfaction derived from consuming one more unit. While one measures the overall value (total utility), the other measures the values of added consumption (marginal utility).

2. B. Every choice creates a cost and a benefit. When making a decision, the benefit is the chosen solution while the cost becomes the forgone solution.

3. C. An inverse relationship exists between prices and quantity demanded. As prices rise, consumers reduce their quantity demanded. As prices fall, consumers increase their quantity demanded. Prices can act as both a positive and negative incentive to consumers.

4. A. An external preference is not a factor that helps consumers make choices.

5. C. Surpluses are a rise in the inventories of goods. When this occurs, quantity rises and prices fall. Prices act as an incentive for consumers.

Production Costs

In previous chapters, we've explored the behavior of consumers; let's now turn our attention to the behavior of producers. Variety and selection are factors that help businesses succeed in a market economy. Businesses offer a selection of goods to appeal to the various tastes and preferences of consumers. When producing goods, firms use a range of resources, such as labor, land, and capital. The price of these resources affects the price of the finished product. The monetary payments and opportunity costs firms experience comprise a firm's production costs. This chapter focuses on the production costs of a firm and how firms continually try to reduce their production costs to increase revenue. Our main goal in this chapter is to examine the way firms attempt to achieve economic efficiency.

A simple circular flow diagram (see Figure 9-1) shows how money flows from the household sector to the business sector in payment for goods and services. The flow of money to businesses represents that sector's total revenue. In turn, money flows from the business sector to households as payment for the use of their resources—land, labor, and capital. After the resources have been paid off, the owner of the firm receives or gets to retain what is called a **profit**. The profit ultimately depends on what the firm paid for its resources and how much the firm received in revenue. A firm's goal is to produce its units at the lowest possible cost without compromising the value or quality of its product. Doing so requires a firm to compare all combinations of inputs that can be used to produce output.

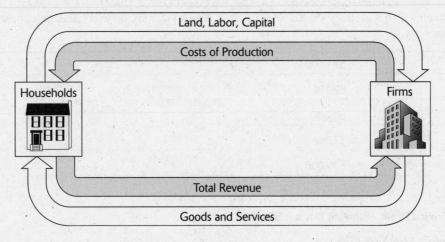

Figure 9-1

Diminishing Marginal Returns

The relationship between quantities of a variable resource and quantities of output is called the **law of diminishing marginal returns**. According to this law, when successive equal amounts of a variable resource are combined with a fixed amount of another resource, output will initially accelerate, then decelerate, and eventually decline.

Implicit and Explicit Costs

Explicit costs are monetary payments a firm makes for its costs. Labor, raw materials, rent, and power are all explicit costs. Firms make these payments for resources owned by another person or entity. Although explicit costs are used to determine a profit, they are not the *only* costs to be considered.

Implicit costs are trade-offs and opportunity costs that arise from a firm's decision to pay for its own resources. When firms have implicit costs, they forgo resources owned by other entities. The decision to use self-employed resources creates a trade-off. Implicit costs are anything external resources could have generated in monetary and nonmonetary value.

Consider this example: suppose you work for a shoe store and you are earning $20,000 a year in wages. After some time at the shoe store, you decide to become an entrepreneur and open your own shoe store. You invest about $30,000 in savings that had been earning you $1,000 in interest a year. Your new shoe store will be in a shopping center and will cost you $8,000 a year in rent. You also hire someone to help you with the work at the shoe store, and you pay that individual an annual salary of $15,000. You total up your accounting after a year in business, and here's what you find:

Total Sales Revenue	$150,000
Cost of Shoes	$40,000
Clerk's Salary	$15,000
Building Utilities	$6,000
Total Explicit Costs	**$66,000**
Explicit Cost Profit	**$84,000**

It would appear that your store is a success; however, you have not yet tabulated all the figures. You still haven't considered the implicit costs, which need to be factored in to determine the pure profit. By using your own capital, building space, and labor, you have created implicit costs. The implicit costs in this scenario are the $1,000 in interest you could have earned with your savings account, the $20,000 a year in wages you gave up to be an entrepreneur, and the $8,000 a year in rent you're paying:

Explicit Profit	$84,000
Forgone Wages	$20,000
Forgone Rent	$8,000
Forgone Interest	$1,000
Total Implicit Costs	$29,000
Pure Profit = Explicit Profit – Implicit Costs = $55,000	
Or Total Revenue – Economic Cost	

Economic Profit: Short Run and Long Run

The term **economic profit** is used by economists to illustrate the pure profit or the profit that has all (both implicit and explicit) the costs subtracted from it. Economists often gauge the value of a business venture by determining its total costs. To determine total cost, however, you must first consider revenue. To determine **revenue**, you figure the number of times your product is sold and multiply that number by the product's price. Once you figure the revenue, you can subtract your economic costs from it to derive your pure profit:

Revenue – economic costs = pure or economic profit

The demand for a firm's product can fluctuate from time to time due to market and economic activities. When demand changes, firms are left with no choice but to scramble and adjust to the changes in demand. The number of workers, raw materials, and other resources employed can be easily adjusted to meet the demand of consumers. Firms can adjust these resources in the short run to stabilize business. Other resources, such as building space and machinery, may take a longer time to adjust. The difference in these periods of adjustment makes it necessary for economists to distinguish between the long run and the short run.

The short run is considered a period of time too brief for firms to alter such resources as building space and machinery. However, the short run is long enough for firms to alter raw materials, labor, power, and output. Firms can determine the intensity in which they use their building space and machinery in the short run.

The long run is a period of time that allows for adjustments in all of a firm's resources. The long run can be enough time for a firm to leave an industry and for other firms to enter an industry. The long run is also known as the *variable* period. Nothing is fixed in the long run.

For example, if a company hires an extra 200 workers to increase production, this can be done in the short run. The company's decision to employ additional labor is based on increasing revenue. New labor can be implemented in a relatively short amount of time. If on the other hand the company decides to add more factory space and install more machines in that factory space, we have to look at the long run. Only in the long run can the company implement these resources and see an impact on its production.

It is important to remember the differences between the short run and the long run. They are not periods on a calendar that can be pegged for specific dates. Rather, these conceptual dates are used by firms to determine the relationship between levels of production and time. The long run can be experienced rather quickly by smaller firms relative to larger firms because it takes less time for them to increase capital. A fast food restaurant, for example, can increase its machinery overnight by simply adding another oven or cooker.

Short-Run Production

A firm's decision to alter production depends on the prices of the inputs needed to modify production. The supply and demand of resources determines the prices of resources. If your firm produces cars and there is a steel shortage, your decision to increase production may be put on hold. In this instance, you'll focus on labor resources rather than physical resources.

When examining a firm's output, you must consider three types of output:

- **Total product:** The total quantity of a good produced
- **Marginal product:** The added unit of a variable resource to the production process

  Marginal product = Change in total product / Change in labor input
- **Average Product:** The output per worker

  Average product = Total product / Units of labor

We know that the short run is a period where firms can change labor resources to alter production. Now let's take a closer look at how much a firm's output rises in the face of added labor.

When firms decide to add labor to increase productivity, they do so in a cautious way because more workers does not necessarily mean more output. **Diminishing marginal returns** describes the point when labor is added but yields a decline in marginal product. Essentially, when labor is added firms expect an increase in productivity. But this is not true all of the time. For a period of time, firms will notice increases in output. However, those increases in output will become less with each worker added until there are no increases in output and sometimes even negative growth. The point at which the firm discovers diminishing marginal returns, an adjustment has to be made. The firm can either cut back on labor units or expand capital. A lack of capital sometimes contributes to diminishing marginal returns.

Suppose a donut store has three workers working in limited, often confined kitchen space. To increase productivity, the store may want to employ more workers. For a period of time, the workers will help productivity. Over time with each new worker added, production will begin to increase at smaller intervals. Soon, the workers will start getting in one another's way, and this will result in negative growth for the store. The workers will have to wait in line to use the machinery, walkway spaces will become crammed with people and raw materials, and the store would turn into one giant mess. Consequently, the total product of the store will start diminishing; the marginal product of additional workers will decline because of the amount of labor relative to machinery. In time, if the store continues to hire more employees, the total product will go to zero due to the lack of store space. Figure 9-2 illustrates diminishing marginal returns on a grid.

Labor Units	Total Product	Marginal Product	Average Product
0	0		—
		10	
1	10		10
		10	
2	20		10
		15	
3	35		11.66
		15	
4	50		12.50
		10	
5	60		12.00
		5	
6	65		10.83
		0	
7	65		9.28
		-5	
8	60		7.50
		-8	
9	52		5.77

Figure 9-2

Figure 9-3 is a graphical representation of the data in the grid.

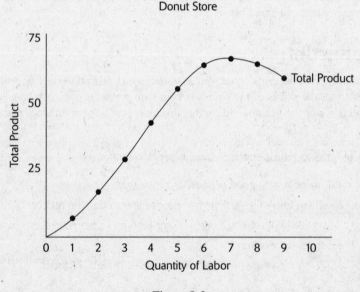

Figure 9-3

The Short-Run Costs of Production

We just examined the effects of diminishing marginal returns. Now let's look at the costs of these inputs. We know that in the short run some resources are fixed while others are variable. With this knowledge, we can safely conclude that short-run costs can be both fixed and variable depending on the resource. Let's focus on three types of costs:

- **Fixed costs:** Costs that do not vary with changes in output. An example of a fixed cost is the rent a firm has to pay for factory space. The rent does not fluctuate each time a firm increases or decreases its output. The rent is an independent cost of production. Costs that do not depend on output are fixed costs.

- **Variable costs:** Costs that change with the level of output. Variable costs are the opposite of fixed costs in that they fluctuate with the production levels. If output rises, then variable costs rise as well. When there is a decrease in output, typically there will be a decrease in variable costs. Variable costs include power, fuel, payments for materials, and most labor. Remember that variable costs do not rise or fall in the same increments as output levels. As production begins, variable costs increase by decreasing amounts, but as production continues, variable costs increase by increasing amounts.

- **Total costs:** The sum of variable costs and fixed costs. Firms must rely on calculating total costs because that calculation gives them a total accounting cost. It is a monetary figure that allows firms to see the combined effects of their variable and fixed costs. Remember that fixed costs are independent of output levels; therefore, firms have to pay them regardless of production levels. Variable costs, on the other hand, depend on the levels of output. Although variable costs may not rise or fall at the same rate of output, they do change depending on output levels. Total costs will always be present regardless of the level of production or output.

Figure 9-4 illustrates fixed costs, variable costs, total costs, average fixed costs, average variable costs, average total costs, and marginal cost.

Output	Fixed Costs	Variable Costs	Total Costs	Average Fixed Costs	Average Variable Costs	Average Total Costs	Marginal Cost
0	100	0	100	0	0	0	0
1	100	300	400	100	300	400	300
2	100	800	900	50	400	450	250
3	100	1400	1500	33.33	466.66	500	200
4	100	2100	2200	25	525	550	175
5	100	2300	2400	20	460	480	40

Figure 9-4

Average Costs

Firms are concerned with the average costs of their operations because they compare that figure with their per-product price. **Average fixed cost** is calculated by dividing total fixed cost by the quantity of output:

$$\text{Average fixed cost} = \text{Total fixed cost} / \text{output}$$

Total fixed cost is the same regardless of output, but average fixed cost declines as output increases. Average fixed costs decline as output increases because the quantity of output minimizes the monetary impact of fixed costs as it rises.

Average variable cost is calculated by dividing the total variable cost by quantity. As resources are added, average variable costs decline at first, then reach a low point, and then begin to increase. The average variable costs curve is U-shaped and reflects this pattern.

At low levels of output, production is inefficient and expensive. It takes more money for producers to yield a smaller amount of product than it does for them to make larger amounts. Take Costco, for example. Costco is a store that sells in bulk. Because Costco buys in bulk, it receives its products from manufacturers at a discounted price. Manufacturers have no problem selling Costco their products in bulk because they find it more cost efficient. This is how Costco is able to charge a relatively lower price for some of its products than other stores.

Average total cost is calculated by dividing total cost by quantity. You can find this cost by adding the average variable cost to the average fixed cost. Total cost invariably means the total sum of the fixed costs and the variable costs.

The **marginal-cost curve** includes the additional cost of producing one more unit. To derive the marginal cost, you must divide the change in total cost by the change in quantity:

$$\text{Marginal cost} = \text{Change in total cost} / \text{change in quantity}$$

When a firm decides to produce one more unit, marginal cost becomes a key factor in its decision. If Rich owns a hot dog stand, he will need to determine the value of making one more hot dog. Will the additional hot dog be worth making?

Marginal cost tells the producer just how much it is going to take to make one more unit of output. Figure 9-5 illustrates the curves we just mentioned. Notice the shapes of each curve.

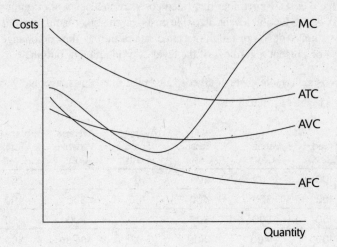

Figure 9-5

Mini-Review

1. Which one of the following best describes why the marginal cost decreases and then increases?

    A. Increasing, then decreasing marginal returns
    B. Increasing, then decreasing marginal utility
    C. Diminishing product of labor
    D. Constant marginal revenue
    E. None of the above

2. How are total costs calculated?

    A. By adding marginal costs and variable costs
    B. By adding marginal revenue to total revenue
    C. By adding fixed costs to variable costs
    D. By adding average fixed costs to total fixed costs
    E. By adding average marginal cost to total variable costs

3. What is the main difference between variable costs and fixed costs?

    A. Fixed costs are steady with output and variable costs are not.
    B. Variable costs are steady with output and fixed costs are not.
    C. Variable costs rise with output and so do fixed costs.
    D. Fixed costs follow what variable costs do; variable costs do not follow fixed costs.
    E. Fixed costs are usually more expensive than variable costs.

Mini-Review Answers

1. **A.** Increasing, then decreasing marginal returns define a firm's output returns.
2. **C.** Total costs are calculated by adding fixed costs to variable costs. When the two are added, firms can see what their total output costs will be.
3. **A.** Fixed costs are steady with output and variable costs are not. Variable costs fluctuate with different levels of output.

Marginal Cost and Marginal Product

Remember that the marginal cost curve indicates what occurs when more workers are hired. In the beginning, the added units of labor may decrease the cost of output; however, as more units of labor are added, the cost of output rises. When diminishing marginal returns set in, the cost of output begins to rise, and firms would be wise not to add units of labor. Marginal cost is the change in cost caused by a change in output.

Marginal Cost, Average Variable Cost, Average Total Cost

When the amount added of marginal cost to total cost is less than the current average total cost, the average total cost falls. The marginal cost that is less than the average total cost brings down the cost of output. On the other hand, when the marginal cost is more than the average total cost, the average total cost rises. As long as the marginal cost curve is below the average total cost, the average total cost will continue to fall, and whenever the marginal cost curve is above the average total cost curve, the average total cost will increase.

Cost Curve Changes

When a firm experiences changes in resource prices or technology costs, the firm's cost curves will shift. If the fixed costs increase, the average fixed cost curve and the average total cost curve shift upward. However, if the price of a variable cost (such as labor) increases, then the marginal cost curve, average variable cost curve, and average total cost curve will all shift upward.

Production Costs in the Long Run

In the long run, firms can adjust the resources they use to take advantage of more efficient means of production. Firms can change the amount of all inputs used, alter the building size, or change the machinery capabilities. Improvements in technology make production costs cheaper in the long run.

The Long-Run Cost Curve

As you've seen, short-run cost curves are U-shaped because of diminishing marginal productivity; long-run curves are also U-shaped but not because of fixed output. Long-run cost curves are U-shaped due to economies of scale. **Economies of scale** means that higher production translates into lower average production costs. The more firms choose to produce, the less costly production of units becomes. A firm's ability to decrease its inputs in order to adjust costs is what makes it cheaper for the firm to produce in the long run.

Constant returns to scale is the area where all inputs are increased by the same percentage to maintain the lowest possible per-unit cost. This area is located at the bottom of the long-run average total cost curve.

Diseconomies of scale means that an increase in production yields a higher average cost of production. It refers to the average cost-per-unit increases in the long run despite fixed inputs. Diseconomies of scale occur when firms become too large to operate efficiently. Decision-making problems, inefficient use of resources, and bureaucracy are all examples of factors that could lead to diseconomies of scale. The three long-run costs are depicted in Figure 9-6.

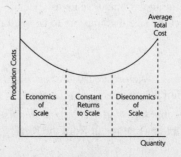

Figure 9-6

It is also important to realize that average total cost curves can take different shapes. In Figures 9-7 and 9-8, the average total cost curve is shown with different returns to scale. Notice the shape of the curve.

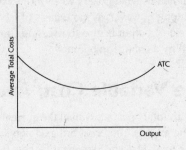

Figure 9-7

In Figure 9-7, the long-run average total cost curve has a longer period of economies to scale than diseconomies to scale. This curve would represent a firm that is lowering its costs rapidly as units are being increased.

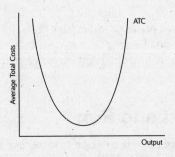

Figure 9-8

In Figure 9-8, the firm has a shorter period of economies of scale and steeper diseconomies of scale.

Reasons for Economies of Scale

It is important for a firm to specialize as it grows larger because specialization improves the firm's chances of realizing economies of scale. Economies of scale may also result from the use of larger machines that are more efficient than smaller ones. Larger machines can produce in mass quantity and sometimes use less power or fuel than a smaller machine while creating the same number of units. Large electrical power generators are more efficient than smaller ones because they provide more output per quantity of resource.

Size does not automatically improve efficiency. The specialization that comes with large size often requires the addition of specialized managers. Each level of supervision requires additional labor inputs, and before you know it, your costs are soaring. A firm can achieve economies of scale by increasing quantities of output while keeping costs at a minimum.

The long run is referred to as a planning horizon because the firm has not committed to a fixed quantity of any resources and has all options available to it. In determining the size or scale to select, the firm must look at expected demand and expected costs of production, and then select the size that appears to be most profitable.

Here are two key points to remember:

- The long-run average total cost curve is U-shaped because of economies and diseconomies of scale. Short-run cost curves get their U shape from diminishing marginal returns.
- Economies of scale can result from technology and specialization. Diseconomies of scale may occur because of coordination and communication problems that result from the firm's growth.

Mini-Review

1. Which of the following is true regarding marginal product?

    A. It is the measure of impact an added unit of input has on output.

    B. It is the measure of how outputs affect inputs.

    C. It lets producers know how much a product is going to cost.

    D. It describes the relationship between average total cost and marginal cost.

    E. None of the above.

2. Why are long-run cost curves U-shaped?

    A. Because they reveal an increasing cost followed by decreasing costs.

    B. Because they describe the impact of economies of scale.

    C. Because as resource prices increase, so does production.

    D. Because resource prices are too cheap.

    E. Both A and C.

3. Which of the following best describes average variable costs?

    A. Variable cost multiplied by quantity

    B. Variable costs multiplied by fixed costs

    C. Variable costs divided by quantity

    D. Variable costs divided by fixed costs

    E. Variable costs divided by marginal costs

Mini-Review Answers

1. A. Marginal product is the measure of impact an additional unit of input has on output.

2. B. Economies of scale explain why long-run cost curves are U-shaped. When the firm initially produces a large quantity, there are economies of scale. As the firm continues to increase its average total cost, there are no returns to scale.

3. C. To derive average variable costs, you must divide variable costs by quantity.

Revenue for Firms

Revenue is calculated by multiplying the price of a product by the number of units sold. Remember that revenue is not the same as profit. Earlier we discussed the differences between implicit and explicit costs. Revenue is simply the amount of monetary flow that is handled by a firm as compensation for its product. Marginal revenue, much like marginal cost, is the difference in revenue when producing one more unit. The marginal revenue should rise as more units are produced.

A firm's profit is determined by subtracting all costs (implicit and explicit) from revenue:

$$\text{Profit} = \text{total revenue} - \text{total cost}$$

Chapter Review Questions

1. Which of the following best describes average total cost?

   A. The relationship between marginal cost and fixed costs
   B. Fixed costs divided by quantity
   C. Variable costs divided by quantity
   D. Marginal product divided by quantity
   E. Average costs divided by fixed costs

2. As Diana eats donuts, which of the following statements regarding Diana's marginal utility is correct?

   A. Her marginal utility from the first donut is greater than her marginal utility from the second donut.
   B. Her marginal utility from the fourth donut is greater than her marginal utility from the third candy bar.
   C. Her marginal utility has nothing to do with donuts.
   D. She initially experiences diminishing marginal utility with the first donut eaten and then gradually increases her utility.
   E. None of the above.

3. Which of the following is true regarding the long-run average total cost curve?

   A. It is U shaped because of diminishing marginal utility.
   B. It is U shaped because of diminishing marginal costs.
   C. It is not U shaped.
   D. It is U shaped because of economies of scale.
   E. The long-run average total cost curve is a down-sloping curve.

4. Which of the following best describes pure profit?

   A. The difference between variable and fixed costs
   B. Total revenue minus total quantity
   C. Total revenue minus implicit and explicit costs
   D. The revenue generated as a result of economies of scale
   E. The revenue generated as a result of quantity sold

5. What is the relationship between increasing quantities of a resource and declining quantities of output?

   A. Increasing returns to scale
   B. Economies of scale
   C. Increasing marginal returns
   D. Diminishing marginal returns
   E. Profit

6. What do economists mean by total cost?

   A. The total of all profits minus revenue
   B. Implicit and explicit costs
   C. The total of all revenue
   D. The total of all quantities minus revenue
   E. Revenue minus monetary costs

7. What happens when marginal cost is added that is less than the total average cost?

    A. Average total cost will rise.
    B. Total cost will rise.
    C. Average total cost and total cost will rise.
    D. Average total cost and total cost will fall.
    E. Both A and B.

8. Which of the following will shift a cost curve for a T-shirt manufacturer?

    A. The price of cotton increases.
    B. The minimum wage level increases.
    C. The price of power increases.
    D. The price of ink increases.
    E. All of the above.

9. How is revenue for a firm calculated?

    A. By taking profit minus all costs
    B. By taking revenue minus costs
    C. By multiplying quantities by product price
    D. By multiplying product price by total costs
    E. By adding fixed costs to variable costs

10. Which one of the following can contribute to diseconomies of scale?

    A. Technology
    B. Specialization
    C. Miscommunication
    D. Decreasing costs
    E. All of the above

11. What is the difference between the long run and the short run?

    A. The difference lies in calendar time periods.
    B. The long run has fixed costs, and the short run has variable costs.
    C. The short run is actually longer than the long run.
    D. The long run is no more than three months.
    E. The long run is when costs are variable, and the short run is when costs are fixed.

12. Which of the following would be considered a short-run cost?

    A. Factory space
    B. Machinery
    C. Labor
    D. Time
    E. None of the above

13. How is average total cost calculated?

    A. By dividing the total cost by quantity
    B. By multiplying variable costs by quantity
    C. By dividing variable costs by fixed costs
    D. By multiplying the fixed costs by quantity
    E. By dividing variable costs by quantity

14. What is marginal cost?

    A. The initial cost of producing one more unit

    B. The initial cost of producing variable costs

    C. The cost of increasing labor

    D. The cost of increasing returns to scale

    E. The overall cost of producing units

15. Which of the following best describes a long-run marginal cost curve?

    A. Initially, costs increase, then decrease to fit production.

    B. Initially costs decrease, then increase because of economies of scale.

    C. The curve slopes downward because costs continually decrease.

    D. The curve slopes upward because costs continually increase.

    E. The curve resembles an individual demand curve.

Answers to Review Questions

  1. **A.** Average total cost is a measure of the impact an additional input has on output.

  2. **A.** As Diana eats donuts, her utility from donut to donut decreases; therefore, her first donut will bring more satisfaction than her second donut.

  3. **D.** It is U shaped because of economies to scale. The curve indicates that in the long run, initially costs will decrease because of increased levels of production and output.

  4. **C.** Pure profit is total revenue minus implicit and explicit costs.

  5. **D.** When the quantities of a resource are increasing and the output is decreasing, we have diminishing marginal returns.

  6. **B.** By total costs, economists are describing the implicit and explicit costs a firm has to consider.

  7. **D.** A marginal cost that is less than the total cost will decrease both total cost and average total cost.

  8. **E.** Cost curves are shifted by resource prices. Cotton, ink, labor, and machines are all resource prices.

  9. **C.** Revenue is calculated by multiplying quantities of a product sold by the price of the product.

10. **C.** Miscommunication can result when a firm becomes too large. Increases in paperwork, labor, and even bureaucracy can result in diseconomies of scale.

11. **E.** Economists describe the long run as being a point where costs are variable because firms have enough time to adjust inputs. The short run is fixed because there isn't enough time to adjust all capital.

12. **C.** Labor is a short-run cost because it can be adjusted relatively quickly.

13. **A.** Average total cost is calculated by dividing total cost by quantity to get the cost per unit.

14. **A.** Marginal cost is the initial cost of producing one more unit.

15. **B.** Initially, costs decrease and then increase because of economies of scale. The initial period is a result of economies to scale, which is followed by constant returns to scale and then diseconomies of scale.

Product Markets and Profit Maximization

We have many firms in the United States, and all of them behave in different ways. Some are extremely competitive, while others are not so competitive. Some companies sell similar products; others sell very different or original products.

Any generalization is difficult because of the number of companies that exist. Without some means of simplification, we'd have to consider hundreds of thousands of firms every time we wanted to discuss the supply side of the market. Economists have devised a classification model based on producing and selling environments. There are four possible categories or market structures: perfect or pure competition, monopoly, oligopoly, and monopolistic competition. In this chapter, we review these market structures in detail and examine the behaviors of firms.

Maximizing Profits

Firms use a combination of resources to produce a good or a service to sell on the open market. A firm's value increases if its resources are paid for and it has monetary value left over. Adding value is an objective for profit as well as nonprofit organizations. The purpose of a profit-oriented firm is to maximize profit. The purpose of a nonprofit organization is to create an output that is more valuable than the cost of inputs. For instance, a temporary aid shelter is a nonprofit organization. The shelter gives needy families food and monetary assistance. The cost of running the shelter is outweighed by the added value of the shelter. The shelter's outputs, or in this case assistance to families, has a higher monetary and nonmonetary value than the costs of its inputs. Adding value is the purpose of business activity. In the long run, organizations that fail to add value will not survive. Inefficient decisions and allocations will eventually be replaced or overturned by more efficient ones.

Measuring added value can be difficult for some firms. Nonprofit firms have a more difficult time measuring added value than do profit-maximizing firms. Added value still remains the goal of both, regardless of the difficulty. Inputs consist of four general groups: land, labor, capital, and entrepreneurship. The cost of each is:

- Rent = Landowners
- Wages and salaries = Workers
- Interest = Owners of capital
- Revenue/profit = Entrepreneurs

With every factor of production there is a monetary and a nonmonetary cost. The nonmonetary cost comes in the form of opportunity costs—the amount necessary to keep the resource owners from moving the resources to an alternative use. If a landowner can rent his land to someone else for a higher price, he will. He has to be paid the opportunity cost of the land. If Joe can earn more money as a waiter rather than as a host, he will choose to become a waiter unless he is paid the opportunity cost of staying a host.

The cost of capital is also an opportunity cost. Capital is usually acquired through loans and sale of ownership. The cost of debt is the interest paid on the debt. Remember that every choice has an opportunity cost and an opportunity benefit. Businesses are no exception to this rule. Like individuals, businesses have to make decisions based on costs and benefits.

Marginal Revenue and Marginal Cost

When a firm decides to produce and supply a product, it is doing so after it has evaluated its costs and benefits. This evaluation is called a **costs and benefits analysis**. To analyze the firm's decisions, we must look at costs and product decisions.

A firm's downward-sloping demand curve lets the firm know that higher prices will lead to lower quantity demanded. This essentially tells firms that total revenue first rises and then declines as the price is lowered down along the demand curve. Maximum revenue is the point at which the price elasticity of demand is 1, but this is not necessarily the profit-maximizing point. We find the profit-maximizing point by comparing marginal cost and marginal revenue.

Recall that marginal cost is the cost of producing one more unit of output. **Marginal revenue** is the additional revenue obtained by selling one more unit of output. If marginal cost is less than marginal revenue, then the firm will make a profit. However, if the firm's marginal cost is higher than its marginal revenue, the firm will lose money. Profit is maximized when marginal revenue equals marginal cost. Figure 10-1 illustrates the marginal cost and marginal revenue relationship with profit and quantity.

Quantity	Total Cost	Total Revenue	Marginal Revenue	Marginal Cost	Profit
0	1,000	0	0	0	-1,000
1	2,000	1,700	1,700	1,000	-300
2	2,800	3,300	1,600	800	500
3	3,500	4,800	1,500	700	1,300
4	4,000	6,200	1,400	500	2,200
5	4,500	7,500	1,300	500	3,000
6	5,200	8,700	1,200	700	3,500
7	6,000	9,800	1,100	800	3,800
8	7,000	10,800	1,000	1,000	3,800
9	9,000	11,700	900	2,000	2,700

Figure 10-1

Figure 10-1 illustrates the profit-maximizing rule of MR = MC with the production and revenues of laptop computers. As output rises, so does revenue because of the quantities sold. Total costs also rise, demonstrating the firm's increasing costs at every quantity. According to our-profit maximizing rule, MR = MC, the point of profit maximization is at eight laptop computers. At this point, our marginal revenue of $1,000 equals our marginal cost of $1,000. Notice our profit and how it has peaked at $3,800. Profit continues to rise as quantity reaches its eighth laptop.

Marginal Revenue

The laptop example demonstrates profit maximization without the marginal revenue curve. The marginal revenue curve is similar to the demand curve in that the demand curve is the average revenue curve. When the average revenue is declining, so is the marginal revenue. Therefore, when the demand curve is downward sloping, the marginal revenue curve is also downward sloping but lies below the demand curve.

The steeper the demand curve, the steeper the marginal revenue curve; the flatter the demand curve, the flatter the marginal revenue curve. Remember that the marginal revenue curve is positive as long as total revenue is rising and that it is negative when total revenue declines. Since total revenue rises in the price-elastic region of the demand curve, marginal revenue is positive in that region. Total revenue then reaches its peak at the unitary point of the demand curve and later falls at the inelastic point of the demand curve.

Criteria for Market Structures

In analyzing the behaviors of firms, economists have created categories to explain the relationship firms have with prices, competition, products, and entrepreneurship. It is important to realize that not every industry fits perfectly into a particular category. The groupings merely represent an effort to consolidate firms to help us understand the market structure. The four categories are perfect or pure competition, monopoly, oligopoly, and monopolistic competition.

The market structure in which a firm produces and sells its product is defined by five characteristics:

- Number of firms
- Type of product

- Price control
- Conditions of entry
- Non-price competition

Pure Competition/Perfect Competition

Perfect competition is a market structure characterized in a distinct way:

- **Number of firms:** There are many perfectly competitive firms. A large number of these firms act independently of one another. These organizations offer their products domestically as well as internationally. Agricultural businesses are one example.

- **Type of product:** Perfectly competitive firms produce an identical or homogeneous product. As long as prices are the same as their competitors, consumers will have no preferences for a product or a firm. Consumers view perfectly competitive firms as perfect substitutes for one another because they all make the same product. Perfectly competitive firms make no attempt to differentiate their products or compete in any fashion because of the existence of a market price.

- **Price control:** Perfectly competitive firms have absolutely no price control. They are referred to as **price takers**. A price-taking firm enters the market accepting the market price rather than setting its own price. If a perfectly competitive firm attempts to set its own price, it will soon fail as a business. Asking a higher-than-market price would not be in the best interest of the firm because consumers would quickly substitute. There would be no reason for the firm to ask for lower than the market price because the firm is already selling all its quantities at the market price. Asking for a lower price would deprive the firm of revenue.

- **Conditions of entry:** The conditions of entry for a perfectly competitive firm are free and easy. A new firm can join the market without barriers or obstacles. New firms can freely enter the market, while old firms can leave without much difficulty in liquidating their assets. No significant monetary, legal, or technological hurdles stand in the way of a perfectly competitive firm.

- **Non-price competition:** In a perfectly competitive market, non-price competition does not exist. Firms are content with the market price and quantities offered.

The Demand for a Perfectly Competitive Firm

The demand for a perfectly competitive firm has little to do with prices. Because a company accepts the market price, the demand for its products varies in quantities at one price (the market price). The perfectly competitive firm has what is called a **perfectly elastic demand**. The firm cannot obtain a higher profit by raising its price or restricting its output. It is important to remember that the *market* demand curve for a perfectly competitive firm is downward sloping and that the individual firm's demand curve is perfectly elastic.

Figure 10-2 illustrates the market and an individual firm's demand curves.

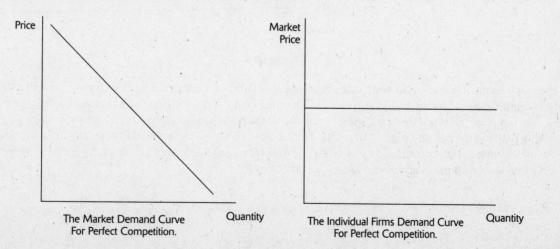

The Market Demand Curve
For Perfect Competition.

The Individual Firms Demand Curve
For Perfect Competition.

Figure 10-2

119

Revenues for a Perfectly Competitive Firm

For a perfectly competitive firm, its revenue schedule is exactly the same as its demand schedule (the demand curve is the same as the revenue curve). Figure 10-3 illustrates the revenue and demand schedules.

Demand Schedule For Firm		Revenue Schedule For Firm	
Price	Quantity Demanded	Total Revenue	Marginal Revenue
$200	0	0	
200	1	200	200
200	2	400	200
200	3	600	200
200	4	800	200

Figure 10-3

The total revenue is calculated by multiplying price by quantity. In our illustration, total revenue increases by the same amount each time: 200. Each unit sold adds exactly its constant price to total revenue. When a perfectly competitive firm decides to change its output, it must consider how this change will affect its total revenue. Marginal revenue (the change in revenue when selling one additional unit of output) will be equal to price for a perfectly competitive firm.

Remember that the price lines in a perfectly competitive firm are horizontal. This demonstrates a market price. The average revenue for a perfectly competitive firm is calculated by dividing total revenue by quantity, and the marginal revenue is the change in total revenue as one more product is sold. If only one price is represented, average and marginal revenue have to be the same. Figure 10-4 shows the firm's graph with average total cost and average variable cost.

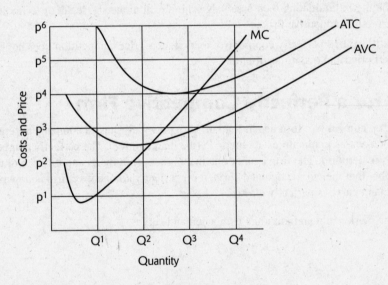

Figure 10-4

This is a graph commonly associated with perfectly competitive firms because of the horizontal price lines that illustrate a perfectly elastic demand for the firm. The four possible prices do not mean the firm has a choice of prices; remember that the firm is a price taker, and these are just four possible scenarios of market prices. Firms determine their profit-maximizing points at the quantity where MR = MC. The long-run condition for a perfectly competitive firm is when you have the minimum point of the average total cost (ATC) curve (productive efficiency) combined with the point where the MC curve intersects with marginal revenue (allocative efficiency).

For a perfectly competitive firm, profit exists in the short run but is eliminated in the long run. In the short run, a firm determines profit by determining whether the average revenue curve is above the average total cost curve. The vertical distance between the two curves indicates the per-unit profit. To get the total profit, we would have to multiply per-unit profit by quantity. The profit range is illustrated in Figure 10-5 figure below in the shaded region of the graph.

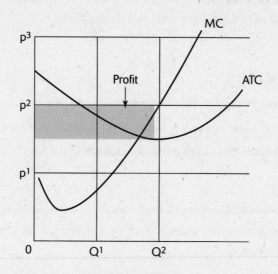

Figure 10-5

We can assume that this is a short-run condition because perfectly competitive firms have no long-run profit. By looking at the graph in Figure 10-6, we can see two things. First, a profit exists; second, the graph is a representation of a perfectly competitive firm. With these two observations, we can assume that the graph is a short-run illustration.

In the long run, other firms become attracted by the profit and, as a result, increase the supply in the industry. When the market supply is increased, the market price declines, thereby eliminating any profit.

A firm can operate with its average cost greater than its average revenue even though it is incurring a loss. As long as the firm's price is higher than its average variable cost, the firm can operate in the short run to minimize losses. If in the long run this continues, the firm will shut down.

Mini-Review

1. Which of the following is a characteristic of a perfect competition?

    A. Few firms in the industry
    B. Many firms in the market
    C. Great degree of price control
    D. Plenty of profit
    E. Many substitutes

2. What is the role of profit in a perfectly competitive firm?

    A. There is never profit.
    B. There is profit in the beginning and no profit in the long run.
    C. There is always profit.
    D. Depending on the firm's ability to set its prices, there will be profit.
    E. There is no profit in the beginning but there is a profit in the long run.

3. How do perfectly competitive firms compete?

    A. They engage in non-price competition.

    B. They engage in price competition.

    C. There is no competition between firms.

    D. They compete through a mix of non-price and price competition.

    E. None of the above.

Mini-Review Answers

1. B. The existence of many firms in the market is a characteristic of a perfectly competitive firm.

2. B. Profit exists in the short run and disappears in the long run because other firms enter the market.

3. C. There is no competition between firms in a perfectly competitive market.

Monopoly

A **monopoly** is when a single seller is the market and has no close substitutes. This is how a monopoly fits into the market structure:

- **Number of firms:** There is only one firm in a monopoly. The monopolist is the market and has no available substitutes or competitors. The firm is the single supplier of the product.

- **Type of product:** The type of product a monopolist sells is original and unique. There are no close substitutes, and if consumers do not buy the product, they are choosing to do without it completely.

- **Price control:** Monopolists are price makers. This means that they set and control their prices for their good or service. They also control the quantity supplied in the market. The demand curve still slopes downward for a monopolist; however, it has the freedom to manipulate the curve by changing quantities.

Conditions of Entry

There is virtually no way into a monopoly's market. No immediate competitors exist because a monopolist has technological or economic barriers. Monopolists enjoy a firm grip on their market and quantities.

Economies of scale play an important role in a monopoly. A monopoly can experience economies of scale in the long run because of the absence of competition. The monopoly's long-run average total cost curve declines because the firm is able to produce quantities at low costs.

Monopolies have legal barriers to entry as well. Patents and licenses are given to pure monopolies (monopolies that the government allows) to protect their market control and product information.

Basic Facts on Monopolies

Let's take a look at a few characteristics of monopolies:

- Monopolies can have long-run economic profits.

- As with other firms, when MR = MC, a monopolist can determine profit.

- In the long run, monopolies do not have to have fair market prices, allocative efficiency, or productive efficiency.

- Monopolists will always produce at the minimum levels and charge at the maximum levels because a monopolist is able to charge a price above the marginal cost of production.

Figure 10-6 shows a graph for a monopoly.

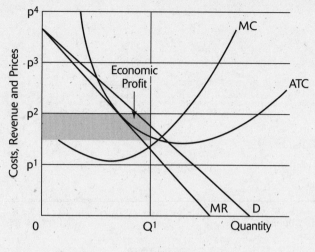

Figure 10-6

The monopolist maximizes profits by producing at Q1, or where MC = MR. Economic profit is realized where the ATC curve reaches its minimum point. Profit per unit is at Q1, and economic profit is the shaded region.

The AP exam expects you to interpret or construct graphs illustrating government intervention. Where ATC = P is considered the fair market price by the government.

Price Discrimination

Price discrimination is when a monopolist charges different prices for a product to different buyers even though the production and transaction costs remain unchanged. To price-discriminate, a firm must have market power. Price discrimination can take place only when certain conditions are met:

- **A monopolist has to have power:** The seller must have outright monopoly power or, at the very least, possess an original product or idea to be able to control output and price.

- **Separation of market must be attainable:** The monopolist must be able to sway buyers into becoming dependent on its product. Elasticities of consumers will vary, but all consumers in the monopolist's market will need to rely on the monopolist's product.

- **Redistribution of product must be forbidden:** When buyers purchase the product from a monopolist, they must not be able to resell the product or service. The reselling of the product or service compromises the power of the monopolist, and it undermines the strategy of cornering the market.

A monopolist can take part in different types of price discrimination. From movies ticket discounts for students to golf courses that offer senior discounts for the elderly, price discrimination is present in the U.S. economy—and not just at a monopolist's level.

Price discrimination works by appealing to different elasticities. How much is someone really willing to pay for your product? Senior citizens have a typically more elastic demand curve than the general public. This is mainly because seniors live on a fixed income. This fixed income gives them less flexibility when it comes to dealing with prices. So when something becomes too expensive, seniors either find a close substitute or simply do without it. A monopolist may want to offer seniors a lower price because of their high elasticity. While offering the general public the exact same product at the exact same costs of production, the monopolist may elect to charge the general public a higher price because of a more flexible income.

Figure 10-7 shows two demand curves with varying elasticities.

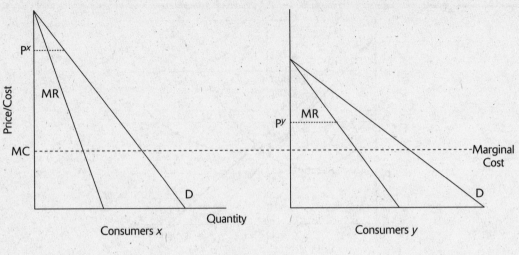

Figure 10-7

In these figures, x consumers are paying a higher price than y consumers because of price discrimination. Marginal cost remains the same for both illustrations; the only thing that is changing is consumer groups and pricing. Y consumers have a more elastic demand curve than x consumers.

Price discrimination, or "dumping," is a strategy used by many domestic firms in the international market. Price discrimination occurs when an identical product is sold internationally for a lower price than what is charged domestically for the same product. Domestic producers do this to reduce excess and maximize profits.

Monopolistic Competition

Monopolistic competition is a little like a monopoly in that each firm in this market organization produces a somewhat unique product. This uniqueness gives the monopolistically competitive firm a "mini-monopoly" over its competitor. So, like a monopolist, the monopolistically competitive firm has a downward-sloping demand curve. Marginal revenue for this type of firm is below the demand curve, and price is greater than marginal cost. The main distinguishing point between monopolistic competition and a monopoly is the ease of entry. Anytime firms in a monopolistic competition are earning above normal profit, ease of entry continues until the profit level returns to normal in the long run.

Firms in a monopolistic competition use product differentiation more so than price as a form of competition. They attempt to provide a product for all tastes and preferences. Even though the market may not be thriving at the moment, monopolistically competitive firms continue to introducing variety. Monopolistically competitive firms can thrive when the market is not expanding by simply introducing new variations of products.

When a new product is available for consumers, the demand curve for close substitutes shifts to the left because less of the total market is available for each product. To counteract this effect, other firms must first accept the new market demand structure and then introduce variations of their own, pulling the demand curve back to the right.

Number of Sellers

Monopolistically competitive firms have a large presence in the U.S. economy, although not as large a presence as perfectly competitive firms. These firms have small market shares that allow them to fluctuate in product variety. While collusion is unlikely, firms are forced to compete using price and non-price methods. These methods are decided upon by the monopolistically competitive firm and do not require market consideration.

Type of Product

Monopolistically competitive firms can produce products with slightly different physical features. For example, clothing stores offer clothes; however, they offer a large *variation* of clothes. This variation is what provides monopolistically competitive firms with leverage in making economic decisions.

Price Control

Because there is differentiation in products for firms in a monopolistically competitive firm, as a result there is some control over their prices. Despite the large number of firms present, the fact that these firms act independently of one another allows them to set output quantities and pricing.

Entry and Exit of Market

Entry for a monopolistically competitive firm is fairly easy because firms in this market are relatively small. The smaller a firm, the less market share a firm has in this case. Economies of scale are few, and the capital needed to start a monopolistically competitive firm is low. Compared with perfect competition, however, it is a little tougher to enter the market because of product differentiation and product information.

Basic Points

Remember these basic points:

- Firms have some price control, which results in their ability to set prices above marginal cost.
- The short run yields profits for a monopolistically competitive firm.
- The long run can only yield "normal profit."
- The demand facing this type of firm is very elastic because of the existence of many competitors with close substitutes.

Graphing the Monopolistically Competitive Firm

In Figure 10-8 we see the short-run and long-run monopolistically competitive firm. In the short run, firms can earn a profit by introducing a new variety of a product. But in the long run, when other firms join the market as a result of new varieties, profits will decline and eventually return to normal.

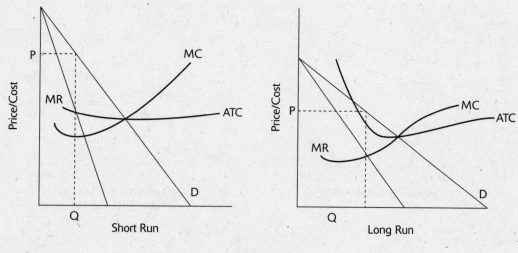

Figure 10-8

Examining the graphs in these figures, we would not be able to tell what type of market structure is being depicted. The only thing we could tell is that it is an imperfect market structure because of the existence of profit. If we were told it was a monopolistically competitive market, then we would be able to distinguish between the long run and the short run by looking at profit levels.

Oligopolies

Oligopolies are interdependent, meaning that each firm takes into account and reacts to what its rivals are doing. Rivalry and competition can be intense in an oligopolistic market. Because of a variety of behavior, the safe way to label an oligopolistic firm's behavior is *strategic*.

Strategic behavior occurs when what is best for Y depends on what X does and what is best for X depends on what Y does. This behavior is such a variable that economists have applied what is called **game theory** to an oligopolistic market. Game theory describes oligopolistic behavior as a series of moves that involve strategy and assumptions.

The Kinked Demand Curve

The law of demand applies to all firms. A firm knows that if it decreases its price, quantities sold should increase. But the firms in an oligopoly may not know the shape of the demand curve for their product because it depends on the reaction of their rivals. They have to predict how their competitors will react to a price change in order to know what the demand curve will look like.

Consider this example with Coke and Pepsi in the beverage industry. Suppose Coke's costs have fallen and the company is deciding whether or not to lower the price of its products. If Coke did not have to consider how Pepsi would respond, it would lower the price to be sure that the new MC curve intersected the new MR curve. But Coke suspects that lowering its prices will not reflect a true gain because Pepsi will soon follow with a price adjustment. If Pepsi does lower its price, the substitution effect will not occur for Coke, thereby eliminating a gain it would have experienced by lowering its price. Ultimately, Coke's strategy is to do nothing because a shift in price could trigger long-run inefficiencies.

Figure 10-9 illustrates an oligopolistic firm's demand curve when firms follow price changes and when they do not follow price changes, respectively.

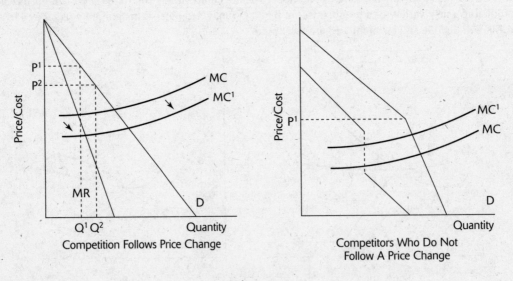

Figure 10-9

Game Theory

Game theory is a common way of explaining oligopolistic behavior. It examines the strategic moves oligopolies make in their decisions regarding pricing, output, and advertising.

The most popular game theory illustration is called "prisoners' dilemma." Two people have been arrested for a crime; however, the evidence against them is weak. The sheriff keeps the prisoners separated and offers each a special deal. If one prisoner confesses, that prisoner can go free as long as only he confesses, and the other prisoner will get 10 or more years in prison. If both prisoners confess, each will receive a reduced sentence of 2 years in jail. The prisoners know that if neither confesses, they will be cleared of all charges and will be released in 2 days. The problem here is that neither prisoner knows what deal the other is being offered or if he will take the deal.

Figure 10-10 shows the options each prisoner has.

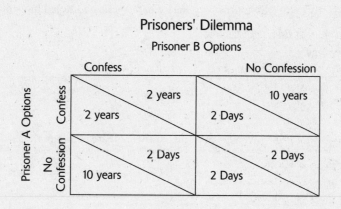

Figure 10-10

Cartels and Collusions

Collusion is an informal agreement between firms to set output and prices with the intention of controlling the market. A **cartel** is a formal agreement between producers to set output and prices to control the market and maximize profits. An example of a cartel is the Organization of the Petroleum Exporting Countries (OPEC). Collusion and cartels are illegal in the United States.

Chapter Review Questions

1. Which of the following is true regarding perfectly competitive firms?

    A. There are very few firms in the market.
    B. They have slightly differentiated products.
    C. It is difficult to start a business in this type of market.
    D. There is no long-run profit.
    E. There is a gradual profit margin.

2. Monopolies compared to perfectly competitive firms are inefficient because:

    A. They produce output with costs exceeding revenue.
    B. They produce more output than is demanded by consumers.
    C. They charge a price that is less than marginal revenue.
    D. They charge a price that is greater than marginal cost.
    E. They charge a price that is less than average total cost.

3. A profit-maximizing firm will:

  A. Hire until workers wages will equal average revenue product.
  B. Set its price above marginal cost.
  C. Employ capital until the interest rate equals wages.
  D. Set its price where marginal cost is equal to marginal revenue.
  E. None of the above.

4. What happens to a perfectly competitive firm's revenue when it sells additional units of output?

  A. It will increase rapidly at first, then decline.
  B. It will remain the same.
  C. It will increase at a slowly decreasing rate.
  D. It will increase at a constant rate.
  E. It will rise at an increasing rate.

5. Which of the following is true if the revenues of orange growers increase when the price of oranges increases?

  A. The supply of oranges is elastic.
  B. The demand for oranges is elastic.
  C. The supply of oranges is inelastic.
  D. The demand for oranges is inelastic.
  E. The demand for oranges is unitary elastic.

6. What is a market with an interdependence of firms called?

  A. A labor market
  B. A monopoly
  C. An oligopoly
  D. Perfect competition
  E. A pure monopoly

7. Which of the following is a characteristic of an oligopoly?

  A. The existence of many firms in the market
  B. Only one firm in the market
  C. Strategic competition
  D. No long-run profits
  E. No competition

8. Which one of the following best describes a perfect competition's profit?

  A. There is no profit.
  B. There can be short-run profit, but in the long run, profit is gained at a greater rate.
  C. There can be short-run profit, but in the long run, new firms restore revenue.
  D. There is no profit in the short run, but there is profit in the long run.
  E. None of the above.

9. Which type of market structure can use price discrimination to its advantage the most?

  A. Oligopolies
  B. Perfect competition
  C. Monopolies
  D. Monopolistic competition
  E. All of the above

10. An increase in which of the following will result in a long-run surplus?

A.   The number of people who supply the product
B.   A legally mandated price floor
C.   An increase in demand
D.   Costs of raw materials
E.   Future expectations of prices

11. In a perfectly competitive market, how is price adjusted?

A.   Each firm decides on price.
B.   Firms with the help of competition decide on prices.
C.   Firms ask the government to set prices.
D.   The forces of supply and demand dictate a market price firms use.
E.   Firms use non-price competition.

12. What type of demand is associated with a perfectly competitive firm?

A.   Income inelastic
B.   Income elastic
C.   Inelastic demand
D.   Elastic demand
E.   Unitary elastic

13. What is the main similarity between a monopolistically competitive firm and a monopoly?

A.   They both have one firm in the market.
B.   They both have extreme price control.
C.   They both have a downward-sloping demand curve.
D.   They both have no competitors.
E.   They both have many competitors.

14. If a perfectly competitive firm decides to increase its price to obtain a profit, which of the following is likely to occur?

A.   The firm will enjoy massive profits.
B.   The firm will enjoy profits at first but no profits in the long run.
C.   The firm will soon go out of business.
D.   Other firms will follow the price increase.
E.   Other firms will follow the price increase with non-price competition.

15. Which of the following is a characteristic of an oligopoly?

A.   A kinked supply curve
B.   No product differentiation
C.   No competition
D.   Existence of many firms
E.   Strategic competition

Answers to Review Questions

1. D. Perfectly competitive firms have no long-run profit. These firms cannot afford to set their prices above the market price because their products have perfect substitutes.

2. **D.** Monopolies charge a price that is greater than marginal cost. To maximize efficiency in a perfectly competitive market, firms must have MR = MC.

3. **B**. A profit-maximizing firm will set its price above its marginal cost to create a profit.

4. **D.** When perfectly competitive firms have excess product, they can sell the product and receive revenue at an increasing constant rate. This remains true as long as the firm is selling excess. If the firm had no excess and tries to increase its price to increase revenue at a constant rate, then the firm will suffer because of the availability of perfect substitutes.

5. **D.** If the revenue for oranges increases despite an increase in price, the demand for oranges will be considered inelastic.

6. **C.** Oligopolistic firms are interdependent of one another because of strategic competition. Firms speculate on what their competitors' next move is going to be, and they make their decisions based on their prediction.

7. **C.** Strategic competition is a characteristic of oligopolies. Firms speculate on their rivals' next move.

8. **A.** Perfectly competitive firms have no profit because they are price takers that sell a homogeneous product. Any variation in price would eliminate growth.

9. **C.** Monopolies can benefit the most from price discrimination because they control pricing and output. Monopolists can get away with charging different groups different prices because of the levels of elasticity demand.

10. **B.** An increase in a legally mandated price floor would create a surplus in the long run.

11. **D.** Prices are adjusted by supply and demand. If the forces of supply and demand fluctuate, market prices fluctuate as well. Firms cannot adjust their own prices in a perfectly competitive market.

12. **D.** A perfectly competitive firm's demand curve is perfectly elastic. There is one price, the "market price," that all quantities are purchased at.

13 **C.** The main similarity between a monopolistically competitive firm and a monopoly is that they both have a downward-sloping demand curve. The law of demand applies to both markets, at separate price ranges.

14. **C.** If a perfectly competitive firm raises its price above the market price and stays there, in the long run the firm will go out of business. The firm cannot afford to have its marginal revenue above its marginal costs.

15. **E.** Strategic competition is a characteristic of oligopolies. When an oligopoly makes a decision, it is usually based on what its competitors are going to do in reaction to that decision. Oligopolies are dependent on one another because of the strategic competition that is present among firms.

The Government's Role, Externalities, and Efficiency

Our free-market system is run on basic human nature. Self-interest is a guiding force in the free market that allows buyers to create demand and suppliers to set prices. This economic freedom is not present, however, without the guidance of the government. Although the government does not control the economy, the structure it gives the economy helps it run more smoothly.

The two main tools the government uses to intervene in the market place are antitrust policy and regulation. *Antitrust policy* is the principal behind the notion of fair competition. The government promotes competition to create efficiency in the economy. If a company were to monopolize a market, it would be eliminating competition. Economic regulation involves a larger role for the government. It ranges from prescribing output and pricing in certain industries that are failing on their own, to temporarily running and operating a business. Normally, the government's role is to allow the forces of supply and demand to regulate the free market. But there are instances when supply and demand needs a nudge from the government.

The September 11, 2001, terrorist attacks left the economy reeling from a lack of spending and confidence. One industry that was affected the most was the airline industry. This industry suffered huge and insurmountable losses that threatened the survival of the largest airline companies. Without air travel, businesses became slower, less efficient, and less reliable. In this instance, a lack of demand wasn't necessarily indicative of consumers' true feelings toward air travel. Rather, this lack of demand was created by an extreme disaster. So the question became, what should be done? Should the government have let the forces of supply and demand take over and eventually revamp the airline industry? Or should the government have taken a more proactive approach? The answer depended on time. If the government stood by and let the economy regulate itself in this situation, the airline industry may have recovered, but in the process, countless more jobs would have been lost. So the government intervened and put together a monetary aid package to keep the airline industry alive.

It is important to remember that it is not the government's responsibility to revive failing industries or businesses. Rather, it is the responsibility of the government to do what is best for the economy as a whole. If an individual business is failing, this is a normal occurrence of the free-market structure. Failing businesses are replaced by new businesses, and the cycle continues in a free-market environment.

The Government's Role

In our economy, the role of the government consists of six major components:

- **Promote and secure competition:** When competition is present in a market, producers are forced to become more efficient. Competition also protects the consumers. It improves the quality and price of goods and services for consumers. Whether the government should ensure competition in all instances is debatable; however, the need for competition in a free-market system is a given.

- **Protect private property rights:** When there is no market failure, we have social benefits equaling social costs. This allows the government to create laws to protect the interests of private citizens. Property rights should be clearly defined because they create efficiency. It is the government's responsibility to clearly define and protect property rights.

- **Provide equity:** The government's responsibility to close the widening gap between the poverty threshold and the middle class is becoming more important every day. The disparity of income in the U.S. economy is part of capitalism; nevertheless, too large a gap affects productivity. The government's responsibility to redistribute income is not at issue; rather, how *much* of income should be redistributed can be questioned.

- **Provide public goods:** Public goods exist because these goods could not be efficiently allocated in a private market. A good example is national defense. Excluding non-taxpayers from protection of an invasion may not be the brightest idea. Aside from it being nearly impossible to do, excluding individuals from national defense would be too costly and inefficient.

- **Protect against externalities:** It is the responsibility of the government to protect society from negative externalities. Externalities are negative or positive events that have an impact on individuals outside a transaction. If pollutants exist in the air or water, the government's role is to put an end to and clean the pollutants through taxation and laws.

- **Stabilize growth in the economy:** Through fiscal policy, the government examines different phases of the business cycle and acts to secure long-term growth in the economy.

Market Failure and Costs

Markets work best when two things occur: First, producers are responsible for all of their costs, and these costs are paid for by the goods and services firms supply. Second, consumers who pay for these goods and services are the only beneficiaries of the goods and services. If either condition is not met, the result is called market failure. **Market failure** is the inability of a market to sufficiently allocate resources that best fit the needs and wants of a society. When there is market failure, who bears the cost?

- **Marginal private cost:** The cost paid by the producer of producing an additional unit of a good or service.

- **Marginal social cost:** The cost paid by society to produce an additional unit of a good or service.

- **Marginal private benefit:** The benefit or utility a consumer has for a good or service.

Supply and demand depend heavily on costs to the consumer (demand) and costs to the supplier (supply). When the supplier is responsible for all costs by the pricing of its goods and services, the supply curve represents the marginal cost of producing additional units. Conversely, when consumers who purchase goods and services become the only beneficiaries of those goods and services, the demand curve represents the marginal benefit of consumers. Essentially, producers are responsible for what they produce, and consumers benefit from goods and services they pay for. The market runs efficiently and equilibrium production takes place at the point where marginal social benefit is equal to marginal social cost (see Figure 11-1).

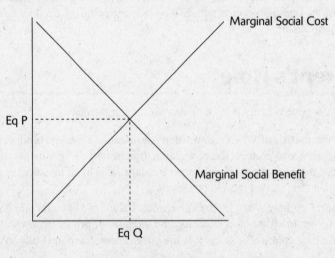

Figure 11-1

The graph in Figure 11.1 illustrates the relationship between social costs and benefits when additional units are produced. The market is at equilibrium when the costs equal the benefits.

The Impacts of Positive and Negative Externalities

A negative externality is an example of market failure. In such a situation, the full private cost is not recognized by the producers. In this case, firms' private costs are not all present in the price of their product, and they spill out to society, forcing consumers to bear some, most, or all of the cost.

Spillover Costs

When firms have spillover costs, they shift some of their costs onto the community. When this occurs, a firm's marginal cost decreases, thereby reflecting an inaccurate supply curve. The spillover costs underestimate the costs of production, and the eventual outcome may be overproduction of the good and overuse of the resources. The firm's spillover costs also create nonmonetary costs. These types of costs are usually associated with health problems or environmental pollution that result from a firm's overuse or overproduction of resources.

Consider this example: Dan lives in a house that has a wonderful view of the city skyline. Dan enjoys coming home every day and taking in the beautiful view. One day a building contractor notifies Dan that his firm will construct a new high school in front of his home. Dan initially digests the news with little concern, but over the next few months, he begins noticing that his precious view is beginning to disappear. Once the construction is complete, Dan's view will no longer be of a skyline; rather, it will be a view of the side of the gym. This is an example of a negative externality.

Pollution is another example of a negative externality. If a firm begins producing a good and is polluting the water in its area and ignoring its costs, this firm is creating a negative externality. Negative externalities in this situation can be graphed as shown in Figure 11-2. The graph illustrates the marginal cost curve above the supply curve. The reason for this is because the firm is not incurring all of the costs. Some of its costs are borne by society, and this actually allows the firm to produce more because of a low monetary cost.

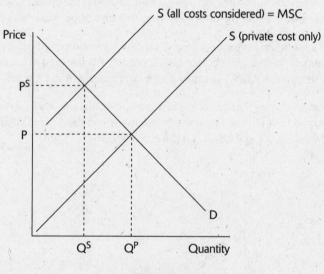

Figure 11-2

The graph in Figure 11-2 shows that if the producer is creating a negative externality, the price to make its product is relatively low because it is not paying all of the costs. This is indicated at Qp and P on the graph. If the producer were to bear all costs, the cost of production would rise and the quantity of the good would decrease.

The government can sometimes regulate what and how much is produced by a firm. If that is the case, you would use the graph to illustrate the government regulation. The graph in Figure 11-3 illustrates another government option for limiting production: taxation.

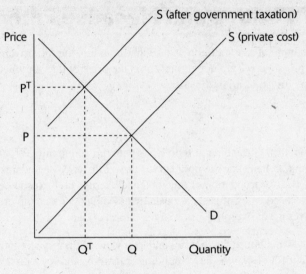

Figure 11-3

The graph in Figure 11-3 reveals the same result as the previous one, but for a different reason. In this scenario, the government has decided to levy a tax on a firm's output. This drives up the cost of production and decreases output while increasing price. The government can use this money to clean up the negative externality.

Positive Externalities or Spillover Benefits

Spillover benefits are benefits received by those who did not pay for them. The demand curve is located below the marginal social benefit. The demand curve illustrates the utility of all who paid the costs to receive the benefit from the good. However, it does not take into account the utility and benefit received by those who did *not* pay for the good.

Consider this example: Andy goes to the doctor to receive a vaccine for various viruses. Andy pays the cost for this benefit; however, people with whom he comes into contact also benefit by his decision because they are less likely to catch the viruses for which he was vaccinated. Andy has created a positive externality as a result of his decision.

When illustrating a positive externality on a graph, you must remember that the demand curve is located to the left of the marginal benefit curve. Figure 11-4 illustrates a positive externality; in the figure, MSB stands for **marginal social benefit** which is the additional positive social effects on the economy.

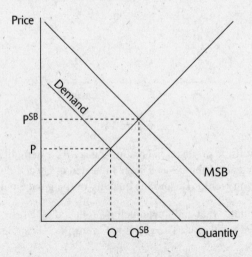

Figure 11-4

Figure 11-4 illustrates the impact of a positive externality on quantity and price. In our example, when Andy decided to get his shot, he paid for his vaccine as a private benefit. His private benefit becomes a social benefit when he comes into contact with society. If the costs of the benefit were realized by society, the benefit would have a higher price and a higher quantity.

If the government mandated the vaccine, then all members of society would have to get one as well. This would cause the demand curve to shift to the right because all members of society would now bear the cost of the benefit (see Figure 11-5).

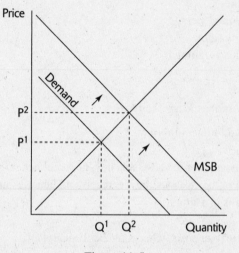

Figure 11-5

The demand curve shifts toward the marginal social benefit curve because society is now forced to pay the costs to receive the benefits of the vaccinations.

Public Goods

Public goods are goods that are funded by taxpayers for the public. Public goods do not exclude anyone from using them. Whether or not someone is a taxpayer, that individual can still drive the highways, go to the park, and take advantage of other public goods. Public goods create a dilemma for government officials: Would the government be better off spending the money in the private sector? Or should it spend the resources on the public sector? Remember that every decision has an opportunity *cost* and an opportunity *benefit*. To find a resolution, the government performs a cost-benefit analysis to decide what sector to spend the money on.

Tragedy of the Commons

Some things in this world are nonexclusionary; in other words, they can be used by anyone and everyone. Rivers, trees, and oxygen are examples of nonexclusionary things because the rights to them are held by everyone. The downside to this is that as long as everyone can use them, anyone can destroy them—this is known as the **tragedy of the commons**.

We normally take care of things we pay for. Think about it; when was the last time you worried about damage to a public good? You are more likely to be concerned about damage to your own property before worrying about anything else because you have directly paid for it. When individuals directly pay for and directly receive benefits from goods, they tend to take better care of that good.

Consider this example of a public good: Freeways are often littered with trash because individuals do not directly bear the costs to drive on the freeways. One way some governments have tried to counter this dilemma is through the use of incentives. Some states have an adopt-a-highway program. This program allows the private sector (firms and individuals) to "adopt" a certain portion of a highway. The adoption of the highway entails giving the paying party the responsibility to clean its portion of the highway, and in return, the paying party gets to post its name on the side of the freeway. The incentive for the paying party is free advertisement or just simple recognition.

Mini-Review

1. Which of the following is part of the government's role in a free-market system?

   A.   To control the stock market
   B.   To regulate the output of producers
   C.   To protect private property rights
   D.   To save every business that is failing
   E.   Both B and C

2. Which one of the following describes market failure?

   A.   When supply and demand form equilibrium
   B.   When inflation takes place
   C.   When producers do not bear all of the costs and buyers do not benefit from all of the benefits
   D.   When producers bear all of the costs and buyers receive all benefits they paid for
   E.   When there are no benefits in a situation

3. If social costs are higher than private costs, what could be the cause?

   A.   There is a positive externality.
   B.   Producers are paying too high a cost to make their product.
   C.   Producers are not bearing enough of a cost to make their product.
   D.   Buyers are not bearing enough of the cost.
   E.   Both buyers and producers are not bearing enough of a cost to make the product.

Mini-Review Answers

1. **C.** The government's role is to protect and to clearly define private property rights.

2. **C.** Market failure is a situation in which producers are not bearing all of the costs to make their product (spillover costs) and buyers are not receiving the utility they have paid for.

3. **C.** When social costs are higher than private costs, a producer is not bearing enough of the cost to make its product. Some of the cost is being paid by society in the form of pollution, for example.

Income Equity and the Lorenz Curve

The rich and poor exist in every country. There are various distinctions of income based on the rich, the poor, and the middle class. Although each country's class distinction varies, all countries have distinctions. Incomes are not distributed equally, and this degree of inequality varies from country to country. To compare income distributions, economists need a measure of income equality. The Lorenz curve is an illustration of how income is distributed among members of a population.

Equal incomes on the graph can be plotted along a 45-degree line that stretches from left to right. This line splits the axis equally and represents the various levels of equal incomes. The horizontal axis measures the total population in cumulative percentages. As you examine the horizontal axis from left to right, you are viewing an increasing percentage of the population. The vertical axis measures real GDP in cumulative percentages. As you move up the vertical axis, the percentage of real GDP becomes larger and larger, capping at 100 percent. Each point on the 45-degree line represents an equality between real GDP and population.

Points that are off the line are indicators that there is an inequality of income. Sometimes points are to the left of the line, which indicate that total income is greater than population. On the other hand, if the points are to the right of the line, this indicates that total population is greater than total income. Whenever total population is greater than income, you have a declining total income; whenever total income is greater than total population, you have an increasing total income. The farther any point strays from the line of equality, the more of an inequality in the distribution of income we have. Figure 11-6 is an illustration of the Lorenz curve.

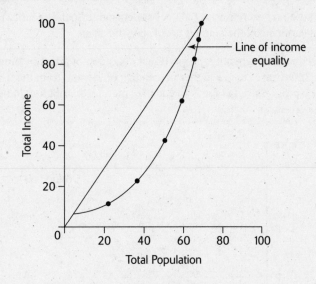

Figure 11-6

In Figure 11-6 we can see that the distribution of income is not equal until the last point on the curve. We know that there is an inequality because the plot points are straying from the line of equality. The farther they stray, the farther we are from an equal income distribution. Our graph shows that the income distribution seems to be declining as a result of less GDP and more population.

The government has a responsibility to limit the number of inequalities through some specific areas:

- **Cyclical changes in the economy:** The government can limit unemployment through government spending and taxation.

- **Job skills:** The government can reinforce the structure of education, thereby increasing the knowledge and skills of the current and future workforce.

- **Social shortcomings:** The government can offer transfer payments to those who are experiencing unemployment or disabilities. Social security payments, food stamps, and unemployment compensation are all types of transfer payments that can redistribute income in the United States.

It is important to remember that the Lorenz curve does not indicate who the poor are or what their quality of life is. The Lorenz curve is a relative measure of income distribution. The saying "one man's shack can be another man's castle" is true when describing the relative measure of income distribution. What is considered poverty here could be considered middle or even upper class in another country.

Economists can measure income before any government intervention affects the distribution of income, although the process is extremely difficult. This measurement gives us a more accurate figure of the distribution of income.

Taxation

One way to reduce poverty is to increase the level of disposable income people have. Some economies adopt an approach that taxes the rich heavily and taxes the poor lightly. You will need to know about three types of taxes for the AP exam:

- **Progressive tax:** A tax that rises as income rises. As an individual's income rises, the percentage of income that goes to taxes also rises.

- **Proportional tax:** A tax whose rate does not change as the tax base changes. If the proportional tax rate is 25 percent, then no matter what income an individual earns, she pays 25 percent of her income to taxes. The percentage stays the same but the amount varies. Twenty-five percent of $100,000 is a lot less than 25 percent of $1,000,000.

- **Regressive tax:** A tax whose rate decreases as the tax base changes. Social security tax is an example of a regressive tax. As an individual earns more, the amount taxed stays the same.

Progressive taxes tend to reduce income inequality; proportional taxes do not affect income distribution; and regressive taxes increase inequality. Progressive taxes take a higher percentage of income from the rich or upper class than it takes from the middle or the poor. The progressive tax tends to equalize income distribution in the United States. Figure 11-7 shows the impact a tax has on a producer.

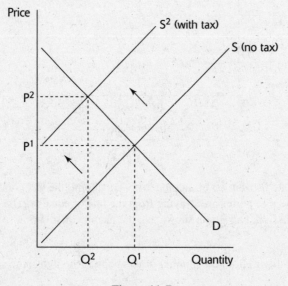

Figure 11-7

The tax on a supplier lowers its quantity produced and increases its price. The government can use taxation to limit the production of a specific good, or it can use taxation to increase the production of a certain good. Depending on its impact on society, the government can regulate a firm's or industry's output.

Review Points

- The economy experiences efficiency when producers are responsible for all costs; if they are not, spillover costs are created.

- Externalities are considered market failure because either producers are failing to bear all of the costs or buyers are not the only beneficiaries of the goods and services produced.

- Public goods are nonexclusionary. People who pay as well as those who do not pay have access to the public good.

- *Tragedy of the commons* is a phrase used to describe the ownership of resources such as air, trees, and water.
- Externalities can be both positive and negative; either one is considered market failure.
- The government can try to eliminate an externality through output regulation or taxation.
- The Lorenz curve is an illustration of income distribution. It measures the relationship between real GDP and population.
- The 45-degree line on the Lorenz curve illustrates equality between real GDP and population.

Chapter Review Questions

1. What will a firm do if a positive externality exists?

    A. Increase the number of resources for production
    B. Charge a higher price
    C. Increase the labor force
    D. Reduce the number of resources for production
    E. None of the above

2. What will the government do if a negative externality exists?

    A. Increase the amount of transfer payments to society
    B. Decrease taxes for firms
    C. Increase taxes for firms
    D. Subsidize a competing firm
    E. Tax a competing firm and leave the negative externality creating firm alone

3. Which of the following are the best example(s) of a positive externality?

    A. Smog
    B. Traffic
    C. Vaccines
    D. Water pollution
    E. Both A and C

4. What does the term "free rider" mean?

    A. A taxpayer who uses the highway system
    B. A nontaxpayer who uses the public park
    C. Anyone who uses the freeway
    D. All taxpayers
    E. Both A and D

5. Which of the following is consistent with market failure?

    A. When a producer bears all the costs
    B. When a buyer benefits from what he pays for
    C. When society's cost is equal to private cost
    D. When the cost to society is greater than private costs
    E. When all markets benefit as a result of a decision

6. Income tax would fall under which of the following categories?

    A. Progressive tax
    B. Regressive tax
    C. Proportional tax
    D. Sales tax
    E. Both B and D

7. Which of the following is true regarding the Lorenz curve?

    A. It measures real GDP.
    B. It illustrates the relationship between inflation and unemployment.
    C. It measures the relationship between unemployment and GDP.
    D. It measures the quality of life for members of society.
    E. It measures the relationship between real GDP and population.

8. Which of the following would be considered a transfer payment?

    A. A payment to a federal employee
    B. A payment to a babysitter
    C. A payment to the Federal Reserve
    D. Unemployment compensation
    E. Taxation

9. Which of the following best describes the 45-degree line in the Lorenz curve?

    A. A point of inequality
    B. A point of equality
    C. The relationship between inflation and unemployment
    D. The line that represents the total number of poor people in the United States
    E. The line that illustrates the number of unemployed people

10. What does the term *nonexclusionary* refer to?

    A. Private goods
    B. Public goods
    C. Government-owned goods
    D. Goods owned by the city government
    E. The right to prevent someone from using a good

11. How can the government improve income distribution?

    A. By increasing taxes
    B. By increasing subsidies for education
    C. By decreasing subsidies
    D. By decreasing transfer payments
    E. None of the above

12. Which one of the following is true regarding spillover costs?

    A. They shift the burden of cost from the firm to society.
    B. They shift the burden of cost from society to the firm.
    C. They are positive externalities.
    D. They are a result of a balanced market.
    E. They are present in every market transaction.

13. Why would the government want to close the gap between the poor and the upper class?

    A. To increase payments to the economy

    B. To increase efficiency

    C. To increase the national debt

    D. To decrease efficiency

    E. None of the above

14. Which of the following best describes a remedy for negative externalities?

    A. Increase taxes on the firm producing them.

    B. Decrease taxes on the firm producing them.

    C. Provide subsidies to the firm's competitor.

    D. Decrease competition for the firm that is responsible for the negative externality.

    E. Increase transfer payments to society.

15. Which of the following will result in the reduction of the poverty level?

    A. Increased taxes

    B. Decreased taxes

    C. Increased subsidies for firms

    D. Increased transfer payments

    E. None of the above

Answers to Review Questions

  1. D. If a positive externality exists, this means that people are benefiting from things they did not pay for. As a result, the firm will decrease its productive resources to be more efficient and less wasteful.

  2. C. The government will increase the tax rate for a firm that is causing a negative externality. The negative externality will be harder to produce because the firm's production costs will rise as a result of the tax increase.

  3. C. Vaccines are a positive externality because people who pay for them externalize a benefit to people who did not pay for them. Every time people come into contact with someone who has received a shot, they are benefiting from that individual's decision to get that shot.

  4. B. A free rider is a term used to describe someone who benefits from something they did not pay for. Any nontaxpayer can be considered a free rider if they are using a public good.

  5. D. When the cost to society is greater than the private cost, we have a market failure. Market failures exist because either costs are not consumed by the responsible party or paying parties do not receive full benefits.

  6. A. Income tax is a progressive tax because the more you earn, the more you're taxed (percentage). Income is separated into different brackets; with each increase in pay, an individual may enter a new bracket that commands a higher tax percentage.

  7. E. The Lorenz curve measures the relationship between real GDP and population. It is the relative measure of GDP and population; it cannot evaluate quality of life.

  8. D. Unemployment compensation, social security, and food stamps are all considered transfer payments. Transfer payments are used by the government to increase the amounts of disposable income.

  9. B. The 45-degree line on the Lorenz curve illustrates equality between real GDP and population. Every point along the line is an illustration of an equal distribution of income.

  10. B. Nonexclusionary refers to public goods. Public goods are nonexclusionary because society has access to them.

  11. B. Increasing subsidies for education improves the distribution income because more workers become skilled. Skilled workers will earn more money, thereby improving human capital.

12. A. Spillover costs shift the burden of cost from the firm to society. This is also an example of a negative externality.

13. B. Closing the widening gap between the poor and the upper class would increase efficiency in the economy. More people would have jobs, thereby increasing productivity.

14. A. Increasing taxes is one way to reduce the levels of negative externalities because it increases the cost of production for firms.

15. B. A decrease in taxes increases the level of disposable income. This increase in disposable income elevates people from the poverty threshold.

International Economics

Over the last 20 years, the world has become an increasingly interdependent group of countries. The new buzzword of the twenty-first century is globalization. **Globalization** refers to the interdependence of goods and resources that belong to various countries. We realize more so now than ever before that no single country is self-sufficient. Countries may be self-sufficient to a certain extent, but they would be better off with the existence of trade.

This chapter examines and reviews the impacts and benefits of world trade and the nature of connections between countries. Trade occurs because of specialization in production. No single individual or country can produce everything better than others can. The result is specialization in production based on comparative advantage. Remember that comparative advantage is based on relative opportunity costs and how much a country has to "give up" to produce a good. A country will specialize in the production of a good if the opportunity cost of producing that good is lower relative to other countries. Nations then trade what they produce in excess of their own consumption to acquire new or needed products.

The world price for goods and services is determined by the individual countries' demand curves and supply curves. If the world demand for coffee surpasses the world supply for coffee, then the price of coffee will be on a steady incline. Just like an economy's equilibrium price, the world's equilibrium price is derived from the forces of supply and demand. Who has what, how much of what, and at what price are all questions that depend on the world's supply and demand for goods and services.

Trade exists because people's needs and wants are unlimited. Trade improves the condition of both people and countries because it provides goods and services at lower opportunity costs. Because countries differ in their comparative advantages, they export different goods. Countries also have different tastes and technological needs, and differ in what they import. The existence of variety is the very reason for trade. Variety appeals to the human trait of self-interest. When the world can provide a variety, individuals needs and wants have to be met. To meet the demand, countries trade to obtain goods that would otherwise be unavailable to its citizens.

World Equilibrium

The world economy is complex because each country has a unique pattern of trade. A country's trading partners and types of goods traded vary from country to country. It's almost as if you have to look at the world as one giant puzzle of trade. Countries have to find other countries that have what they are looking for in terms of goods and services. That's just half the battle. The other half is finding a country that needs what you produce. While some countries trade a great deal, the countries that trade very little are the ones that feed into the changing world equilibrium forces. The determinants of world equilibrium shape the existences of comparative advantages in the world.

Comparative Advantage and Absolute Advantage

Comparative advantage is derived by examining the relative costs of production in each country. Economists measure the costs of production through opportunity costs, which entails looking at what must be given up in order to produce a certain good.

Absolute advantage is calculated by tallying the resource costs of producing a product. We derive absolute advantage by comparing these resource costs to other countries producing the same good.

Suppose the United States and Canada are two isolated nations in our example. Each nation can produce both candy and wheat. The difference is that each nation can produce each product at different opportunity costs. Figure 12-1 illustrates the production possibilities for each country when producing wheat and candy.

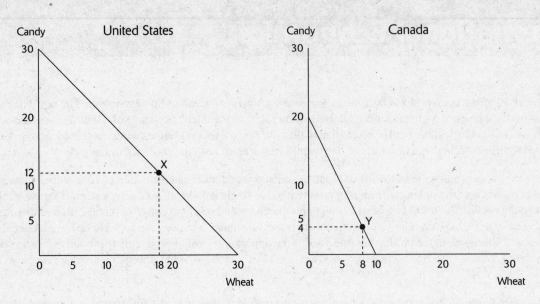

Figure 12-1

The United States can operate efficiently on its production possibilities curve by trading off one unit of wheat for one unit of candy or one unit of candy for one unit of wheat. The domestic exchange ratio in the United States is 1 for 1. In Canada, 20 units of candy must be given up to get 10 units of wheat. This means that the ratio or opportunity cost of candy and wheat is two units of candy for one unit of wheat.

Canada and the United States will have to choose a level of output that is beneficial to both countries. Each country selects an output that provides the greatest utility for the country's economy. Let's assume that points X and Y in the figures are the best production possibilities for both countries. This assumption simply means that each country's most desirable output of candy and wheat is located at X and Y. The domestic equilibrium is located at X and Y for each country.

The idea of comparative advantage states that total output will be greatest for the countries if each specializes in the good for which it has the lowest opportunity cost. In our example, we can see that the United States has the lower opportunity cost if it specializes in wheat (U.S.: one unit of wheat for one unit of candy; Canada: two units of candy for one unit of wheat). It would not be in Canada's best interest to specialize in wheat because it would be giving up two units of candy for one unit of wheat, when the United States could be used as a trading partner. The whole idea here is to let a country produce a good that is in demand for you because they have an easier time producing it. Why would Canada employ valuable resources to produce a good that could be attained more easily with a trading partner?

Canada has the lower opportunity cost when it comes to producing candy because they are giving up only half a unit of wheat when producing one unit of candy. The United States has to give up one unit of wheat for one unit of candy, which makes the United States' opportunity cost higher than Canada's.

In our analysis, we have discovered that the United States should specialize in wheat and Canada should specialize in candy. If the United States specializes in wheat, then it will be able to make 30 units of wheat at capacity and 0 units of candy. If Canada specializes in candy, then it will be able to make 20 units of candy and 0 units of wheat. People in both countries are still going to want wheat (in Canada) and candy (in the United States), so what should the countries do? Trade!

Trading Terms

The United States and Canada must come to an agreement with the terms of trade. They already know that they need each other's good. What they need to determine is what will it take to get the goods for trade. In the United States, the domestic opportunity cost is one unit of candy for one unit of wheat. For the United States to benefit from trade, it must obtain more than one unit of candy for each unit of wheat exported or it will not benefit from exporting wheat in exchange for candy. The whole point here is for the United States to get a better deal internationally than it does domestically for its products.

In Canada, one unit of wheat is equal to two units of candy; therefore, Canada would like to get one unit of wheat by exporting anything less than two units of candy. Canada's goal is to get a better deal internationally than its domestic rate for wheat and candy. The Canadians can make two units of candy for each one unit of wheat. This ratio has already told us that Canada should specialize in candy; however, at what exchange rate will Canada benefit the most for wheat? The terms of trade will fall between:

U.S. = 1 unit of wheat = 1 unit of candy

Canada = 1 unit of wheat = 2 units of candy

Canada prefers the terms of exchange to fall closer to its ratios, and the United States prefers the terms of exchange to fall closer to its ratios. The goal for the Canadians is to get as much wheat for their candy because that's what the Canadians specialize in. The goal for Americans is to get as much candy for their wheat because that's what the United States specializes in.

In actuality, the exchange ratio depends on the international forces of supply and demand. If the world supply for wheat is high, then the United States will have to give a little on its price for wheat when trading to Canada. Similarly, if the world supply for candy is high, the Canadians will lose price leverage on their candy and will have to give a little when trading with the United States. This does not mean each country cannot benefit from trade—it just means that according to the international forces of supply and demand, one country may have to benefit a little less than the other. Both countries still benefit from trade.

For the sake of our example, let's try to find some middle ground for the terms of trade between the United States and Canada. Assume that the exchange rate for candy and wheat is one unit of wheat for one and one-half units of candy. Figure 12-2 illustrates the gains both countries have as a result of trade.

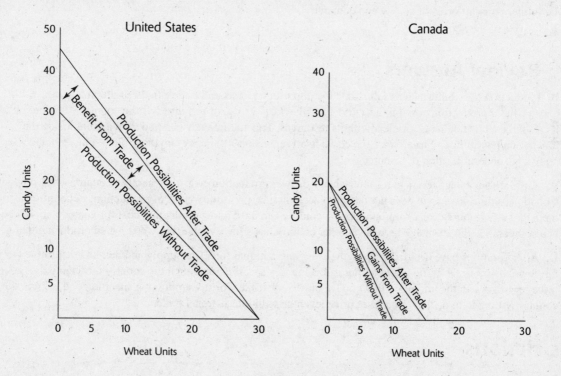

Figure 12-2

By examining the graphs, we can see that the production possibilities for each country have increased due to trade. Both parties have benefited as a result of trade. Canada has more wheat for its candy, and the United States has more candy for its wheat.

For the AP exam, you will be expected to discover the absolute and comparative advantage for the entities involved. You will then be expected to construct production possibilities graphs that illustrate gains from trade for each country.

Mini-Review

1. What does a production possibilities curve illustrate?

   A. The inflation rate of a country
   B. The opportunity costs and trade-offs of production
   C. The aggregate supply in an economy
   D. The aggregate demand in an economy
   E. Both the aggregate supply and demand in an economy

2. Absolute advantage refers to:

   A. A country having lower opportunity costs than another country
   B. A country having lower production costs than another country
   C. Two countries determining that they will not benefit from trade
   D. Two countries determining that they will benefit from trade
   E. A country having a higher production cost than another country

3. After specialization, what determines exchange rates for countries?

   A. Domestic output and demand
   B. International governments
   C. Domestic governments
   D. International forces of supply and demand
   E. None of the above

Mini-Review Answers

1. **B.** Production possibilities curves illustrate the opportunity costs and trade-offs of producing goods. Each country has a production possibilities curve that illustrates its use of resources. If the country is underemploying its resources, it is not being efficient with its resources. This inefficiency is noted with a point inside the production possibilities curve. Since the curve itself represents efficiency, anything plotted inside the curve represents underutilization of resources.

2. **B.** Absolute advantage refers to a country having lower production costs than another country when producing a good. Absolute advantage does not take into account the opportunity costs of production; rather, it measures monetary and resource costs of production. A country can have a low production cost for a good and still be at a comparative disadvantage because another country has a lower opportunity cost when producing that good.

3. **D.** After countries have decided to specialize, the international forces of supply and demand determine the values of the goods for trade. If the world output is lacking in a specific good, then the country producing that good has price leverage with the trading of that good. Conversely, if the world's supply of a specific good is high, the country willing to trade that good loses price leverage with international trade.

Restrictions

The existence of restrictions comes about as a result of governments' desire to protect domestic producers from foreign competition. Although some cases of government intervention are needed, most of the time when the government intervenes it harms the consumer. Comparative advantage maximizes world output, providing variety and efficiency to the world's consumers. If government intervenes and restricts trade, consumers end up paying higher prices for a lower quality of goods. First, let's look at some arguments against free trade.

Protecting Domestic Jobs

The premise behind this idea is if foreign goods are kept out of the economy, more U.S. jobs will be preserved. If there are fewer foreign competitors, American firms can increase output and employ more workers. This would cause the unemployment rate to decline and consumer spending to rise. The downside to this argument is that only the protected industry benefits in terms of employment from the elimination of foreign competition.

Because domestic consumers will be paying higher prices for the protected output, they will have less money to spend on other domestic goods and services. In time, this will reduce the purchasing power of consumers and in fact increase the unemployment rate. Another downside to this argument is that other countries may retaliate in reaction to the U.S. decision to restrict trade. If foreign countries do restrict U.S. exports, domestic firms' production will decrease and unemployment will rise. Essentially, if we were to restrict trade to save jobs, we would only be redistributing employment into the protected industry. Our economy would not be experiencing any growth.

Equal Opportunity

The argument of equal opportunity comes from some protectionists who complain that the inclusion of foreign goods and services takes away from the demand of domestic goods and services. But if you examine this argument closely, you'll notice that it goes against the very foundation of our economy: competition. Doesn't competition force firms to be efficient? Won't the inclusion of foreign products force domestic firms to provide variety and better quality? The argument for equal opportunity is a touchy subject to some, but for the AP exam you will need to know the basis behind trade restrictions to form better arguments for a free-response question.

Tools of Trade Restriction

A **quota** is designed to limit the number of goods that may be imported to a country. If the United States wanted to limit the number of foreign cars imported, it could place a quota on the number of cars allowed per year. A **tariff** is a tax placed on imported goods. Although tariffs do not limit the number of foreign goods outright, they do make it more costly for foreign producers. Tariffs tend to benefit the government more so than a quota does. With a quota, the foreign producer can raise its per-unit price, thereby making up for any lost sales because of the quota.

Tariffs and quotas are tools used to limit trade in an economy. Both of these tools lead to higher prices and less consumption by domestic buyers. The basis for these tools lies in the government's effort to control prices and output.

Effects of a Tariff

A tariff has four possible effects:

- **A decline in imports:** International producers are hurt by an increase in production costs. Volume may rise for the product domestically, but foreign producers do not see the rise in volume because the revenue goes to the government that is imposing a tariff.

- **Consumption declines:** Prices of imported goods rise when a tariff is imposed. When tariffs are present, producers have no choice but to raise their prices in efforts to sustain revenue.

- **Revenue for the government:** Tariffs redirect revenue that would have gone to the international producer to the government instead. The government gets a share of revenue in the form of a tariff placed on either each unit or a lump-sum tariff.

- **An increase in production for domestic producers:** Domestic producers increase production of goods and services because individuals are substituting the expensive foreign goods for the less expensive domestic goods. Demand increases, thereby forcing suppliers to step up production.

Effects of a Quota

A quota has the following effects:

- **Transfer of revenue:** A quota transfers revenue from the government to international firms. Quotas are established to limit the number of international goods in the economy; they do not yield any revenue to the imposing government.

- **Higher domestic prices:** Much like a tariff, quotas lead to higher domestic prices. Producers are forced to charge higher prices for goods and services because of the increased tax.

Open and Closed Economies

An **open economy** is one that considers exports and imports. Economists use the term "open" to describe the inclusion of trade when analyzing such data as GDP and the price level. An open economy considers consumption, investment, government, and exports minus imports. Open economies allow trade to flow freely with consumers, who have the ability to choose among a variety of goods. Open economies are forced to compete with foreign firms for goods and pricing. The pricing in an open economy is called the **world price**.

Let's consider an example involving the production of steel. Once upon a time, steel was produced in the United States at high levels. Steel companies produced steel to feed world and domestic demand. Over time, the U.S. steel companies were outbid by European steel companies because they found cheaper ways to produce steel. To protect the steel workers in the United States, the government could have done a couple of things: first, it could have established an import quota, restricting the amount of imported steel. Or, the government could have used tariffs as a negative incentive for international steel producers. Let's take a look at both options in Figure 12-3 and see the difference.

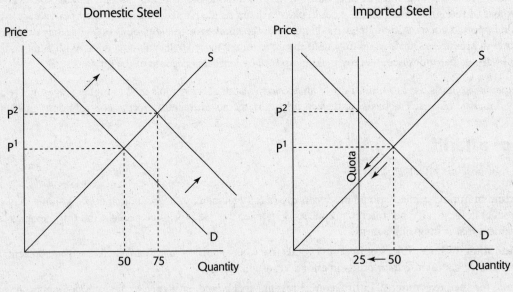

Figure 12-3

As you can see, once the quota has been placed on a specific good, the international supplier is limited to the amount of good supplied to the U.S. economy. The quota has limited the supply and increased the price, thereby making it less enticing to domestic consumers.

Meanwhile, domestic producers of steel benefit because demand for their steel increases as a result of the substitution effect. Domestic consumers see that U.S. steel is cheaper; therefore, demand increases for the domestic steel. With this increase in demand, producers increase the price for steel.

The downside is that while jobs and firms are being saved in the steel industry domestically, other industries will suffer from an increase in the price of steel. The price increase may trigger a price level increase and/or an increase in unemployment in other industries.

Recall that the United States government's other option is to impose tariffs on imported steel. A tariff is a tax on imported goods and services. Tariffs are used to limit the supply and create revenue for the government. Figure 12-4 illustrate the impacts of tariffs on price and quantity.

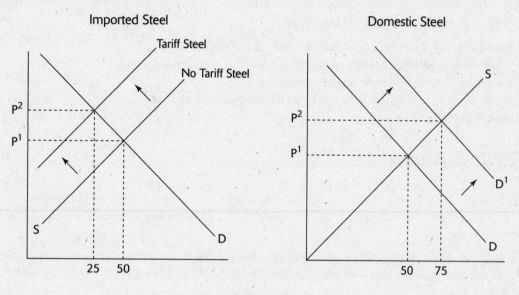

Figure 12-4

We can see that the effects on supply and demand are similar to when a quota is placed on imported goods. In Figure 12-7, a tariff is placed on imported steel. This makes it more expensive for international producers of steel to sell steel in the United States. The supply curve for the international firm decreases, causing an increase in price and a decrease in quantity available. Tariffs also generate revenue for the government. International firms are forced to pay the tax to the government on either a per-unit or lump-sum basis.

As a result of a tariff, the domestic demand shifts to the right because once again consumers are substituting international steel for U.S. steel. An increase in demand means an increase in the price of domestic steel.

The downside is that, as with a quota, tariffs may be only a temporary way of saving employment. Jobs may be saved in the steel industry; however, other industries may experience negative effects because of the steel industry's high prices. Other industries may lose employment and demand as a result of the increase in steel prices.

What it all means is that with quotas, the government is giving the international firm the right to increase the price of its product. Depending on its quality relative to domestic quality, the international firm may still capture enough demand despite having a higher price than the domestic firm. With a tariff, the government is able to increase its revenue while directly charging international firms for making their products available in the United States.

Mini-Review

1. What impact on domestic demand does a tariff have?

    A.   It decreases domestic demand for the substitute good.
    B.   It increases demand for international goods.
    C.   It decreases demand for domestic complements.
    D.   It increases the demand for domestic goods.
    E.   It has no impact on demand.

2. What will happen to the price of a protected good after a quota?

    A. It will rise.

    B. It will fall.

    C. Depending on inflation, it may rise or fall.

    D. There will be no change in price.

    E. None of the above.

3. What is the difference between a quota and a tariff?

    A. Tariffs limit supply while quotas create revenue for the government.

    B. Quotas limit supply while tariffs create revenue for the government.

    C. There is no difference between quotas and tariffs.

    D. Tariffs are used only with durable goods; quotas are used with all goods.

    E. Both A and D

Mini-Review Answers

1. D. Tariffs increase the demand for domestic goods because people substitute the foreign (more expensive) good for the domestic good. International firms are forced to increase their prices because of an increase in taxes. This increase in price decreases their quantity demand and shifts the domestic firms' demand curve to the right, thus triggering a higher price.

2. A. The price of a protected good after a quota will rise because the supply of that good will be limited in the economy. Anytime a good is limited in quantity, chances are the price of that product will rise because it will become rarer.

3. B. Quotas are designed to limit supply while tariffs are designed to limit supply and increase revenue for the government. Today, the use of tariffs and quotas is discouraged because of the emphasis on free trade. The lower the trade barriers, the higher the chance of trade between countries.

Equilibrium World Price

Think of the world as a box of sand. The sand symbolizes all the goods and services available. When there is more sand available in one area than another, the sand comes at a cheaper price. If we were to examine a location in the sandbox that had little sand available, then the price of sand would rise. This is much like the supply and demand for goods and services on an international scale. When the world has too much of a good in supply—meaning too many countries can easily produce a particular good—the country/countries producing that good cannot command a high international value. But if we are talking about something that is produced by only a handful of countries, like oil, then those countries have a good amount of control over their prices because of high demand.

When the world is open to trade, the many forces or factors that affect supply and demand can be seen and understood. To simplify our discussion, let's include only two countries in our explanation. International equilibrium occurs for these two countries when supply and demand intersect. One nation's import demand curve has to intersect the other nation's export supply curve for an international equilibrium to exist. At the point where the two curves intersect, the import demand curve and the export supply curve, we have a world market price. This world market price (between the two countries we are examining) is the prevailing price for the good. Both countries have agreed to this price through their supply and demand. After trade occurs, this world price still prevails due to the involvement of other countries.

Exchange Rates

Currency exchange is used by nations to pay for goods and services. The value of currency fluctuates as imports and exports are shifted and as world equilibrium shifts. The dollar, for example, is relatively strong in some markets and not so strong in others.

Financing international trade becomes a critical part of the value of the dollar. Because international trade involves the participation of other countries, the value of the dollar and exchange rates become crucial when calculating trade values. When U.S. firms export to foreign countries—for example, Japan—the U.S. firm wants to be paid in dollars while the Japanese importer prefers the yen. The importer must exchange the yen for dollars before the U.S. export transaction can occur.

The problem of different currencies can be resolved in foreign exchange markets where any one currency can purchase another currency. International banks back the purchases of various currencies and facilitate the foreign exchange market. Suppose a U.S. firm agrees to export $100,000 of television sets to a Japanese firm. Let's also suppose that the exchange rate is $2 for 1 yen. This means that the Japanese importer must pay the equivalent of 50,000 yen for the $100,000 in television sets. Let's also assume that all buyers of yen and dollars are in the United States and Japan. These are the steps that must be taken to form this transaction with exchange rates:

1. To pay for the television sets, a Japanese buyer writes a check for 50,000 yen and sends it to its U.S. exporter.
2. To pay for its costs, the U.S. exporter must convert the yen into dollars by selling the Japanese check to a U.S. bank, which then gives the exporter $100,000 (the equivalent in yen).
3. The U.S. bank deposits the 50,000 yen check in a Japanese bank for future sale to a U.S. buyer who needs yen.

The process the exchange market follows is tedious and precise. Banks can make money off currency as rates fluctuate on a daily basis. The U.S. banks are willing to buy foreign currencies because they can make money from such transactions. If the U.S. exporter sold the check at a time when the dollar was weak, then the bank would benefit from any future strength the dollar gained on the yen. Banks make money off exchange market fluctuations. Conversely, banks can also lose money as a result of exchange market fluctuations.

The Balance of Payments

The **balance of payments** is basically the sum of all transactions that occur between a country's residents and the residents of international countries. Transaction examples include tourism, the import and export of goods and services, and any interest or dividends received or paid internationally. The balance of payment statements for a country include all internationally originated income and expenditures.

The **current account** describes a country's trade in currently produced goods and services. The current account includes all imports and exports a country is making and receiving. U.S. exports typically have a plus sign next to them on a balance sheet because they are considered income. U.S. exports typically have a minus sign next to them because they are considered expenditures in the economy.

A balance of goods describes the relationship between imports and exports. If a nation's imports outweigh its exports, then there is an imbalance of goods. The imbalance arises from an unequal monetary value for imported items and exported items. A country's exports must earn enough revenue to finance its imports or there will be an imbalance of trade.

Flexible Exchange Rates

When a nation has an imbalance of trade, the adjustments it makes to correct the imbalance depends on the exchange rate system in use. The two common exchange rate systems are:

■ **Flexible exchange rate system:** Guided by the forces of supply and demand. Supply and demand determine the exchange rates without government intervention.

■ **Fixed exchange rate system:** Guided or determined by the government. The government is responsible for maintaining and supervising the country's exchange rate system.

Exchange Rate Determinants

Exchange rate determinants are factors that would cause a nation's currency to depreciate or appreciate in value. They are the principles that guide the understanding of exchange markets, and they help producers gauge or predict exchange rate occurrences. Here are three key factors to keep in mind when considering determinants:

1. The first factor to remember is rather simple and is based on the law of demand: If the demand for a nation's currency increases, that currency will appreciate in value. If the demand for a nation's currency decreases, that currency will depreciate in value.

2. The second factor is based on the law of supply. The supply of a nation's currency is inversely related to the value of that nation's currency. If a nation increases the amount of its currency, the currency depreciates. If a nation decreases the quantity of its currency, then the currency appreciates.

3. The third factor to keep in mind is based on the connection currencies have to each other. If one country is benefiting from an increasing or appreciating currency, then another country is experiencing a depreciating currency. It is not possible for all currencies to be appreciating at the same time. Currencies become interdependent of one another; therefore, as one rises in value, it is benefiting from the depreciation of another currency.

The three factors above help illustrate the concept of a determinant. The following sections discuss specific determinants.

Changes in Interest Rates

If two countries are trading, they are likely to become accustomed to the exchange rates they are using. If interest rates in the countries fluctuate, that may alter the exchange rate between the two countries. If the interest rates increase in country A and stay the same in country B, country B will find country A a beneficial place to make a financial investment. As country B makes investments, it will have to convert its currency into country A's currency. This increases the quantity of country B's currency, thereby depreciating it. Country A's currency appreciates relative to country B.

Price Level Changes

If the purchasing power of one nation's currency declines, the result could be a reevaluation of exchange rates with its participating countries. Whenever the price level fluctuates considerably, countries that are trading with one another must realign their exchange rates. The price level can determine the exchange rate between trading partners.

Income Changes

When a nation's national income grows too quickly, it is likely to depreciate. When the economy is growing rapidly, incomes are growing at a rapid rate as well. When national income rises, individuals increase their consumption of foreign and domestic goods. A country's demand for international goods increases, and in turn this depreciates the dollar because of its international availability.

Taste and Preference Changes

Changes in tastes and preferences of a good or service alter the demand of that good or service. When the demand is altered, the demand for the country's currency is also altered. If Japanese televisions become more attractive to U.S. buyers, then exchange rates will favor the Japanese because of American consumers flooding the international market with the U.S. dollar.

Before current exchange policies were developed, countries used a universally valued form of currency. Gold was used to back currencies and regulate money supplies. Countries used gold as a universally valuable tool to trade and exchange. Here are some facts regarding the international exchange of gold:

- Countries used gold to back their currencies up until the 1930s.
- Countries gauged their money supply with the amount of gold they possessed.
- Countries imported and exported gold, thereby appreciating and depreciating their currencies.

Chapter Review Questions

1. What does the word *globalization* refer to?

   A. The increasing amount of tariffs used around the world
   B. The idea of being self-sufficient in production and use of resources
   C. The idea of specialization occurring between nations that are increasingly interdependent
   D. When countries are using gold for trade and exchange
   E. None of the above

2. Which of the following could contribute to the U.S. balance of trade deficit?

   A. China pays interest on its debt to a U.S. bank.
   B. An Egyptian builds a large estate in the United States.
   C. U.S. tourists travel in large numbers to Japan.
   D. Exports to Russia are increased.
   E. Toyota builds a motor plant in Iowa.

3. Which of the following describes a barrier to trade in the form of laws forbidding trade in certain goods?

   A. A tariff
   B. An embargo
   C. A quota
   D. Import taxes
   E. A voluntary trade agreement

4. An increase in U.S. tariffs on foreign produced steel would benefit all of the following except:

   A. Domestic steel producers
   B. U.S. steel workers
   C. Domestic steel users
   D. Domestic iron producers
   E. Related steel-producing firms

5. The following table gives the number of tons of wheat and corn that can be produced in country A and country B by using the exact same amount of productive resources:

	Wheat	*Corn*
Country A	10	5
Country B	8	2

The theory of comparative advantage suggests that under these conditions, country B would find it beneficial to:

   A. Export wheat and import corn
   B. Export corn and import wheat
   C. Export both wheat and corn
   D. Import both corn and wheat
   E. Neither import nor export wheat or corn

6. In a free market system, the government:

    A. Is not needed

    B. Directs production and distribution plans

    C. Only establishes and protects property rights

    D. Regulates key production industries such as oil and utilities

    E. Redistributes all economic profit earned

7. If California and New York both produced wine and cheese, how would we be able to determine production advantages?

    A. We would need to know the tax rate in both states.

    B. We would need to know what opportunity costs each state has in producing wine and cheese.

    C. We would need to know how much wine and cheese each state produces in a day.

    D. We cannot determine any production advantages for these states.

    E. We would need to know if California imports its wine.

8. If total exports exceed total imports, what is the United States experiencing?

    A. A balance of payments deficit

    B. A balance of payments surplus

    C. A balance of trade deficit

    D. A balance of trade surplus

    E. A budget surplus

9. If Americans decide to buy less English tea:

    A. The demand for England's pound will shift to the right.

    B. The demand for England's pound will shift to the left.

    C. The supply of England's pound will shift to the left.

    D. The demand for U.S. dollars will shift to the left.

    E. The supply of U.S. dollars will shift to the right.

10. Labor-intensive products are likely to be exported by countries:

    A. With a small population

    B. With a highly skilled labor force

    C. With many unskilled workers

    D. That have few raw materials

    E. That have abundant capital resources

11. The main reason behind creating barriers for the importation of goods and services from abroad is to:

    A. Increase economic efficiency

    B. Reduce the prices of domestically produced goods

    C. Help expand the exportation of goods

    D. Benefit from special interest groups

    E. Lower the cost of producing goods

12. All other things constant, if there is an increase in U.S. exports, then there will be:

    A. An increase in U.S. demand for foreign currencies

    B. A decrease in the supply of foreign currencies

    C. Upward pressure on the U.S. price level

    D. A decrease in the United States' GDP

    E. A decrease in U.S. interest rates

13. Which of the following is true regarding a flexible exchange rate system?

    A. There is no government involvement.

    B. The government only controls the forces of supply and demand.

    C. The government controls all aspects of the exchange rate system.

    D. The system can only be used with gold.

    E. The system depends on the geographical location of the country.

14. Which of the following describes what happens to the dollar if demand for imports rises?

    A. Eventually the dollar will lose its value internationally.

    B. The dollar will initially have low value, but it will get stronger eventually.

    C. Imports have no impact on the dollar.

    D. The dollar will appreciate only if imports and exports decrease.

    E. The dollar will depreciate only if imports and exports increase.

15. Which of the following is a main guiding force in the flexible exchange market?

    A. The government

    B. Supply and demand

    C. Inflation

    D. Currency

    E. Specialization

Answers to Review Questions

  1. C. Globalization is a term that refers to the increasing interdependency between nations. As specialization becomes more common in the world, countries learn to depend on one another for goods they cannot specialize in. This dependency translates into efficient and lower production costs.

  2. C. U.S. tourists traveling in large numbers to Japan contributes to a trade deficit because the dollar is being spent in large amounts abroad. The dollar is not being spent on domestic goods; rather, it is being spent on international goods that will contribute to a trade deficit.

  3. B. An embargo is a law that forbids the trade of certain goods. Embargoes do not limit or tax the amount of goods traded; they simply stop the availability of a good in an economy. Embargoes are created and lifted by the government.

  4. C. An increase in tariffs would benefit all of the choices except for U.S. steel users. A tariff would eliminate competition for domestic steel producers. With less competition, domestic steel producers can increase their price, benefiting the company, workers, and even related industries. However, this increase in the price of domestic steel would come at the expense of consumers, who would have no choice but to pay for a more expensive product.

5. A. It would be most beneficial for country B to export wheat and import corn because it would have an easier time specializing in wheat. Remember that countries will specialize in goods that have the lowest opportunity cost in producing.

6. C. In a free market or capitalistic system, the government's role is to establish and protect property rights. Property rights become unclear when dealing with different sectors, such as the public sector and the private sector. With the government's direction, individual property rights can be defined and protected.

7. B. To determine production advantages, we would need to know the opportunity costs each state faces in its production of wine and cheese. With this knowledge, we can determine who should specialize in what product.

8. D. If U.S. exports exceed imports, the country is experiencing a trade surplus.

9. B. If Americans decide to buy less English tea, the demand for the English pound will shift to the left because fewer dollars are being converted into pounds for the sale of tea. Whenever the demand for a product decreases, the demand for the currency that represents that product also decreases because less currency is being exchanged for the purchase of that product.

10. C. Countries with many unskilled workers use labor-intensive production. This is because with little skill, workers have limited capabilities in the production of certain goods. Machines and other production methods cannot be maximized because workers do not possess the skills to use them.

11. C. When governments elect to use a protectionist method, they are doing so to expand the level of exports for the country.

12. B. All other things held constant, if U.S. exports increase, then the supply of foreign currency will decrease because foreign countries are converting their currencies to the dollar to purchase U.S. goods.

13. A. Flexible exchange systems have no government involvement. The exchange rates are determined by the forces of supply and demand. These forces reveal exchange rates, prices, and distribution. They also allow a nation to decide whether it should specialize in the production of a certain good or service.

14. A. If the U.S. demand for imports rises, eventually the dollar loses its value internationally because more dollars are being spent to purchase foreign currencies and products. As the dollar becomes increasingly present abroad, its value decreases.

15. B. Supply and demand are the main guiding forces in a flexible exchange market. The government has no involvement, and it is the forces of supply and demand that dictate exchange rates in this system.

PART IV

AP MACROECONOMICS AND MICROECONOMICS TESTS

Section I

- 60 multiple choice questions 70 minutes

Section II

- 1 long free-response question and
- 2 short free-response questions 10 minutes for planning
  50 minutes for writing

Total Time: 2 Hours and 10 Minutes

Macroeconomics Section I: Multiple-Choice Questions

Directions: You have 70 minutes to complete the 60 multiple-choice questions in this section of the exam.

1. Circular flow models:

   A. Illustrate firms as the buyers in a product market

   B. Illustrate firms as the sellers in a factor market

   C. Are only used by business owners

   D. Show no government involvement

   E. Illustrate firms as the suppliers in a product market

2. Which one of the following statements is true regarding classical economists?

   A. The market needs government intervention.

   B. The government does not need to intervene in every situation and should do so only when the economy is in trouble.

   C. The market is not self-correcting.

   D. The market is self-correcting.

   E. None of the above.

3. What will an increase in corporate taxes do to aggregate supply?

   A. Increase it.

   B. Decrease it.

   C. Have no impact.

   D. Increase only if firms pay taxes.

   E. Have no impact if aggregate demand decreases.

4. Which of the following increases the nation's GDP?

   A. Mr. Lane purchases a share of stock in an automobile company.

   B. A clothing storeowner increases her stock of clothing.

   C. The government increases its domestic purchases of clothing for the military.

   D. A soda company sells its soda from last year's inventory.

   E. A father sells his water skis to his son.

5. Which of the following is likely to occur to an economy when it is experiencing a shortage of goods?

   A. The amount of investment spending by firms and the government increases.

   B. Interest rates increase.

   C. Interest rates decrease.

   D. The demand for money increases.

   E. The demand for money decreases.

6. Inflationary gaps can be covered by:

   A. A decrease in personal income taxes

   B. An increase in the money supply

   C. An increase in spending

   D. An increase in personal income taxes

   E. An increase in the minimum wage

7. According to Keynesians, expansionary monetary policy means:

    A. Lower interest rates and more investment

    B. Lower prices

    C. Higher prices

    D. Higher real income and higher interest rates

    E. No change in the economy

8. In what way can the Federal Reserve increase the money supply?

    A. Selling gold to banks

    B. Selling bonds to firms

    C. Buying international bonds

    D. Buying gold from foreign countries

    E. Buying government bonds on the open market

9. If a bank receives a deposit of $400 and its excess reserves increased by $350, what is the reserve requirement?

    A. 13 percent

    B. 10 percent

    C. 5 percent

    D. 25 percent

    E. 2 percent

10. According to Keynesians, what happens to savings when aggregate income increases?

    A. Savings increase by less than the amount of the increase in income.

    B. Savings decrease by less than the amount of the increase in income.

    C. There is no change in savings.

    D. Savings exceed the amount of the increase in income.

    E. None of the above.

11. Which of the following is true when the demand for holding money increases because of an expectation of increased interest rates?

    A. Individuals are holding money for transactions.

    B. Individuals are holding money for exchange.

    C. Individuals are holding money for liquidity.

    D. Individuals are holding money for speculation.

    E. Individuals are holding money for emergencies.

12. If the federal government is currently experiencing a budget deficit, which of the following is likely to occur?

    A. Interest rates will fall.

    B. Investment will decline.

    C. Taxes will decrease.

    D. The nation's debt will rise.

    E. State governments will cover the national government's spending gap.

13. An increase in Italy's demand for U.S. goods will cause the U.S. dollar to:

    A. Depreciate because of inflationary expectations

    B. Depreciate because of Italy's demand

    C. Appreciate because Italy would be buying more U.S. dollars

    D. Appreciate because Italy would be selling more U.S. dollars

    E. None of the above

14. Contractionary supply shocks produce:

    A. Increases in aggregate demand

    B. GDP increases

    C. Net national product increases

    D. Deflation

    E. An increase in unemployment

15. If nominal GDP is increasing and real GDP is decreasing, which of the following could be the reason?

    A. A rising unemployment level

    B. Inflation

    C. Imports that are less than exports

    D. A period of economic contraction

    E. Government deficits

16. Why is the official unemployment rate not an accurate assessment of unemployment?

    A. Because government spending is not taken into account.

    B. Full employment is greater than the natural employment rate.

    C. Structural employment never exists.

    D. Discouraged workers are not accounted for.

    E. None of the above.

17. To reach its goal of full employment in an economy experiencing a recession, the Fed should:

  A. Increase spending
  B. Buy open market bonds from the government
  C. Sell open market bonds
  D. Increase the reserve ratio
  E. Increase the price level

18. What best describes a recession?

  A. Two consecutive quarters of increasing GDP
  B. When investment is too high
  C. When firms decide to hire more workers
  D. Two consecutive quarters of declining GDP
  E. When the stock market is not performing well

19. The spending multiplier can decrease as a result of:

  A. A reduction in taxes
  B. A decline in exports
  C. A decline in imports
  D. An increase in government spending
  E. An increase in the marginal propensity to save

20. Which of the following is part of M1?

  A. Gold
  B. Silver
  C. Checkable deposits
  D. Savings accounts
  E. Large certificates of deposit

21. The value of the multiplier will decrease because:

  A. The velocity of money is increasing.
  B. Interest rates are high.
  C. Unemployment is low.
  D. The government is in a budget deficit.
  E. People are holding their money in currency.

22. Which of the following would require a restrictive monetary policy?

  A. High employment
  B. High inflation
  C. High unemployment
  D. Low interest rates
  E. A budget deficit

23. What is the purpose of automatic stabilizers?

  A. To reduce public spending
  B. To help balance the federal government's budget
  C. To stabilize the unemployment rate
  D. To produce more jobs
  E. To reduce the inflation rate

24. Which of the following would be responsible for a decline in GDP?

  A. Negative net investment
  B. Introduction of new technology
  C. Deflation
  D. A decrease in the death rate of foreigners
  E. A decline in wages

25. Unexpected increases in inventories precede:

  A. Price level increases
  B. Import increases
  C. High unemployment and price levels
  D. Decreases in production
  E. A decline in unemployment

26. The short-run aggregate supply curve will decline when:

  A. The government increases spending.
  B. Productivity becomes more expensive.
  C. The money supply increases.
  D. The federal budget deficit increases.
  E. Imports increase.

27. Economists believe that unemployment is:

  A. Overstated
  B. Understated
  C. All cyclical
  D. All structural
  E. All seasonal

28. Which one of the following will not cause a shift in aggregate demand?

  A. Consumption
  B. Investment
  C. Exports
  D. Corporate income taxes
  E. Government spending

GO ON TO THE NEXT PAGE

29. What occurs when full employment is reached?

    A.   There is no unemployment.

    B.   Only teenagers are counted as unemployed.

    C.   There is about a 5 percent rate of unemployment.

    D.   Only seasonal and cyclical unemployment exist.

    E.   None of the above.

30. Which of the following is true when the economy is operating at productive capacity?

    A.   Aggregate demand can increase aggregate supply by having firms employ more workers.

    B.   Aggregate demand can decrease the price level by hiring more workers.

    C.   The price level will rise if demand continues to increase.

    D.   There will be no price level increase.

    E.   Deflation will occur.

31. If Jill lost her job because the economy is in a recession, this is an example of:

    A.   Structural unemployment

    B.   Cyclical unemployment

    C.   Seasonal unemployment

    D.   A discouraged worker

    E.   Frictional unemployment

32. Which of the following is an example of a contractionary fiscal policy?

    A.   A decline in spending and taxes

    B.   Tax increases; a decline in spending

    C.   A rise in spending; a decrease in taxes

    D.   An increase in spending and taxes

    E.   An increase in interest rates

33. What is a possible reason for tax cuts failing to stimulate the economy?

    A.   The tax cut is permanent and raises disposable income.

    B.   The tax cut is temporary and the price level is rising.

    C.   The tax cut increases production of goods and services.

    D.   The tax cut makes it easier for consumers to purchase goods.

    E.   None of the above.

34. To an economist, investment means:

    A.   Purchasing bonds

    B.   Purchasing capital

    C.   Purchasing stocks

    D.   Purchasing mutual funds

    E.   Putting your money in a savings account

35. Which of the following discourages exports?

    A.   Increasing the reserve requirements

    B.   Increasing the tax on imports

    C.   Decreasing the tax on imports

    D.   Increasing government spending

    E.   Decreasing a tax on domestic firms

36. The purpose of monetary policy is to:

    A.   Control government spending

    B.   Shift aggregate demand

    C.   Increase GDP

    D.   Alter the money supply

    E.   Increase taxes

37. Which of the following explains why the long-run Phillips Curve is vertical?

    A.   The inflation rate is always the same.

    B.   The natural rate of unemployment never changes.

    C.   Any level of inflation can occur at the full-employment rate in the long run.

    D.   Any level of unemployment can occur at the full-employment rate of inflation in the long run.

    E.   None of the above.

38. What step does the Fed take when it decides to decrease the money supply?

    A.   Reduces interest rates

    B.   Increases interest rates

    C.   Increases private spending

    D.   Sells government bonds

    E.   Decreases the reserve ratio

39. What impact will a tariff have on imported cars?

    A.   The tariff will make cars more expensive domestically.

    B.   The tariff will decrease unemployment.

    C.   The tariff will increase spending.

    D.   The tariff will encourage investment.

    E.   There will be no impact on imported cars.

40. Which of the following is a tool used by the Federal Reserve?

 A. Stagflation
 B. Natural rate of unemployment
 C. Price changes
 D. Wage changes
 E. None of the above

41. If the nominal interest rate is 6 percent and the expected inflation rate is 4 percent, what is the real interest rate?

 A. 10 percent
 B. 6 percent
 C. 4 percent
 D. 2 percent
 E. –2 percent

42. How does the U.S. government define unemployment?

 A. Individuals who do not hold a paying job
 B. Individuals who have been recently fired
 C. Individuals who work part-time but need full-time work
 D. Individuals without a job but looking for work
 E. Individuals who want a job but are not searching for one because of perceived availability

43. What happens to the economy if there is a major improvement in technology?

 A. Aggregate demand increases.
 B. Aggregate demand decreases.
 C. Aggregate supply increases.
 D. Aggregate supply decreases.
 E. Aggregate expenditures decrease.

44. In response to an increase in investment during an inflationary period, the government should:

 A. Lower taxes
 B. Increase spending
 C. Raise taxes
 D. Decrease interest rates
 E. Increase interest rates

45. Which of the following is an example of structural unemployment?

 A. Schoolteachers unemployed during the summer
 B. A college graduate looking for his first job
 C. A high school student seeking part-time employment at the local grocery store
 D. A worker who just lost her job because she doesn't know how to use the new computer
 E. None of the above

46. Which of the following is true about the product market of the circular flow diagram?

 A. Businesses pay wages, rent, and profits to households in return for use of factors of production.
 B. Businesses purchase goods and services from households in return for money payments.
 C. Households pay wages, rent, interest, and profits to businesses in return for use of factors of production.
 D. The relationship between households and businesses exists only in a command economy.
 E. The relationship between households and businesses exists only in an authoritative economy.

47. Which of the following is a possible cause of stagflation?

 A. Increases in labor productivity
 B. An increase in the price for raw materials
 C. Rapid growth and development of an industry
 D. A decline in labor unions
 E. A low growth rate of the money supply

48. Fiscal policy could be used to aid which dilemma most effectively according to a Keynesian?

 A. Low aggregate supply
 B. Inflation
 C. Low aggregate demand
 D. Homelessness
 E. World hunger

GO ON TO THE NEXT PAGE

49. Which of the following is true if a country is operating its resources inside the production possibilities curve?

    A. It has a market economy.

    B. It has a centrally planned economy.

    C. It is in the early stages of industrial development.

    D. It is underutilizing its resources.

    E. It is using its resources efficiently.

50. What type of policy is most likely to encourage long-run economic growth?

    A. A reduction in government spending

    B. An increase in taxes

    C. An increase in tariffs

    D. An increase in government spending

    E. Both A and C

51. Which of the following is a tool of monetary policy?

    A. Adjusting interest rates

    B. Adjusting savings rates

    C. Selling securities

    D. Adjusting taxes

    E. None of the above

52. The sum of which of the following expenditures is equal to GDP?

    A. Consumption, unemployment transfer payments, and taxes

    B. Government spending, consumption spending, investment, and taxes

    C. Consumption spending, interest rates, taxes, and exports

    D. Exports/imports, consumption spending, government spending, and investment

    E. Exports and imports, consumption spending, government spending, and inflationary spending

53. To fight a recession, the Federal Reserve should:

    A. Buy government bonds

    B. Sell government bonds

    C. Increase government spending

    D. Decrease government spending

    E. Decrease taxes

54. If the economy is performing below its capacity, which of the following is true?

    A. Aggregate demand can rise without a substantial increase in the price level.

    B. Aggregate supply can increase without a substantial increase in the price level.

    C. The unemployment rate is low.

    D. Investment is too high.

    E. None of the above.

55. Which of the following is not a phase of the business cycle?

    A. Peak

    B. Expansion

    C. Contraction

    D. Unemployment

    E. Trough

56. What step(s) is the government likely to take to fight demand-pull inflation?

    A. Increase government spending and decrease taxes.

    B. Decrease spending and increase taxes.

    C. Increase both spending and taxes.

    D. Decrease both spending and taxes.

    E. Increase interest rates.

57. Classical economists argue that:

    A. The economy needs government spending to grow.

    B. The economy needs increases in taxes to grow.

    C. The economy needs decreases in taxes to grow.

    D. The economy should be left alone.

    E. The economy needs the government to create laws protecting the economy from a decline.

58. What step(s) can the Federal Reserve take to reduce a federal budget?

    A. Increase government spending.

    B. Decrease spending and increase taxes.

    C. Decrease taxes.

    D. Increase interest rates.

    E. None of the above.

59. What is the main reason the Fed requires commercial banks to keep reserves?

    A. To provide banks with extra money for their vaults

    B. To give the Federal Reserve more control over the money-creation operations of banks

    C. To ensure that banks do not make excessive profits off loans

    D. To help the U.S. Treasury reduce the federal government's debt

    E. To allow the government to borrow money at lower interest rates

60. When a foreign country increases its demand for U.S. goods, what impact does that have on the value of the dollar?

    A. Eventually the dollar will fall in value.

    B. Eventually the dollar will rise in value.

    C. The dollar will not change in value.

    D. The gold standard in the U.S. will increase.

    E. Foreign countries will have more U.S. dollars.

Macroeconomics Section II: Free-Response Questions

Directions: You have one hour to answer all three free-response questions: one long and two short questions. Spend the first 10 minutes for planning, and in the remaining 50 minutes construct your responses. Explain your answers thoroughly with examples and illustrations where appropriate.

1. Assume the United States is experiencing growth and that inflation is approaching high levels.

   A. Draw a correctly labeled graph illustrating this.
   B. Which governmental policy will have an impact on this condition and why? Illustrate the impact of this fiscal policy on aggregate demand.
   C. Which monetary policy might be appropriate in this situation?

2. Let's say there is a sudden increase in demand in the United States for Italian products. Explain how this increase will have an impact on the following:

   A. The money supply
   B. The value of the dollar

3. Assume that a bank is left with no excess reserves and that someone makes a deposit in the amount of $1,000.

   A. What will happen to the money supply?
   B. What is the maximum effect that this deposit can have on the money supply with the reserve requirement at 20 percent?

Multiple-Choice Answers and Explanations

1. **E.** The circular flow model illustrates firms as the suppliers in a product market. In a product market, the physical flow of goods and services goes from firms to households and, in return, households send a monetary flow for the goods and services. This is called a product market.

2. **D.** According to classicalists, the market is self-correcting when it enters disequilibrium. Classicalists believe that if abnormal circumstances (such as war, domestic crisis, and supply shocks) take place, the economy will be able to automatically adjust and return to full-employment output.

3. **B.** An increase in corporate taxes will affect aggregate supply because firms will be forced to cut back on production. Higher taxes cause production costs to rise for firms. As production costs rise, firms decrease production, thereby decreasing aggregate supply.

4. **C.** Remember that GDP does not include stock market transactions, such as the purchasing of stock, so that rules out A. GDP does not include nonmarket transactions, such as the selling of water skis to a family member. GDP is affected when the government spends money on goods and services because the government is acting as a consumer. The money being spent goes directly to firms for goods and services and may be used in the current year's calculation.

5. **B.** If the economy is experiencing excessive demand, then interest rates increase because of the demand for money. As people demand more money, interest rates rise for two reasons: First, an inverse relationship exists between interest rates and the demand for money, and second, the economy might be approaching dangerous inflation and so higher interest rates will help curb demand.

6. **D.** An increase in personal income taxes takes away purchasing power from the consumer. Since inflation is caused by excessive demand, an increase in purchasing power curbs the excessive demand and either slows down the rate of inflation or halts it.

7. **A.** Keynesians believe that lower interest rates promote more investing. As interest rates fall, investment rises. Remember that investment is not the buying of stock; rather, it is the purchase of capital. When interest rates decline, more firms increase their purchases of capital.

8. **E.** When the Fed wants to increase the money supply, it has a variety of tools it can use. The most common tool the Fed uses is the buying and selling of open-market securities. When the Fed wants to increase the money supply, it buys government bonds. Conversely, when the Fed wants to decrease the money supply, it sells securities.

9. **A.** If there is an initial deposit of $400 and the bank's excess reserves expand by $350, then the reserve requirement is 13 percent. The difference between $400 and $350 is $50. You can divide the $50 by the $400 to get 13 percent. The bank, in this example, must keep 13 percent of the deposit in its reserves while 87 percent of the deposit can go to its excess reserve (where that money can be lent out).

10. **A.** When there is an increase in income, there is an increase in spending by consumers. The propensity to consume is always higher than the propensity to save. Whenever there is an increase in income, savings rise but not at the rate of the increase in income because most of the increase in income is going to consumption.

11. **D.** Individuals choose to hold money instead of investing in bonds because they are anticipating a rise in interest rates. If interest rates are low, there is no incentive for individuals to hold money in a bank. Therefore, individuals keep money on hand to deposit into interest-bearing accounts when interest rates rise. They are anticipating the rise of interest rates.

12. **D.** If the federal government is experiencing a budget deficit, the deficit will soon turn into debt because the government will need to spend money. When the government realizes a deficit, it covers that deficit by borrowing money. When it borrows money, the government creates debt.

13. **C.** When foreign countries demand increases for U.S. goods, the value of the dollar increases because of that demand. Italy will cause the demand for the dollar and U.S. goods to rise, thereby strengthening the dollar. An eventual impact of this scenario might be that the U.S dollar gains too much strength, thus causing exports to decrease.

14. E. Whenever there is a contractionary supply shock, aggregate supply decreases. Whether it is a natural disaster or the result of human activity, supply shocks hurt the economy because they limit the quantity of units firms can produce. When a firm's production is limited, it is forced to cut back on labor. As a result, the unemployment rate rises because of a contractionary supply shock.

15. B. If the nominal rate of GDP is increasing while real GDP is decreasing, one possible effect could be inflation. Remember that nominal GDP is not inflation adjusted; therefore, any increases in inflation may distort nominal GDP relative to real GDP.

16. D. The official unemployment rate is understated because people who are able but not willing to work are not counted as unemployed. Discouraged workers—workers who have given up on looking for a job for one reason or another—are not counted in the unemployment rate. Remember that the definition of an *unemployed* person is someone who is willing and able to work but does not have a job.

17. B. To help an economy that is underachieving, the Federal Reserve can buy open-market securities to increase the money supply. This is an example of expansionary, or "loose," monetary policy.

18. D. A recession is defined as two consecutive quarters of declining GDP. However, some economists believe that this definition is too cut-and-dried. The economy tends to bounce back and forth from declining GDP, making it difficult at times to gauge a recession.

19. E. When the marginal propensity to save increases, it causes the spending multiplier to decrease because less money is being spent and more money is being saved. In order for the multiplier to gain strength, individuals have to increase consumption relative to savings.

20. C. The largest portion of the money supply is M1, and checkable deposits are a part of M1. Paper money, coins, checkable deposits, and travelers checks are all a part of M1.

21. B. When interest rates are high, more people keep their money in interest-bearing accounts. This reduces the impact of the spending multiplier because more money is being saved than spent. As consumption increases, the multiplier increases.

22. B. High levels of inflation require attention from the Federal Reserve. The Fed can implement a contractionary monetary policy that will reduce the money supply. The most common way the Fed can go about this is by selling open-market securities. The selling of open-market securities helps reduce the money supply, thereby decreasing the rate at which the price level is rising.

23. B. Automatic stabilizers or built-in stabilizers help balance the government's budget because they are designed to increase tax revenue at a point where government spending is creating debt. They can either increase tax revenue (to help reduce debt) or decrease tax revenue (to help control surpluses).

24. A. Negative net investment reduces GDP. Investment (the purchase of capital) is a key component of GDP. When investment decreases, firms begin to lose revenue, and the amount of goods and services produced in a year declines.

25. D. Unexpected rises in inventories come before a decrease in production. When firms realize their inventories are increasing in size, they cut back on production. When production is curtailed, the next step is to reduce a firm's labor force. The rise in inventories means that producers are supplying more than what is being demanded.

26. B. When productivity becomes more expensive, firms have no choice but to cut back on production. A decline in production translates to a decrease in aggregate supply.

27. B. Economists believe that the unemployment rate is understated because it does not include such factors as discouraged workers. Unemployed individuals who have given up looking for a job (for one reason or another) are not accounted for in the unemployment rate.

28. D. Corporate income taxes do not cause a shift in aggregate demand; shifts results from changes in consumption, government spending, exports, and investment. Corporate income taxes are designed to affect aggregate supply through the costs of production.

29. C. When full employment is reached, there is about a 5 percent rate of unemployment. Full employment is reached when the economy is at its productive capacity. At any point after full employment, there is little growth and only increases in the price level.

30. C. When the economy is at productive capacity, any increase in demand causes the price level to increase further and offer no growth to the economy.

31. B. Cyclical unemployment is a result of the economy experiencing contractionary elements. If Jill loses her job because she does not possess the skills to accomplish certain tasks assigned to her, then she is considered structurally unemployed. But because Jill loses her job in the midst of a recession, she is classified as cyclically unemployed.

32. B. Contractionary fiscal policy is a combination of increased taxes and decreased spending. The government does this to fight inflation. Contractionary fiscal policy is using either of the tools (spending or taxes) or using both tools simultaneously.

33. B. A tax cut that is temporary during a period of rising price levels will not have a significant impact on growth. Tax cuts are used to stimulate disposable income, thereby encouraging consumers to spend more money. If a tax cut is implemented and the price level is rising, the goal of growth could be compromised. Goods and services would become more expensive at a time when disposable income is temporarily being increased.

34. B. To an economist, investment means the purchase of capital. The term *investment* is used to describe a firm's decision to borrow money to buy machines, raw materials, and labor. When investment increases, firms are choosing to buy more factors of production.

35. C. Decreasing the tax on imports discourages exports because foreign goods in the United States become cheaper. When goods become cheaper, consumers buy more foreign goods, thereby increasing the demand for imports relative to exports.

36. D. The main purpose of monetary policy is to influence the money supply. The Fed does not control government spending, nor can it increase GDP or influence taxes. The Fed's purpose is to influence the money supply, and it can do this by using three tools (the reserve requirement, open-market securities, and the discount rate).

37. C. Any level of inflation can occur at the full-employment rate in the long run. The Phillips Curve illustrates the relationship between inflation and unemployment. In the long run, the inflation rate does not have an impact on employment.

38. D. The Fed decreases the money supply by selling government bonds. When bonds are sold, the money supply decreases. This is an example of contractionary monetary policy.

39. A. When a tariff is placed on an import, the cost of that good increases. Cars that are imported to the United States will become more expensive because dealers will initially have to incur the costs of the import. Once the dealer pays the tariff for the import, it will increase the cost of the car to compensate for the tariff.

40. E. The Fed cannot induce or control stagflation, wage changes, unemployment, and price changes. The Fed has three tools it works with (the reserve requirement, open-market securities, and the discount rate), and those three tools help it control the money supply.

41. D. If the nominal rate of interest is 6 percent and the inflation rate is 4 percent, then the real rate of interest is 2 percent because inflation erodes interest. For example, if you take out a $100 loan at 3 percent interest per year and the inflation rate is 1 percent, the real or actual amount you will be paying back is only 2 percent. Inflation helps borrowers with their debt.

42. D. The United States defines unemployment as those individuals without jobs but who are looking for work. The unemployment rate is calculated without considering those who choose not to actively seek work.

43. C. A major improvement in technology will make it less expensive for firms to produce goods and services. The aggregate supply curve will shift to the right, indicating an increase in production because of cheaper production costs. For example, if a new machine were able to convert water into fuel, fuel costs would decrease significantly.

44. C. In response to an increase in investment in an inflationary time, the government (in an effort to reduce consumption) should increase taxes. When taxes are increased, the purchasing power of consumers is weakened. An increase in taxes decreases the amount of disposable income individuals have.

45. D. Structural unemployment refers to an individual not having the necessary skills to perform a required task. When an individual loses his job because he does not know how to use a new computer, he is lacking the skills necessary to perform his job. Structural unemployment usually occurs as a result of new technology. Technology creates growth; however, the full impact of its growth cannot be felt until the long run because people need to acquire the skills to use the new technology.

46. A. In a product market, businesses pay or send a monetary flow to households for land, labor, and capital. Households are the beneficiaries of a monetary flow in this instance and give businesses aid in production.

47. B. An increase in the price for raw materials would trigger a twofold problem. First, it would initiate a rise in the price level because producers would have to increase prices to compensate for expensive raw materials. Second, it would force producers to cut back on labor and thus add to the unemployment rate.

48. C. According to Keynesians, fiscal policy could most effectively remedy low aggregate demand. When aggregate demand is lacking, government spending increases consumption and disposable income.

49. D. The production possibilities curve represents efficiency. Every point on the curve is a representation of being efficient with resources. If a country is underachieving or underutilizing, the country's production possibilities are located inside the line of efficiency.

50. D. An increase in government spending encourages long-run economic growth because it creates employment and increases disposable income. When more resources are employed, the economy has a better chance of attaining efficient use of its resources.

51. C. Selling securities is a tool of monetary policy. It is also the most common tool used by the Fed because it can quickly be altered. Also, the effects of buying and selling securities on the money supply can be felt almost immediately.

52. D. Consumption spending, exports/imports, government spending, and investment are all calculated as the nation's income. Total income is measured for GDP.

53. A. To fight a recession, the Fed should buy securities to increase the money supply. When the money supply is increased, individuals are given the incentive to consume more. This is an example of "loose" monetary policy.

54. A. If the economy is performing below its capacity, aggregate demand can increase without a substantial impact on the price level. The economy can welcome growth because resources are not fully employed. When the economy reaches its productive capacity, it has reached a point where resources are fully employed; after this point, there is little or no room for growth.

55. D. Unemployment is not a phase of the business cycle. Unemployment may be a result of the contraction or trough phase of the business cycle, but it is not a phase itself. The four phases are expansion, peak, contraction, and trough.

56. B. To fight demand-pull inflation, the government will decrease spending and/or raise taxes. Decreasing spending slows economic growth. Raising taxes decreases disposable income, which in turn decreases aggregate demand. A decrease in aggregate demand stabilizes the price level.

57. D. Classical economists argue that the economy is self-correcting and should be left alone. Any governmental intervention is considered detrimental to an economy.

58. E. It is not the responsibility of the Fed to reduce the government's budget debt. The Fed's responsibilities are to monitor and control the money supply.

59. B. The main reason the Fed requires reserves for banks is to give the Fed more control over the money supply. With control over the money-creation process, the Fed can monitor bank activities and ensure that transactions are being handled properly.

60. B. When foreign countries increase their demand for U.S. goods, the value of the dollar increases because demand for the dollar increases. In time, however, U.S. exports could become too expensive for Italy and the demand for U.S. exports would decrease, lessening the power of the dollar.

Free-Response Answers and Explanations

1. A. There are two ways to handle this solution. If you drew either of the following graphs, then you are correct.

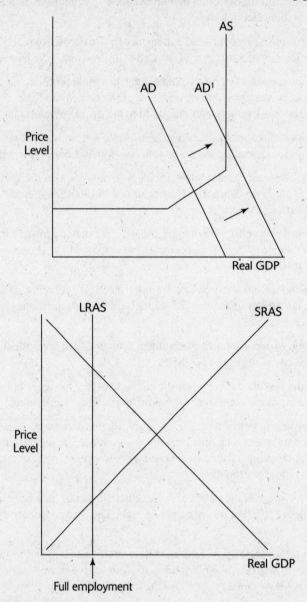

B. There are also two ways to handle this solution:

- A decrease in government spending will have an impact on a rising price level. A decrease in government expenditures will slow private sector growth.

- An increase in personal taxes will help stabilize the price level by decreasing disposable income.

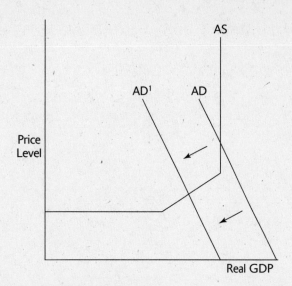

C. The monetary policy that is appropriate in this situation is restrictive monetary policy. For example, selling government bonds or increasing the discount rate.

2. A. An increase in demand for Italian products will lead to an increase in the supply of dollars to purchase Italian currency. The increase in the supply of dollars will decrease the value of the dollar abroad.

B. The domestic value of the dollar will rise because there will be a reduced supply of dollars in the U.S. to convert to Italian currency.

3. A. The $1,000 deposit will increase the money supply because banks will be loaning out portions of the deposit.

B. The maximum amount of an increase is $4,000. The money multiplier is 1/RR:

$$1/.2 = \text{multiplier (5)}$$

Remember to deduct the original amount of the deposit to determine the true impact the deposit has on the money supply:

$$5 \times \$1,000 = \$5,000$$
$$\underline{-\$1,000} \text{ (original deposit)}$$
$$\$4,000 \text{ increase in money supply}$$

Macroeconomics Full-Length Practice Test 2

Section I
- 60 multiple choice questions — 70 minutes

Section II
- 1 long free-response question and
- 2 short free-response questions — 10 minutes for planning
  50 minutes for writing

Total Time: 2 Hours and 10 Minutes

Macroeconomics Section I: Multiple-Choice Questions

Directions: You have 70 minutes to complete the 60 multiple-choice questions in this section of the exam.

1. Which of the following would cause the production possibilities curve to shift outward (to the right)?

   A. Reopening an oil factory that had been closed
   B. Rehiring oil workers
   C. Using machinery for steel production instead of oil production
   D. Becoming more efficient at making oil
   E. Using machinery for oil production instead of steel production

2. If in 1976, nominal GDP grew by 11 percent and real GDP grew by 5 percent, what would be the inflation rate for this year?

   A. 2 percent
   B. −6 percent
   C. 6 percent
   D. 3 percent
   E. 16 percent

3. Of the following types of unemployment, which one is structural unemployment?

   A. A software engineer who leaves his job to move to Spain
   B. A worker who loses his job during a recession
   C. An assembly line worker who is replaced by a machine
   D. A teacher who is unemployed during the summer months
   E. A worker who is unproductive

4. If there were a large labor productivity increase, what would be the effect on GDP and the price level?

   A. An increase in GDP, an increase in the price level
   B. An increase in GDP, a decrease in the price level
   C. No effect on GDP, an increase in the price level
   D. A decrease in GDP, an increase in the price level
   E. A decrease in GDP, a decrease in the price level

5. Which of the following could be attributed to an increase in the spending multiplier?

   A. An increase in the supply of money
   B. An increase in GDP
   C. An increase in personal income taxes
   D. An increase in the marginal propensity to consume
   E. An increase in the required reserve ratio

6. According to Keynesians, which of the following could be attributed to an increase in aggregate demand?

   A. An increase in investment
   B. An increase in interest rates
   C. A decrease in transfer payments
   D. A decrease in government expenditures
   E. A decrease in consumer spending

7. *Question 7 refers to the following graph.*

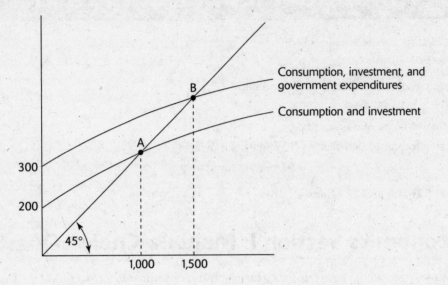

In the graph above, equilibrium A is indicated for an economy without government spending. With the addition of government spending resulting at equilibrium B, which of the following must be true?

A.   Government spending is $500 and the spending multiplier is 5.
B.   Government spending is $100 and the multiplier is 5.
C.   Government spending is $100 and consumption increases by $500.
D.   Government spending has no effect on GDP.
E.   Consumption increases government spending by $300.

8. How can commercial banks increase the money supply?

A.   By transferring funds to the Federal Reserve
B.   By buying bonds from the Federal Reserve
C.   By transferring money to other banks
D.   By keeping all deposits in reserves
E.   By lending out excess reserves

9. If the reserve requirement is 20 percent, the existence of $100 in excess reserves can create how much money in the money supply?

A. $20
B. $100
C. $300
D. $500
E. $750

10. If the Federal Reserve lowers the reserve requirement for banks, which of the following is true?

A.   There will be an increase in the money supply.
B.   Interest rates will rise.
C.   There will be a decrease in the money supply.
D.   Banks will be forced to keep more money in their vaults.
E.   Businesses will purchase less capital equipment.

11. If the transaction demand for money increases, what is the impact on the banking system?

A.   The Fed can decrease unemployment.
B.   The Fed can decrease aggregate supply.
C.   The Fed can decrease taxes.
D.   Banks will have a difficult time loaning excess reserves.
E.   Banks will have an easy time loaning excess reserves.

12. According to Keynesians, what will an increase in spending and a decrease in taxes do to consumption and unemployment?

    A. A decrease in consumption, an increase in unemployment

    B. A decrease in consumption, no change in unemployment

    C. An increase in consumption, a decrease in unemployment

    D. An increase in consumption, an increase in unemployment

    E. No change in consumption, a decrease in unemployment

13. Which of the following is the best solution for a recession?

    A. Increased taxes, increased spending

    B. Decreased taxes, increased spending

    C. Decreased taxes, decreased spending

    D. Increased taxes, decreased spending

    E. None of the above

14. If the economy is functioning at full employment, and an increase in income tax with a reduction of government spending is implemented to reduce government debt, which of the following is most likely to occur?

    A. An increase in employment

    B. An increase in the inflation rate

    C. A decrease in employment

    D. An increase in government debt

    E. A decrease in the price level

15. To protect domestic producers, a country poses a tariff on an imported good (X); which of the following is likely to occur?

    A. An increase in the production of X

    B. A decrease in the price for X

    C. An increase in the price for X

    D. A decrease in the quantity of X

    E. Both C and D

16. When two countries decide to specialize and trade, which of the following will occur?

    A. The goods the countries are trading become more expensive.

    B. The goods the countries are trading become scarcer.

    C. Unemployment will increase in both countries.

    D. There will be more efficient production of the traded goods.

    E. Both countries will be producing at less efficient rates.

17. Which of the following situations would have a positive impact on GDP for the United States?

    A. An increase in the production of Canadian chairs

    B. An increase in domestic consumption spending

    C. A decrease in foreign trade

    D. An decrease in quotas

    E. A decrease in tariffs

GO ON TO THE NEXT PAGE

18. *Question 18 refers to the following graph.*

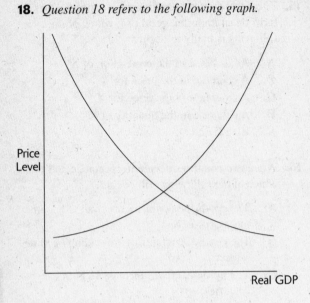

According to the graph above, which of the following will result in a decrease in output?

- **A.** A shift to the left of the aggregate supply curve and a shift to the left of the aggregate demand curve
- **B.** A shift to the right of the aggregate supply curve and a shift to the left of the aggregate demand curve
- **C.** An increase in government spending and a decrease in taxes
- **D.** A decrease in taxes only
- **E.** None of the above

19. Which of the following will cause the biggest increase in aggregate demand?

- **A.** A $200 million decrease in taxes
- **B.** A $100 million increase in taxes
- **C.** A $500 million increase in government spending
- **D.** A $500 million increase in government spending and a $100 million decrease in taxes
- **E.** A $500 million increase in government spending and a $100 million increase in taxes

20. Which one of the following fiscal policies would be most effective for an economy in a severe recession?

- **A.** An increase in government spending
- **B.** A decrease in government spending
- **C.** An increase in personal income taxes
- **D.** The Fed's decision to sell open-market securities
- **E.** The Fed's decision to buy open-market securities

21. If an increase in the income tax rate is implemented in an economy experiencing a recession, which of the following will occur?

- **A.** An increase in unemployment
- **B.** A decrease in unemployment
- **C.** A decrease in the price level
- **D.** An increase in consumer spending
- **E.** Both A and C

22. Which of the following is a tool of the Federal Reserve?

- **A.** Taxes
- **B.** Selling of bonds
- **C.** Spending
- **D.** A reduction of interest rates
- **E.** An increase in employment

23. What determines the value of the dollar in the United States?

- **A.** Governmental regulations
- **B.** The amount of gold the United States possesses
- **C.** The goods and services the United States will buy
- **D.** The multiplier
- **E.** The marginal propensity to save

24. As national income increases, the demand for money increases due to:

- **A.** An increase in consumption of goods and services
- **B.** An increase in interest rates
- **C.** An increase in the money supply
- **D.** A change in consumer confidence
- **E.** An increase in demand for foreign currency.

25. Which of the following best describes why the aggregate supply curve is horizontal over a certain range?

A. Higher price levels lead to higher interest rates.

B. Changes in the aggregate price level do not induce substitution.

C. Output cannot increase unless the price level and interest rates increase.

D. Rigid prices prevent employment from fluctuating.

E. Resources are underemployed in the economy; an increase in spending can occur without any price level pressure.

26. Which of the following would be an appropriate combination of fiscal and monetary policy?

A. An increase in the reserve requirement and a decrease in taxes

B. A decrease in government spending and a decrease in the reserve requirement

C. The purchase of open-market securities and an increase in government spending

D. The purchase of open-market securities and a decrease in government spending

E. A decrease in spending and an increase in taxes

27. What does a Phillips Curve illustrate?

A. Unemployment and inflation

B. Unemployment and government spending

C. Inflation and government spending

D. Price level and aggregate demand

E. Aggregate demand and aggregate supply

28. Which of the following could cause a simultaneous increase in inflation and unemployment?

A. A decrease in government spending

B. A decrease in the money supply

C. A decrease in the velocity of money

D. An increase in inflationary expectations

E. An increase in the overall level of productivity

29. What will an increase in U.S. imports do?

A. Cause the dollar to appreciate

B. Cause the dollar to depreciate

C. Cause no change in the value of the dollar

D. Cause the price level to rise

E. Cause the price level to fall

30. Which of the following would increase the standard of living in an economy?

A. An increase in taxes

B. An increase in the number of banks

C. An increase in federal regulations

D. An increase in labor productivity

E. An increase in the labor force

31. Which of the following could shift the long-run aggregate supply curve to the right?

A. An increase in the price of product resources

B. An increase in productivity

C. An increase in the federal budget deficit

D. A decrease in the money supply

E. A decrease in the labor force

32. What does the CPI measure?

A. Unemployment

B. Price level

C. A change in the price of heavy machinery

D. Taxation

E. Government spending

33. If the economy is currently experiencing full employment, which of the following must be true?

A. There is zero unemployment.

B. There is only cyclical unemployment.

C. There is equilibrium with imports and exports.

D. There is frictional unemployment.

E. There is a high level of inflation.

34. A classical economist would support which of the following?

A. Saving should be greater than investment.

B. The economy can be in equilibrium even though it is not experiencing full employment.

C. Inflation is not a serious economic problem.

D. Prices of products are inflexible.

E. The economy self-corrects itself when disequilibrium is reached.

35. If the government decides to decrease spending, which of the following is most likely to occur?

A. An increase in aggregate demand

B. An increase in output

C. A decrease in aggregate consumption

D. A decrease in aggregate supply

E. An increase in taxes

GO ON TO THE NEXT PAGE

36. If current unemployment is at 10 percent and the price level is stable, what would a Keynesian recommend?

   A. An increase in interest rates
   B. A decrease in interest rates
   C. A decrease in taxes
   D. An increase in government spending and taxes
   E. An increase in government spending and a decrease in taxes

37. The government can reduce an inflationary gap by:

   A. Increasing spending
   B. Increasing the supply of money
   C. Decreasing the money supply
   D. Increasing personal income taxes
   E. Decreasing the reserve requirement

38. What does the circular flow include?

   A. Businesses buying from households in a factor market
   B. Households buying from businesses in a factor market
   C. Households buying from the government in a factor market
   D. Government regulation over what is sold and bought
   E. Only a monetary flow of goods and services

39. If the required reserve ratio is 20 percent and Marty's bank has no excess reserves, what impact will a $100 deposit have on the bank's excess reserves?

   A. $50 in excess reserves
   B. $100 in excess reserves
   C. $500 in excess reserves
   D. $80 in excess reserves
   E. $120 in excess reserves

40. If more people decide to hold currency as opposed to keeping it in the bank, which of the following is likely to occur?

   A. An increase in interest rates
   B. An increase in the reserve requirement
   C. An increase in employment
   D. An increase in disposable income
   E. An increase in the price level

41. Which of the following would be most effective in stimulating aggregate demand?

   A. Increased taxes
   B. Decreased taxes
   C. Increased government spending
   D. Decreased government spending
   E. Decreased money supply

42. What happens to the price level when there is an increase in taxes?

   A. It decreases.
   B. It stabilizes.
   C. It increases.
   D. There is no impact on the price level.
   E. None of the above.

43. Which of the following best describes a supply shock?

   A. It changes the price level in the economy.
   B. It affects only the general price level.
   C. It can always be anticipated.
   D. It can change the short-run aggregate supply curve into the long run aggregate supply curve.
   E. It does not harm the economy.

44. If from 2003–2004 the unemployment level decreased from 6.5 percent to 5.9 percent and the inflation rate fell from 2.9 percent to 1.3 percent, which of the following could explain these changes?

   A. The aggregate demand curve shifted to the left.
   B. The aggregate demand curve shifted to the right.
   C. The aggregate supply curve shifted to the right.
   D. The aggregate supply curve shifted to the left.
   E. The production possibilities curve shifted to the left.

45. What occurs to autonomous investment when there is an increase in interest rates?

   A. It increases because investors want to earn more for their money.
   B. It increases because less people want to spend.
   C. It decreases because businesses have less incentive to borrow money.
   D. It decreases because the government increases spending.
   E. Interest rates do not influence autonomous investment.

46. Which of the following best describes comparative advantage?

A. When one country can produce a good or service at a cheaper price than another

B. When one country is less capable than another at producing a good or service

C. When both countries decide to specialize in the production of one good

D. When one country can produce a good or service at a lower opportunity cost than another country

E. When neither country can specialize because of trade barriers

47. When inflation is unanticipated, which of the following groups would benefit from it: savers, borrowers, or lenders?

A. Savers only
B. Borrowers only
C. Lenders only
D. Savers and borrowers only
E. Savers and lenders only

48. What is the result if there is an increase in the labor force?

A. Investment increases and savings decrease.
B. Investment decreases and savings increase.
C. There is no impact on investment or savings.
D. It will be easier to reduce the unemployment rate.
E. It will become more difficult to reduce the unemployment rate.

49. Which of the following do the Keynesians believe?

A. Savings depends on interest rates.
B. Government spending depends on interest rates.
C. The economy returns itself to full employment.
D. Macroeconomic equilibrium can occur at less than full employment.
E. Wages are more flexible than prices.

50. If the government increases its total spending by $10 billion yet it has no impact on GDP, what could be the reason for this?

A. The price level is rising.
B. There is high unemployment already present in the economy.
C. The spending multiplier has increased.
D. The economy is in equilibrium.
E. There has been an increase in aggregate supply.

51. What is the most important factor in saving and consumption according to Keynesians?

A. The interest rate
B. The inflation rate
C. The income of individuals
D. The level of employment
E. The price level and wages

52 through 54. *Questions 52 through 54 refer to the following graph.*

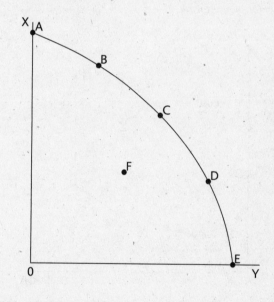

52. What does each plot point on the graph above represent on the production possibilities curve?

A. Quantity demanded
B. Quantity supplied
C. Supply and demand
D. Opportunity costs
E. All of the above

GO ON TO THE NEXT PAGE

53. What does point F represent?

   A. An unattainable point
   B. Underutilization
   C. Trade-offs
   D. Opportunity cost
   E. Where firms can produce most efficiently

54. What does a production possibilities curve illustrate?

   A. The relationship between price and quantity demanded
   B. The relationship between price and quantity supplied
   C. The various combinations of how resources can be applied efficiently
   D. The various combinations of how supply and demand can be applied efficiently
   E. The various combinations of unemployment and inflation

55. through 57. *Questions 55 through 57 refer to the following graph.*

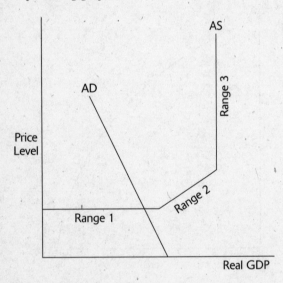

55. In what range is full employment located on the graph above?

   A. Range 1
   B. Range 2
   C. Range 3
   D. Ranges 1 and 2
   E. Ranges 2 and 3

56. According to aggregate demand on the graph, what is the economy experiencing?

   A. Low unemployment
   B. High inflation
   C. High unemployment
   D. High levels of government spending
   E. High levels of growth

57. According to Keynesians, what fiscal policy would help aggregate demand shift into full employment?

   A. Increased taxes and decreased spending
   B. Decreased interest rates
   C. Increased interest rates and decreased spending
   D. Increased spending and decreased taxes
   E. Decreased reserve requirement

58. An increase of which of the following is likely to help the long-run growth rate in the economy?

   A. Population
   B. GDP
   C. Education for the public
   D. The supply of goods and services
   E. Interest rates

59. What effect will an increase in the money supply have on the economy?

   A. It will cause interest rates to rise.
   B. It will increase the amount of money banks hold in primary reserves.
   C. It will decrease interest rates.
   D. It will decrease unemployment.
   E. It will increase unemployment.

60. If the economy were experiencing high levels of inflation, which of the following would be proper monetary policy?

   A. Lowering interest rates
   B. Increasing interest rates
   C. Decreasing the reserve requirement
   D. Selling open-market securities
   E. Raising taxes

Macroeconomics Section II: Free-Response Questions

Directions: You have one hour to answer all three free-response questions: one long and two short questions. Spend the first 10 minutes for planning, and in the remaining 50 minutes construct your responses. Explain your answers thoroughly with examples and illustrations if appropriate.

1. The U.S. economy is currently experiencing the following conditions:

   - Inflation is at 7 percent.
   - Unemployment is at 4.2 percent.
   - Real GDP is growing at 4 percent.

   A. Examining the data, what is the main problem in this scenario? Explain.

   B. Describe the appropriate actions the Federal Reserve should take to provide a solution to this scenario. Use an aggregate supply and demand curve to illustrate the impact of the Fed's policy on the following:
   - Interest rates
   - Price level

   C. Describe the appropriate actions Congress would take to remedy the scenario. Illustrate the effects of your answer on an aggregate demand and aggregate supply model.

   D. Why is it important for Congress and the Federal Reserve to work together?

2. Assume a closed economy with business, households, and the government:

   A. Draw and correctly label a circular flow diagram for the headline above.

   B. Identify two methods of calculating GDP and explain how each works.

   C. Identify the determinants of aggregate demand and the determinants of aggregate supply.

3. Assume the economy is experiencing a recession:

   A. Identify possible remedies the Federal Reserve would implement.

   B. Identify possible remedies Congress would vote on implementing.

Multiple-Choice Answers and Explanations

1. **D.** D is the only answer that describes efficiency. All other possible choices are interchangeable and too ambiguous. The production possibilities curve shifts outward when there is an increase in productive resources or a more efficient means of using productive resources.

2. **C.** The inflation rate in 1976 would be 6 percent because that is the difference between nominal and real GDP. Remember that nominal GDP is the unadjusted version of output, whereas real GDP is adjusted for inflation. The difference between the two will give us the inflation rate.

3. **C.** A worker who is replaced by a machine is an example of someone who is structurally unemployed. The worker's skills have become obsolete for the required job.

4. **B.** As labor productivity rises, so does GDP; however, the price level decreases because there is an increase in supply. When there is an increase in aggregate supply, the price level decreases. This essentially happens in order to decrease supply.

5. **D.** An increase in the marginal propensity to consume increases the value of the spending multiplier. When people consume more of their additional income, the spending multiplier is increased because more transactions are taking place in the economy. The higher the marginal propensity to consume, the stronger the impact of the multiplier becomes.

6. **A.** Keynesians hold that an increase in investment will increase aggregate demand. Remember that investment to an economist is not holding money in an account; rather, investment is when firms purchase capital to expand. When firms purchase capital, they typically borrow money from banks. When more money is borrowed, the economy benefits from an increase in consumption and aggregate demand thus increases.

7. **A.** Government spending is $500 and the multiplier is 5. With the addition of government spending, the expenditures curve increases in value because we now have investment, consumption, and government expenditures.

8. **E.** Commercial banks can increase the money supply by lending out excess reserves. When banks have large amounts of excess reserves, the interest rate on their loans drops to entice investors. Once the interest rate falls, the public can borrow money for consumption.

9. **D.** $500 can be created as a result of $100 in excess reserves in a bank that has a 20 percent reserve requirement. The $100 eventually turns into $500 because of the money multiplier (1/reserve requirement).

10. **A.** When the Federal Reserve lowers the reserve requirement for banks, it is attempting to increase the money supply. The money supply can increase because banks are allowed to loan excess funds to borrowers. Borrowers will borrow money at a low interest rate and use it for consumption. The reserve requirement tells banks how much they have to keep in reserves and how much they may have in excess reserves (loanable funds).

11. **E.** If the transaction demand for money increases, banks have an easier time lending out excess reserves. When the public wants more money for transactions (buying goods and services), the demand for loans increases and banks have an easier time lending their excess reserves.

12. **C.** An increase in spending coupled with a decrease in taxes stimulates growth in the economy. Unemployment decreases because firms employ more resources (including labor), and consumption increases because disposable income is increased as a result of a tax cut.

13. **B.** A recession can be remedied by decreasing taxes and increasing spending. This is an example of fiscal policy. Remember that a recession is at least two consecutive quarters of declining GDP.

14. **C.** A decrease in the employment level is likely to occur if the government reduces spending and increases taxes. The contractionary decision by the government may slow or even halt growth. These particular policies are typically used when the economy is growing too quickly, risking high inflation.

15. **E.** Both C and D are correct answers. Depending on producers' reaction to a tariff, the good will increase in price, and may decrease in quantity because it becomes more expensive for producers to create the good.

16. **D.** More efficient production of the traded goods will result because of specialization. Countries that specialize will concentrate resources on the production of a specific good. This concentration will allow producers to increase efficiency and minimize costs.

17. **B.** An increase in consumption spending will have a positive impact on GDP because consumption is one of the components of the GDP expenditure approach. Consumption increases aggregate demand, which helps the economy grow.

18. **A.** When aggregate supply and aggregate demand decrease, we have a decrease in output. Quantity or output decreases because there is a decline in aggregate supply. To better understand this, draw an aggregate supply and aggregate demand curve on your own and draw decreasing shifts. Notice what occurs with quantity or output. Output declines to a decrease in aggregate supply.

19. **D.** A $500 million increase in spending along with a $100 million decrease in taxes will affect the economy the greatest. When the government spends money, the impact due to the multiplier will be greater than the tax break. However, coupled with a tax break, government spending becomes that much more effective.

20. **A.** An increase in government spending is the appropriate fiscal policy for a recession. Recessions occur because money is not being spent and the economy is not growing. For growth, the government injects money into the economy, producing opportunities for firms and households. The other two answer choices are examples of monetary policy.

21. **A.** If there were an increase in taxes during a recessionary period, the effects of this decision could have a major negative impact on the economy. Unemployment would soar because firms would have to pay higher taxes. Higher taxes means less money for wages and resources.

22. **B.** The selling of bonds is a tool that the Federal Reserve uses often because of its subtle effects on the economy. The Fed does not directly control all interest rates; however, it can manipulate interest rates by adjusting the discount rate or electing to alter the money supply. An alteration of the money supply forces interest rates to rise or fall according to the level of money banks have in reserve.

23. **C.** The value of the dollar is determined by the goods and services it will buy. Long ago, the amount of gold in reserve determined the value of money, but the United States no longer uses that policy.

24. **A.** An increase in the consumption of goods and services occurs when national income increases. This is called the *income effect*. When income increases, so does the marginal propensity to consume.

25. **E.** Over the horizontal range, any increase in demand can be facilitated by the economy without any pressure on the price level. The price level is not influenced because the economy's resources are underemployed. Any rise in demand increases employment but will be in no danger of increasing the price level significantly.

26. **C.** The purchase of open-market securities and increased government spending are the appropriate combinations of monetary and fiscal policy for an economy that is experiencing a recession.

27. **A.** The Phillips Curve illustrates the relationship between unemployment and inflation. Normal inflation (1 percent–3 percent) helps the economy grow and increases unemployment. However, high levels of inflation decrease unemployment and growth.

28. **D.** An increase in inflationary expectations leads to a simultaneous increase in inflation and unemployment. The price level rises because consumers are bracing for a higher price level, and the unemployment level rises because producers are bracing for a higher price level.

29. **B.** An increase in U.S. imports will tend to cause the U.S. dollar to depreciate because of an increased supply of dollars internationally. When U.S. consumers purchase international goods, the international supply of the dollar increases, causing the decline of the value of the dollar.

30. **D.** An increase in the productivity of labor increases the standard of living in an economy. When workers are more productive, costs per unit fall and more goods and services are available for consumers.

31. **B.** An increase in productivity shifts the long-run aggregate supply curve to the right. An increase in productivity increases the economy's capacity for production. When the capacity improves, more goods and services can be provided without pressure on the price level.

32. B. The CPI is used to measure the price level. It examines a particular amount of goods, called a *market basket*, to reveal any changes in the average price for those goods. If the average price rises, the price level rises (inflation).

33. D. If the economy is experiencing full employment, it does not mean that the unemployment level is zero. It simply means that the economy is performing at its productive capacity, where most of its resources are employed. In this condition, structural unemployment still exists because people graduate from school and search for jobs and people are still unhappy with their jobs and search for new ones. No matter how healthy the economy is, there are always some instances of unemployment simply due to matriculation and normal market activity.

34. E. Classical economists believe that the economy is self-correcting when disequilibrium occurs. The basic principle that is outlined by classical economists is that the economy needs no government intervention because it is capable of returning to equilibrium on its own.

35. C. If the government were to decrease spending, initially aggregate expenditures would decline because there would be fewer jobs available due to a lack of spending. This lack of spending would diminish the purchasing power of individuals and in turn decrease aggregate consumption.

36. E. If the unemployment level reached a high point while the price level remained stable, Keynesians would recommend an increase in government spending and a decrease in taxes. This would stimulate growth as well as increase purchasing power for the public. Firms could then employ more resources because taxes would be lower. Individuals would spend more money because disposable income would be increased.

37. D. Inflationary gaps are the result of too much disposable income. When individuals have extra money, they tend to spend it, causing the price level to rise. When the price level rises, the value of the dollar falls and an inflationary gap is created. An increase in the income tax rate can curb disposable income, forcing consumption to decrease and the price level to stabilize.

38. A. A circular flow chart includes businesses paying for factors of production from households in a factor market. Some examples of factor markets include labor (wages) and payments to households for land.

39. D. A deposit of $100 in a banking system that has a 20 percent reserve ratio will have an $80 impact in excess reserves because 20 percent is kept in reserves while excess reserves are exposed to the remaining 80 percent—in this case, $80.

40. A. If the public's desire to hold money in the form of currency increases, demand for loanable funds rises. This demand causes interest rates to climb.

41. C. Government spending is the most effective option for stimulating aggregate demand because of the multiplier effect. Consumers spend only a portion of a tax cut; a greater portion is dispersed into the economy with government spending.

42. B. When an increase in taxes occurs, the price level is stabilized because disposable income declines. When people have less money to spend, the price level is stabilized because of decreased consumption.

43. A. Supply shocks change the price level in the economy because they have a ripple effect on goods and services. When one industry is influenced by a supply shock, interdependent industries are affected as well. When enough industries are affected by a supply shock, the price level rises because of a lack of available goods and services in the economy.

44. D. If the unemployment level and the price level fall, it can be attributed to an increase in the aggregate supply curve. The aggregate supply curve is an indicator of the economy's productive capacity. When the aggregate supply curve increases, so does the economy's productive capacity. Avoiding an increase in the price level and increasing employment is the result of an increased aggregate supply curve.

45. C. When interest rates increase, incentives for autonomous investment decrease because of the increased cost to borrow money. Firms borrow less money, buy less capital, and employ fewer workers. An increase in interest rates has a contractionary impact on the economy.

46. D. Comparative advantage describes one nation's ability to produce a good or service at a lower opportunity cost than another nation producing that same good or service. Comparative advantage outlines opportunity costs, not necessarily monetary costs.

47. B. When inflation is unanticipated, borrowers benefit because the value of what they owe is actually decreasing as a result of inflation. Inflation decreases purchasing power and lowers the value of currency. If a borrower is lent money and the inflation rate increases, the payback amount for the borrower remains the same; however, the ability to obtain the amount becomes easier.

48. E. If there is an increase in the labor force, it becomes more difficult to reduce the unemployment rate because more jobs have to be created to satisfy the increased labor force. As the number of labor force participants grows, the number of jobs has to increase with it or we will experience an increase in unemployment.

49. D. According to Keynesians, macroeconomic equilibrium can occur at less than full employment. Where short-run aggregate supply meets aggregate demand, we have macroeconomic equilibrium.

50. A. When government spending has no impact on GDP, one reason could be that the price level is rising. This means that the economy has reached its productive capacity and that GDP can no longer increase. All that's left for producers to do is to increase the price level.

51. C. According to Keynesians, the most important factor of savings and consumption is the level of income for individuals. The more people receive in income, the more they spend and save. The marginal propensity to consume and save rises as income climbs. Consumption and savings are dependent on the level of income.

52. D. Each plot point on the production possibilities graph represents an opportunity cost. As you move from one plot point to another, you have to give up one good for another. The production possibilities graph is designed to illustrate available resources and describe their allocative possibilities.

53. B. Point F on the graph represents underutilization. Underutilization occurs when a country is producing inside the production possibilities curve. Any point inside the curve illustrates a country that is not being efficient with its available resources. The production possibilities curve represents allocative efficiency; any point on the curve represents efficient use of resources.

54. C. A production possibilities curve illustrates the various combinations of resources that can be applied or allocated. The combination of the vertical and horizontal axis is the sum of resources in the scenario. The production possibilities curve illustrates the allocative efficiency of the goods on the horizontal and vertical axes.

55. B. Full employment is located in range 2. Range 2 has a slight increase in price level (growth) and is the optimum level of performance for applied resources in the economy. In range 2, the economy is at or near productive capacity, meaning that resources are being used efficiently for production.

56. C. The graph illustrates the economy's aggregate demand in range 1. In range 1, there are high levels of unemployment and any increase in spending can satisfy aggregate demand without any pressure on the price level. Range 1 illustrates an economy that is lacking spending and disposable income.

57. D. Increased spending and decreased taxes are the fiscal policy options a Keynesian would recommend for an economy that is lacking growth. Spending helps increase employment whereas lower taxes increase disposable income and allow firms to produce at lower costs.

58. C. Education is considered human capital. Human capital helps the economy in the long run because the labor force becomes more productive with increased education. When workers are educated, skills become more advanced and firms can produce more goods and services and increase quality.

59. C. An increase in the money supply results in a decline in interest rates. Lenders will have more money to lend, and to make it more enticing for consumers to borrow, they will lower interest rates. The relationship between money supply and interest rates is an inverse one.

60. D. If the economy experiences high levels of inflation, the appropriate monetary policy is to sell open-market securities in order to decrease the money supply. When the money supply decreases, the price level becomes stabilized.

Free-Response Answers and Explanations

1. A. The main problem in this scenario is inflation. At a 7-percent rise in the price level, the economy has reached and started to surpass its productive capacity. A 4.2-percent unemployment rate indicates that the economy has fully employed its labor resources, further indicating a problem with inflation as aggregate demand continues to grow. The growth in real GDP is not a problem; however, it is expected due to the low rate of unemployed people in the labor force and a growing price level.

B. To combat inflation, the Federal Reserve should implement a "tight" monetary policy—the Fed decreases the money supply with the intension of increasing the value of the available dollars in the economy. To accomplish this, the Fed could use any one of its monetary policy tools: increasing the reserve ratio, increasing the discount rate, or, most likely, selling open market securities. Refer to the following illustration:

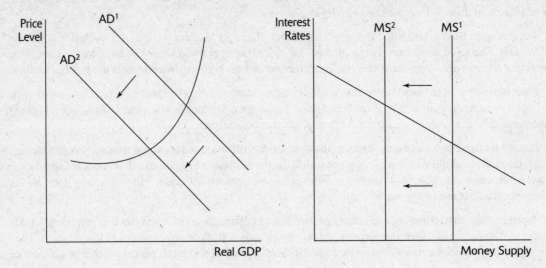

C. Congress would partake in a contractionary fiscal policy with the objective of halting the price level by decreasing disposable income. To do this, the government could increase taxes and/or reduce spending. Refer to the following illustration:

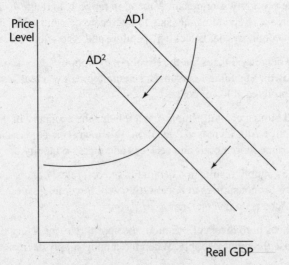

D. It is important for Congress and the Fed to work together because they are the two most influential entities on the economy. If the Fed and Congress do not work together, the effectiveness of policies enacted by either of the two would be diminished significantly.

2. A. Refer to the following illustration:

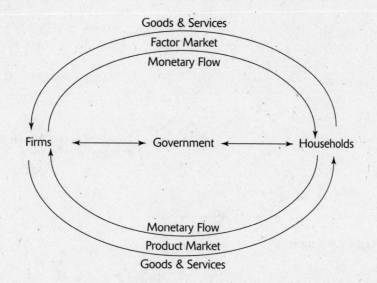

B. Two ways of calculating GDP are the expenditure approach and the income approach. The expenditure approach examines the amount spent on all final goods and services produced in a specific year on a nation's soil. The income approach examines the amount received from the purchases of all final goods and services produced in a specific year on a nation's soil. One examines the amount spent (expenditures), while the other examines the amount received (income).

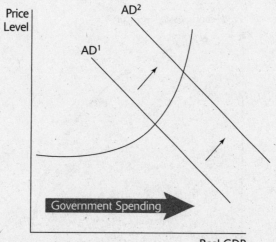

C. The determinants of aggregate demand are:

■ Income

■ Taste and preferences

■ Price of complementary product

■ Price of substitute product

■ Future expectation of price

■ Number of consumers

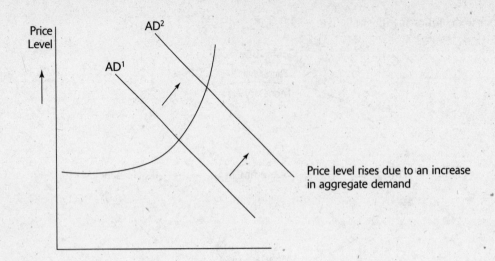

Determinants of Aggregate Supply:

- Resource prices
- Technology
- Government (subsidies and taxes)
- Number of suppliers

3. A. If the economy were experiencing a recession, the Federal Reserve would increase the money supply, which would make more money available at a lower cost for consumption.

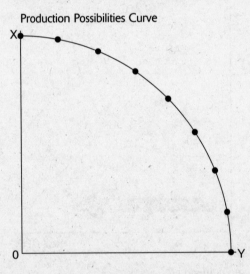

B. Congress would vote on decreasing taxes and/or increasing spending. This would increase disposable income, which would increase aggregate demand to stimulate a sleeping economy.

Microeconomics Full-Length Practice Test 1

Section I

- 60 multiple choice questions   70 minutes

Section II

- 1 long free-response question and
- 2 short free-response questions   10 minutes for planning
                                         50 minutes for writing

Total Time: 2 Hours and 10 Minutes

Microeconomics Section I: Multiple-Choice Questions

Directions: You have 70 minutes to complete the 60 multiple-choice questions in this section of the exam.

1. In a perfectly competitive market all of the following are true *except*:

- **A.** Producers and consumers are price takers.
- **B.** There are many small firms.
- **C.** Entry and exit into the industry are costless.
- **D.** Firms produce different products.
- **E.** There are no transaction costs.

2. What characteristics are true of an oligopoly?

I. A few large firms.

II. All products are identical.

III. High entry/exit costs.

- **A.** I only
- **B.** II only
- **C.** I and II only
- **D.** I and III only
- **E.** I, II, and III

3. Mrs. Buttermilk enjoys eating maple syrup with her pancakes for breakfast. If one day the price of pancakes increases, which of the following will result?

- **A.** The supply curve for maple syrup will shift to the left.
- **B.** The demand curve for maple syrup will shift to the left.
- **C.** The supply curve for pancakes will shift to the left.
- **D.** The demand curve for pancakes will shift to the right.
- **E.** Nothing will happen to the demand curve for maple syrup since it is vertical.

4. A well-known consumer magazine concludes that SUVs are the safest type of motor vehicles to drive. What effect does this have on the motor vehicle market?

- **A.** An increase in the price of sedans, a substitute for SUVs
- **B.** A decrease in the price of sedans, a substitute for SUVs
- **C.** An increase in production costs for SUVs
- **D.** A decrease in the price of sedans, a complement to SUVs
- **E.** A decrease in the price of SUVs

5. The government wants to take actions to prevent people from smoking. What policy should they enact in order to curb the demand of smokers?

- **A.** Create a price ceiling above the equilibrium price.
- **B.** Create a price floor above the equilibrium price.
- **C.** Increase the property tax for tobacco firms.
- **D.** Decrease the income tax for tobacco firms.
- **E.** Increase the sales tax of cigarettes.

6. If a farmer can produce 1 pound of tomatoes in 2 hours and 1 pound of oranges in 4 hours, what is the opportunity cost of producing 1 pound of oranges?

- **A.** 1/2 pound of tomatoes
- **B.** 1 pound of tomatoes
- **C.** 2 pounds of tomatoes
- **D.** 1/2 pound of oranges
- **E.** 1 pound of oranges

7. When is a producer said to have a comparative advantage in producing a particular good?

   A. The producer requires a smaller number of inputs to produce that good.

   B. The producer requires a larger number of inputs to produce that good.

   C. The producer is getting all it can from the scarce resources available to produce that good.

   D. The producer is producing less than what is available to produce that good.

   E. The producer has the smaller opportunity cost of producing that good.

8. Canned soup is said to be an inferior good when:

   A. The demand rises as income rises.

   B. The demand falls as income rises.

   C. The supply falls as income decreases.

   D. The supply rises as income rises.

   E. The supply rises as income decreases

9. What term is used to refer to a hypothetical situation in which all other factors other than the one being studied are held constant?

   A. *Ceteris paribus*

   B. Fixed costs

   C. Efficiency

   D. Marginal costs

   E. Variable costs

10. An ice cream parlor produces double-chocolate-fudge ice cream, their most popular flavor. All of the following situations will affect the quantity of ice cream they are willing to supply *except*:

    A. The price of ice cream is lowered.

    B. A new machine speeds up production time.

    C. Sugar costs double in price.

    D. The parlor shop expects a huge surge in sales as summer approaches.

    E. A sales tax is placed on ice cream.

11. The price of hotdog (a substitute for pizza) falls, and the price of tomatoes (an input of pizza) increases; what will happen to the market for pizzas?

	The Supple Curve	The Demand Curve
A.	Shift inwards	Shift inwards
B.	Shift inwards	Shift outwards
C.	Shift outwards	Shift outwards
D.	Shift outwards	Shift inwards
E.	Shift inwards	No change

12. Demand is said to be inelastic if:

    A. The quantity demanded responds substantially to changes in the price.

    B. The quantity supplied responds substantially to changes in the price.

    C. The quantity demanded responds slightly to changes in the price.

    D. The quantity supplied responds slightly to changes in the price.

    E. None of the above.

13. What is the percentage change in quantity supplied divided by in order to reach the price elasticity of supply?

    A. Percentage change in price

    B. Change in price

    C. Percentage change in quantity demanded

    D. Change in quantity demanded

    E. Percentage change in income

14. The national government wants to evaluate the effect increasing rent will have on the inner cities. When monthly rent costs $200, 10 people are willing to rent those apartments. If the price were to increase to $300, only 7 people are willing to rent apartments. What is the price elasticity of demand?

    A. 5/3

    B. −5/3

    C. 3/5

    D. −3/5

    E. None of the above

15. The economic depression took its toll on Java Café. Their coffee sales fell from 1,000 coffees sold daily to 500. They reduced their prices from $2.00 per a cup of coffee to $1.00. How much total revenue did they lose?

    A. $2,000

    B. $1,000

    C. $1,500

    D. $500

    E. $100

16. Government imposes a price ceiling of $2 per slice of pizza, which is below the equilibrium price of $3.00. What effect will this have on the market for pizza?

    A. Excess of quantity supply

    B. Excess of quantity demand

    C. Shortage of quantity demanded

    D. Supply curve will shift outwards

    E. Demand curve will shift outwards

17. What is the tax revenue that the government will collect if they impose a price ceiling at $1.20?

A. $900
B. $720
C. $400
D. $360
E. $200

18. A country that produces more than the domestic quantity demanded at the world price will most likely:

A. Export
B. Import
C. Increase prices
D. Decrease prices
E. Increase quantity supplied

19. The consumer surplus after trade equals:

A. A
B. A + B
C. A + C
D. B + C
E. A + B + D

20. When a country allows trade and becomes an importer of a good:

A. Domestic consumers are better off; domestic producers are better off.
B. Domestic consumers are better off; domestic producers are worse off.
C. Domestic consumers are worse off; domestic producers are worse off.
D. Domestic consumers are worse off; domestic producers are better off.
E. No changes in total welfare.

21. What type of tax requires everyone to pay the same amount regardless of income?

A. Lump-sum tax
B. Proportional tax
C. Regressive tax
D. Progressive tax
E. Flat tax

22. Which of the following is the best example of a public good?

A. An ice cream cone purchased at Yolanda's Frozen Yogurt
B. A bomber jet purchased for national defense
C. A salmon caught off the coast of Alaska
D. Christmas presents under the Christmas tree
E. Ice skating rink at the local shopping center

23. Accountant Tina is asked to determine this year's total revenues for a metal company. Tina will include all of the following when measuring the firm's accounting profit *except*:

A. Cost of a new machine
B. Increase in labor supply
C. Decrease in prices
D. Cost of plastic production forfeited to produce metal
E. Damages incurred from the earthquake

24. Under what condition will a firm decide to exit an industry?

A. Total revenue exceeds total cost of production.
B. Total revenue from producing is less than its total cost.
C. Total revenue equals total cost.
D. Profit equals total revenue minus total cost.
E. Price of the good exceeds average total cost of production.

25. In 1999, Kate's Crazy Candy Store sold 500 lollipops at the market price of $2.00. The following year they doubled the quantity sold. What was their marginal revenue that year?

A. $2,000
B. $100
C. $10
D. $4
E. $2

26. If the long-run average total cost falls as quantity produced increases, what is this phenomenon known as?

A. Economies of scale
B. Diseconomies of scale
C. Constant returns to scale
D. Sunk capital costs
E. Efficiency

27. Up until what point do competitive, profit-maximizing firms hire workers?

A. MPL = w
B. VMPL = w
C. VMPL = MPL
D. P = L
E. MPL = 0

GO ON TO THE NEXT PAGE

28. Which of the following are properties of indifference curves?

I. They are downward sloping.

II. They do not cross.

III. They are bowed inwards.

   A. I only

   B. II only

   C. III only

   D. I and III only

   E. I, II, and III

29. If soft drinks and potato chips are inferior goods, what will happen to the budget constraint line if the consumer's income fell?

   A. Will shift out

   B. Will shift in

   C. Will get steeper

   D. Will get flatter

   E. No change

30. Why do deadweight losses occur when taxes are imposed?

   A. They distort the decisions that producers make.

   B. They distort the decisions that consumers make.

   C. They distort the decisions that both producers and consumers make.

   D. They create administrative burdens that taxpayers bear.

   E. They increase government spending.

31. Joe's favorite drink is coffee because it helps him stay alert at work. The following table shows Joe's total utility for each cup of coffee he drinks during a typical day. What conclusion can be drawn using this table?

Cups of Coffee Consumed Per Day	Total Utility
0	0
1	5
2	9
3	12
4	14
5	15

   A. Joe receives no utility from coffee because coffee is not good for him.

   B. Joe's marginal utility from his fourth cup of coffee is greater than his marginal utility from his third cup.

   C. Joe's marginal utility from each additional cup of coffee is constant.

   D. Joe experiences diminishing marginal utility when he drinks his fifth cup of coffee.

   E. The table shows a trend of diminishing marginal utility.

32. The market price of apples is $3 a bushel, and the market price of oranges is $5 a bushel. A farmer can produce 200 bushels of either oranges or apples. If the farmer chooses to produce oranges, what is his opportunity cost?

   A. The farmer's opportunity cost is $1,000, which he can make producing apples.

   B. The farmer's opportunity cost is 200 bushels of apples.

   C. The farmer's opportunity cost is $1,600, which is the maximum amount he can earn growing both apples and oranges.

   D. The farmer's opportunity cost is $400, which is the difference between how much money he can make growing oranges and how much money he can make growing apples.

   E. The farmer has no opportunity cost because he is producing the good that brings him the most profit.

33. What are the intended effects of collusion in the marketplace?

   A. Collusive firms work to increase the supply of goods to the marketplace, effectively reducing the market price for the goods.

   B. Collusive firms are often successful in the long run because they look to please the consumer.

   C. Collusive firms look to decrease industry output to the monopoly level, allowing the firms to charge a monopoly price.

   D. Firms in collusive agreements fail to produce newer and better technologies because they have less incentive to spend money on research and development.

   E. Collusive agreements are used to drive a firm's costs down, thereby lowering the cost of their product for their customers.

34. Which one of the following best describes what the long-run average total cost curve is often referred to as:

    A. planning curve
    B. capital growing illustration
    C. total-product curve
    D. production possibilities curve
    E. None of the above

35. The table below represents points on an economy's production possibility curve.

Apples	Oranges
1000	0
900	100
800	200
700	300

What is the opportunity cost of increasing the production of apples from 700 to 900 units?

    A. 1000 units of oranges
    B. 800 units of good oranges
    C. 200 units of good oranges
    D. 100 units of good oranges
    E. 10 units of good oranges

36. Which of the following best illustrates a monopolistic market?

    A. Over the past 10 years, many small firms have entered the market for medical care.
    B. Demand for athletic shoes increases with income.
    C. The supply for oil is determined by a few countries in the Middle East.
    D. Cable TV keeps the prices for their service above marginal cost and creates an economic profit in the long run.
    E. The price of suntan lotion is determined by the quantity demanded.

37. Assume that a perfectly competitive firm can hire labor for $10 an hour, and that each unit produced sells for $5. According to the following table, how many hours of labor would the firm pay for if labor is the only input considered?

Hours of Labor	Units of Output
0	0
1	5
2	7
3	10
4	11
5	13

    A. 1
    B. 2
    C. 3
    D. 4
    E. 5

38. Suppose that a consumer can purchase two goods: good X and good Y. The price of X is P_X and the marginal utility is MU_X. And assume that the price of Y is P_Y and the marginal utility of Y is MU_Y. Which expression maximizes consumers' utility?

    A. $MU_X = MU_Y$
    B. $P_X = P_Y$
    C. $P_X / P_Y = -MU_Y / MU_X$
    D. $P_X = P_Y MU_X / MU_Y$
    E. $P_X / P_Y = -Y/X$

39. The condition for allocative efficiency holds when:

    A. Short-run profits exist in a competitive industry.
    B. The market demand curve is inelastic in a competitive industry.
    C. The market demand curve is elastic in a competitive industry.
    D. Firms are price makers.
    E. Price equals marginal total cost.

40. When is a Nash equilibrium achieved?

    A. When each firm chooses its best strategy regardless of the other firms' strategies.
    B. Other strategies exist that would better suit the firm given the other firms' strategy.
    C. The firm's strategy maximizes the utility of another firm.
    D. The least desirable strategies for both firms are achieved.
    E. Firms choose their best strategy given the strategy the other firm has chosen.

41. Which of the following explain why the average total cost is U-shaped?

    A. Average fixed costs always decline as output rises.
    B. Average variable cost decreases as output increases.
    C. Total profit increase as output increases.
    D. Average total cost is the difference between average fixed cost and average variable cost.
    E. None of the above.

GO ON TO THE NEXT PAGE

42. Following are two production possibilities curves for Country 1 and Country 2. Both countries produce plastic and metal. According to the graph, what should Country 1 do?

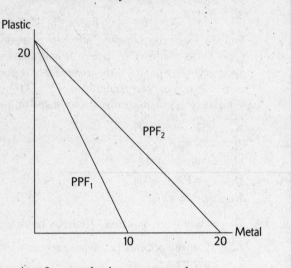

A. Import plastic, export metal
B. Export plastic, import metal
C. Import plastic, import metal
D. Export plastic, export metal
E. Not trade

43. A firm in a perfectly competitive industry is producing at a point where price is below the total cost curve but above the average variable cost curve. If the firm wants to maximize profits, it should:

A. Try to make positive economic profits.
B. Increase quantity supplied.
C. Produce where marginal cost is above marginal revenue.
D. Reduce the amount of inputs.
E. The firm is already earning maximum profits.

44. A negative externality is when:

A. A firm is earning negative economic profits.
B. A firm has an internal cost which it can reduce with new technology.
C. An external cost is imposed on the public.
D. An external benefit is imposed on the public.
E. The price of a product goes up after an increase in demand for that product.

45. A firm who has an elastic demand curve for its product can:

A. Raise the price of its product and expect an increase in profits.
B. Increase output and expect an increase in economic profits.
C. Lower costs by increasing supply.
D. Raise the price of its product and expect a significant decrease in demand.
E. Raise the price of its product and expect a significant increase in demand.

46. Which of the following is true for a good with a price inelastic demand curve?

I. The quantity demanded is constant at any price.

II. The price is constant at all quantities demanded.

III. Producers of the good will have increased revenue if the price increases.

A. I only
B. II only
C. III only
D. I and III only
E. II and III only

47. What best explains why a supply curve is upward sloping?

A. The equilibrium is where the supply curve meets the demand curve.
B. A higher price induces producers to produce a higher quantity.
C. A lower price induces producers to produce a higher quantity.
D. An increase in price will reduce the quantity demanded.
E. An increase in price will raise the quantity demanded.

48. Which of the following ideas best describes the concept of diminishing marginal returns to labor?

A. Each additional worker has a smaller marginal product than the previous.
B. The first worker has the comparative advantage.
C. The first worker has a largest opportunity cost.
D. The wages paid to each additional worker are smaller than the previous.
E. Workers become less productive when they are paid a lower wage.

49. Which of the following statements is true of a monopoly but *not* true of a perfectly competitive firm?

A. Other firms can easily enter the market.
B. The demand for the product is price inelastic.
C. The firm will earn zero economic profit.
D. The market price is affected by decisions made by the firm.
E. The firm is trying to maximize consumer surplus.

50. How would the market price and quantity of tagless t-shirts produced be changed if the competitive market for tagless t-shirts became monopolistic?

	Price	Quantity
A.	Decrease	Stay the same
B.	Decrease	Increase
C.	Increase	Increase
D.	Decrease	Decrease
E.	Increase	Decrease

51. What best describes a situation where the production of a good results in negative externalities and the government does not regulate production?

A. The quantity of goods being produced will be efficient.
B. The government will lose tax revenue.
C. The firm will earn an economic profit.
D. The marginal cost of producing is greater for the firm than for society.
E. The marginal cost of producing is greater for society than for the firm.

52. Assume that time is the only resource required to produce a good. The following table shows the different amounts of time it takes for two individuals to make one paper airplane and one origami swan.

	Bill	*Bob*
Plane	2 minutes	10 minutes
Swan	3 minutes	20 minutes

Which of the following statements is true according to the table?

A. Bill should be self sufficient, because there would be no gains from trade.
B. Bob should give-up because he is slow at both tasks.
C. There would be gains from trade if Bill specializes in planes and Bob specializes in swans.
D. There would be gains from trade if Bob and Bill both specialize in planes.
E. There would be gains from trade if Bill specializes in swans and Bob specializes in planes.

53. Which of the following is true for an ordinary good?

A. As income rises, consumption of good increases.
B. As price of good falls, consumption is not impacted.
C. As price of good falls, consumption decreases.
D. As price of good falls, the demand curve shifts to the right.
E. None of the above.

54. All of the following will cause a shift in the demand curve *except*:

A. The price of a substitute good increases.
B. A change in consumer preferences.
C. Advertising is increased.
D. The price of the good decreases.
E. The number of buyers in the market increases.

55. An increase in the quality of manure allows corn farmers to grow more corn on the same amount of land. If the market for corn is perfectly competitive, what will happen to the equilibrium price and quantity of corn?

	Price	Quantity
A.	Increase	Increase
B.	Decrease	Decrease
C.	Decrease	Increase
D.	Stay the same	Increase
E.	Increase	Decrease

GO ON TO THE NEXT PAGE

56. ABC manufacturing produces widgets, a normal good. Assuming that the widget market is perfectly competitive, which of the following can explain a decrease in the quantity and a decrease in the price of widgets?

    A. A decrease in the price of a substitute and a decrease in the number of firms in the industry

    B. An increase in the average income of consumers and an increase in the price of a major input

    C. A decrease in the average income of consumers and a decrease in the price of a complement

    D. An increase in the number of firms and an increase in the price of a major input

    E. An increase in the number of consumers and an increase in the price of a major input

57. What is the best solution for reducing pollution in a town where a chemical plant pollutes the air?

    A. The government should pass regulation to stop the pollution.

    B. The town should pay the chemical plant to reduce the pollution.

    C. The chemical plant should reduce pollution because it would be more beneficial for society.

    D. The town should lobby against air pollution.

    E. The town cannot stop pollution so they should not try.

58. Which of the following statements is true for an inferior good?

    A. An inferior good is a good that a consumer buys more of when income increases.

    B. An inferior good is a good that a consumer buys more of when price increases.

    C. An inferior good is a good that a consumer buys less of when income increases.

    D. An inferior good is a good that is not the best in quality.

    E. An inferior good is a good that demands a lower price in the marketplace.

59. The elasticity of demand for coconuts is 0.6. If the price of coconuts increases from $2 to $3, what will the impact be on the coconut market?

    A. The demand for coconuts will fall by 30%.

    B. The demand for coconuts will increase by 30%.

    C. The demand for coconuts will fall by 83.3%.

    D. The demand for coconuts will fall by 1.8%.

    E. The demand for coconuts will increase by 1.8%.

60. A study of the tobacco industry revealed that a 10% increase in cigarette prices would cause a 5% decrease in cigarette consumption. What is the elasticity of demand for cigarettes?

    A. 2

    B. 0.5

    C. 0.2

    D. 5

    E. 0.05

Microeconomics Section II: Free-Response Questions

Directions: You have one hour to answer all three free-response questions: one long and two short questions. Spend the first 10 minutes for planning, and in the remaining 50 minutes construct your responses. Explain your answers thoroughly with examples and illustrations if appropriate.

1. Farmer Joe grows peaches and sells them in a perfectly competitive market.

    A. Draw and label farmer Joe's cost curves for growing peaches and the market supply and demand curves for peaches. For the cost curves, include the marginal cost, average total cost, and average variable cost curves. Assume Farmer Joe's marginal revenue is equal to his profit maximizing price.

    B. What is Farmer Joe's profit maximizing output and price? Also, show Farmer Joe's total revenue.

    C. Suppose the market demand for peaches suddenly decreases. Describe the effects of such a change on Farmer Joe's cost curves.

    D. Suppose many peach farmers, not including Farmer Joe, are producing at a point below their average variable cost.

    (i) What will these peach farmers do in the long run?

    (ii) Describe the effects of this choice on the industry supply and how it will effect the other farmers.

    E. Suppose Farmer Joe monopolizes the peach industry. Describe the changes in the quantity supplied, market price, and how these numbers are determined.

    F. Suppose only six farmers, including Farmer Joe, remain in the peach industry, effectively creating an oligopolistic market. The six farmers plan to collude, form a cartel, and charge a monopoly price and quantity. Describe the outcome of the market in the long run.

    G. Suppose that in a perfectly competitive peach industry the government decides to set a price floor.

    (i) Draw and label a diagram showing the price floor set by the government.

    (ii) Discuss the long term effects of a price floor on the peach industry.

2. Assume that California cheese and Wisconsin cheese are close substitutes, both are in their own perfectly competitive markets, and the demand for both is price elastic. Also assume that California cheese and Wisconsin cheese are the only cheeses available in California. What would happen to the cheese markets in California if the California government places a tax on all Wisconsin cheese sold in California.

    A. Draw and label the effects of the Wisconsin cheese tax on the California cheese market in California.

    (i) What will happen to the equilibrium price of California cheese in California?

    (ii) What will happen to the equilibrium quantity of California cheese purchased?

    B. Now draw and label the effects of the Wisconsin cheese tax on the Wisconsin cheese market in California.

    (i) What will happen to the equilibrium price of Wisconsin cheese in California?

    (ii) What will happen to the equilibrium quantity of Wisconsin cheese purchased in California?

    C. Explain what will happen to the total expenditures on Wisconsin cheese in California (remember that the demand for Wisconsin cheese is price-elastic).

3. Assume that pistachios and walnuts are substitutes and both exist in a perfectly competitive long-run market industry that is in equilibrium.

    A. Jack, a small owner of a pistachio grove, engineers a new tool that can reduce the cost of picking pistachios. Discuss in detail how the new tool will affect each of the following:

    (i) The price of production of the final product

    (ii) The quantity of pistachios produced

    B. Jack patents the new tool and makes it available to other pistachio producers for purchase.

    (i) What will happen to the overall market price of pistachios?

    (ii) What will happen to the production of pistachios?

GO ON TO THE NEXT PAGE

C. Manny owns a commercial walnut grove, and he is unable to use Jack's new tool because it cannot pick walnuts.
   (i) What will happen to the price of walnuts in the long run?
   (ii) What will happen to the quantity of walnuts produced in the long run?

D. Using the following chart, answer these questions about the effects of Jack's new tool on the labor market.
   (i) What effects will Jack's new tool have on the labor market for walnuts?
   (ii) Would it be profitable to replant new walnut trees, or would it make more economic sense to replace the old walnut trees with pistachio trees and take advantage of the new pistachio technology?

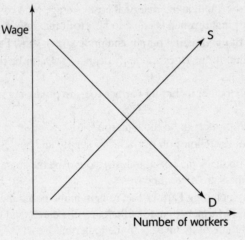

Multiple-Choice Answers and Explanations

1. D. In a perfectly competitive market all the above are true except D. All firms produce an identical product in each industry. If this were not the case, then firms would not be price takers and the buyers' demand for each good would vary. In that case, perfect competition would not be true of that particular market.

2. D. Firms in an oligopoly can produce products that are either identical or different. Since the actions of any one seller in the market can have a large impact on the profits of the entire industry, it is not necessary for the products to maintain homogeneity.

3. B. Maple syrup is a complement to pancakes; therefore, it will react similarly to pancakes if prices were to increase. Increasing the price of pancakes will reduce both the demand for pancakes and maple syrup. This will shift the demand curve for both goods to the left, eliminating choice D. An increase in prices has a positive effect on the supply curve. Because the price of pancakes and maple syrup is high, selling both goods is profitable, so firms will want to produce more and shift the supply schedule outwards. Therefore, choices A and C can be eliminated. Because it can be assumed that the product is a normal good, the demand schedule will not be vertical, or perfectly inelastic. An increase in prices will affect the quantity of goods produced, eliminating choice E.

4. B. Concluding that SUVs are the safest type of car to drive will increase the demand for SUVs, shifting the demand curve to the right. This will increase the price of SUVs, eliminating choice E. If the sedans were a complement to SUVs, this will increase the demand and thereby the price of sedans, eliminating answer D. If sedans were a substitute, it will decrease the demand and the price of sedans, eliminating A. Since this has no effect on production costs, we can ignore choice C.

5. E. If the government wants to decrease consumer demand for cigarettes, they will need to increase the cost of cigarettes to the consumer. An increase in sales taxes of cigarettes will have this desired outcome. A price ceiling or price floor that is above equilibrium prices will create an excess supply and not drive down consumer demand, eliminating choices A and B. Increasing taxes for firms affects the supply curve and does not affect the consumer demand schedule. Therefore, eliminate choices C and D.

6. C. To produce 1 pound of oranges would take 4 hours. In 4 hours the farmer can produce 2 pounds of tomatoes. Therefore the opportunity cost—whatever must be given up to in order to acquire something else—would be 2 pounds of tomatoes, eliminating answers A, B, D, and E.

7. E. Comparative advantage is when a particular country, producer, or individual has a smaller opportunity cost when producing a particular good. Requiring a smaller number of inputs to produce a given item implies that the producer has an absolute advantage, eliminating choices A and B. To maximize production given the available resources means that producer is acting efficiently, eliminating choice C. When the producer is producing less than what is available, the producer is said to be behaving inefficiently, eliminating choice D.

8. B. An inferior good is a good for which, when all other things being equal, an increase in income decreases the quantity of that good demanded. If income were to rise and the quantity demanded rose as well, then the given item would be said to be a normal good. Eliminate choice A. An inferior good deals with the demand side of economics. Therefore, we can eliminate answers C, D, and E because they deal with the supply side of economics.

9. A. *Ceteris paribus* is a Latin phrase, meaning "other things being equal," and is used as a given to remind one that other than the factor being studied, the remaining ones are all held constant.

10. E. Price (A), technology (B), input prices (C), and expectations (D) will all affect the supply curve; therefore, those answers can be eliminated. Sales tax will affect the quantity of a good demanded, which is choice E. Placing a sales tax on ice cream will lower the quantity of ice cream demanded and will shift the demand curve inwards.

11. A. Since hotdogs are a substitute for pizza, a decrease in the price of hotdogs will decrease the demand for pizza, shifting the curve inwards. An increase in the input prices will shift the supply curve inwards as well.

12. C. Demand is said to be elastic when it responds substantially to any changes in the price, eliminating choice A. If demand is said to be inelastic, then it will only respond slightly to a change in the price. Elasticity of demand is the measure of how much demand (not supply) responds to change, eliminating choices B and D.

13. A.

$$\text{Price elasticity of supply} = \frac{\text{Percentage change in the quantity supplied}}{\text{Percentage change in price}}$$

14. D.

$$\text{Price elasticity of demand} = \frac{\text{Percentage change in the quantity demanded}}{\text{Percentage change in the price}}$$

$$(-30\%) / (50\%) = -3/5$$

15. C.

$$\text{TR} = \text{Price} \times \text{Quantity}$$

$$\text{TR (last year)} = \$2000 = \$1000 \times \$2.00 \qquad \text{TR (this year)} = \$500 = \$500 \times \$1.00$$

$$\text{Total revenue lost} = \text{TR (last year)} - \text{TR (this year)} = \$2000 - \$500 = \$1500$$

16. B. If the price ceiling is lower than the equilibrium price, then the policy has a binding constraint on the market. This will cause the quantity demand to be greater than the quantity supply, creating a shortage because of the excess of quantity demanded, thus eliminating choices A and C. This will not shift the supply curve or demand curve, eliminating choices D and E.

17. D.

$$\text{Tax Revenue} = \text{Tax} \times \text{Quantity sold}$$

$$\$0.40 \times 900 = \$360$$

18. A. If the quantity supplied domestically is greater than the quantity demanded, then that country will most likely export its excess goods to markets that demand them. This implies that the world price is greater than the price prior to trading, so exports will equal the difference between the domestic quantity supplied and the domestic quantity demanded at the world price.

19. E. Consumer surplus after trade, given that the price level fell below the price level prior to trading, equals the consumer surplus before trading (A), plus the increase in consumer surplus due to the price fall (B), plus the additional imports from the trade (D).

20. B. Domestic consumers are better off because prior to trade, consumer surplus equaled A;, after trade it includes regions B and D. Therefore, overall consumer welfare has increased. Producer surplus originally included B and C, now only equals region C, so they are worse after the trade. However, trade raises the overall economic welfare of a country because the gains of trade exceed that of the losses.

21. A. A proportional tax occurs when high-income and low-income taxpayers pay the same fraction of their income for taxes, eliminate choice B. Regressive tax is a tax for which a high-income person pays a smaller fraction of their income for taxes than low-income taxpayers, and progressive tax is a tax for which high-income taxpayers pay a larger portion of their income than low-income taxpayers; this eliminates choices C and D. A flat tax is a method developed to simplify the taxing system and can take on many different forms of taxing, such as progressive and proportional tax approaches, eliminating answer E.

22. B. A public good is both non-excludable (no one can be prevented from using the good) and non-rival (one person's use of the good does not diminish another person's enjoyment of that good). National defense is considered a public good because is it both non-excludable and non-rival. Choices A, D, and E are private good because they are both excludable and rival. Choice C is considered a common resource because it is rival but non-excludable—any person can catch salmon, but once that person catches a fish there are fewer fish to be caught.

23. D. An accountant's profit measures the firm's total revenues minus all the explicit costs, so it would not include any implicit costs such as opportunity costs. Since the plastic production forfeited in order to produce metal is regarded as an implicit cost, it will not be included in Tina's determination of this years total revenues. An economist's measurement of profits does take implicit costs into account when determining total revenue.

24. B. A firm will exit an industry if the revenue from producing a particular good is less than its total costs. Therefore, answers A, C, and E can all be eliminated. Although profits do equal total revenue minus total cost, it does not explain why a firm would exit an industry unless it somehow reflects that the profits are in the negative region.

25. E.

$$\text{Marginal Revenue} = \frac{\text{change in Total Revenue}}{\text{change in quantity}} = \frac{(\ \$2000 - \$1000\ )}{(\ \$1000 - \$500\ )} = \$2$$

26. A. Diseconomies of scales occur when the long-run ATC rises and quantity of output rises, eliminating choice B. When the long-run ATC remains the same as quantity produced changes, this is known as constant returns to scale; eliminate choice C. Sunk costs is a cost that has already been committed and cannot be returned; eliminate choice D. Efficiency occurs when resources are allocated to maximize the total surplus received by all members of society; therefore, choice E is eliminated.

27. B. A competitive, profit-maximizing firm will hire workers up to the point where the value of the marginal product of labor (VMPL) equals the wage. Hiring below this point implies that the value of the marginal product of labor exceeds the wage, so the firm could increase profits if they hire an additional worker. Therefore, eliminate answers A, C, D, and E.

28. E. Indifference curves have four general properties. One, higher indifference curves are preferred to lower ones. They are always downward sloping because if the quantity of one good is reduced, the consumer will desire more of the other good in order to be equally happy. Indifference curves cannot cross each other because it is our assumption that the consumer will always prefer more of both good. Lastly, indifference curves are bowed inwards because people are more willing to give up goods they have a greater quantity of than they are to give up those that they have less of.

29. A. Since both goods are inferior in nature, a decrease in income will spur the consumer to consume more of both goods. Therefore, the budget constraint line will shift out. A shift inwards would imply that the consumer is consuming less of both good, so eliminate choice B. Since both goods are inferior, both consumption levels will increase equally, so the slope of the budget constraint will not change, eliminating answers C and D. No change would imply that this would have no effect upon the consumer, which is clearly not the case if there is a decline in the income level; eliminate choice C.

30. C. C is the best answer because the deadweight loss is shared by both the consumers and producers, eliminating choices A and B. Although taxes do create administrative burdens, this is not what creates deadweight losses in the market; eliminate D. Taxes are used for government spending, and although it might imply that government spending has increased, it also does not account for the deadweight loss; eliminate choice E.

31. E. Marginal diminishing utility is when marginal utility is increasing at a decreasing rate, and in the table we can clearly see this trend.

32. B. Opportunity cost is the amount the farmer can earn if he produces the next best alternative; in this case the next best alternative is 200 bushels of apples, or in money terms ((200 bushels)($3 a bushel)) $600.

33. C. Collusive firms try to effectively form a monopoly in a market where they can reduce supply and charge a higher price.

34. A. The long-run average total cost curve is often referred to as the firm's planning curve because it allows the firm to forecast costs in relation to future output. The average total cost curve represents the lowest average total cost at which any output level can be produced after the firm had time to make all adjustments in its capabilities.

35. C. At 700 units of apples, the economy was producing 300 units of oranges. If the economy were to produce 900 units of apples, then production for oranges would fall to 100 units. Therefore, the opportunity cost of increasing the production of apples from 700 to 900 units would be 200 units of oranges.

36. D. Monopolies are price makers. Therefore, they determine their price and usually set it above marginal cost, leading to long run economic profits and deadweight losses for society. A monopoly consists of one firm in the given market, eliminating choice A. A normal good's demand increases with income. This can be true of any market, so it would not be the best illustration of a monopolistic market; eliminate choice B. When there are a few firms in a market it is considered to be an oligopoly, so answer C would not be correct. Monopolies are price makers, and they will not determine prices by quantity demanded, eliminating choice E.

37. C. A perfectly competitive firm will hire labor until the maximum marginal product of labor is achieved.

Hours of Labor	Cost of Labor	Units of Output	Revenue	Marginal Profit
1	$10	5	$25	$15
2	$20	7	$35	$15
3	$30	10	$50	$20
4	$40	11	$55	$15
5	$50	13	$65	$15

The firm will produce 10 units of output at 3 hours of labor. After which point there is diminishing marginal product; it would not be rational for a firm to produce beyond that point.

38. D. A consumer's consumption is optimized when $P_X/P_Y = MU_X/MU_Y$. This is the point at which the consumer's budget constraint and indifference curve is tangent. Choices A, B, C, and E can all be eliminated.

39. A. In order to maintain allocative efficiency there must be no deadweight loss in the market. Therefore, the price and output is determined by supply and demand. In the short-run, competitive industries do produce a profit; therefore, the correct answer is choice A. Choices B and C measure the responsiveness of quantity demanded relative to one of its determinants. If supply and demand determines the price, then the firm is a price taker, eliminating choice D. Answer E is incorrect because price equals average total cost for a market to allocate efficiently.

40. E. A Nash equilibrium is a situation in which all the players involved with one another pick the strategy that would best suit their needs given what the other players have chosen. Choice A reflects a dominant strategy in which the player chooses their best strategy regardless of the other players' actions. In a Nash equilibrium the player chooses their most desirable strategy, eliminating choice B. Maximizing the utility of another player does not concern the actors involved, eliminating choice C. It does not have to be the case that the least desirable strategy is chosen, therefore choice D is eliminated.

41. A. The U-shaped average total cost curve can be explained by the average fixed cost and the average variable cost. Average fixed cost declines as output increases because it is being spread over a larger number of units. Average variable costs increase as output does because of diminishing marginal products, eliminating B. Answer C does not explain the shape of the curve. Average total cost is the *sum* of average fixed cost and average variable cost, eliminating choice D. Since A explains the shape of the curve, choice E can be ignored.

42. B. Country 1 has the comparative advantage in producing plastic because the amount of plastic they have to give up in order to produce one more unit of metal is lower than Country 2. Therefore, they should import metal and export plastic.

43. B. In order for the firm to maximize profits it needs to increase quantity supplied; this will cause the firm to move up the marginal cost curve to a point where profits can be maximized.

44. C. The definition of a negative externality is *external cost*.

45. D. Elasticity means when there is an increase in price; the quantity demanded decreases significantly.

46. D. If the demand is price inelastic, the demand curve is a vertical line, meaning the quantity demanded is constant at any price. Because the quantity purchased is constant, an increase in price will raise a producer's revenue.

47. B. The question is not asking about the demand curve, so we can eliminate choices A, D, and E. The answer is not C because it violates the laws of supply. The answer is B because a higher price gives producers an incentive to produce a larger quantity.

48. A. By definition, A is the correct answer. Diminishing marginal returns to labor is the idea that the first worker you hire will increase productivity more than the second. Total output is increasing at a decreasing rate.

49. D. One of the main differences between a monopoly and a competitive firm is that a monopoly can affect the market price of the good. Choice A is not true of a monopoly. Choice B could be true both of a monopoly and a competitive market. Choice C. is not true of a monopoly. Choice E is false for both monopolies and competitive firms.

50. E. A monopolistic firm produces a lower quantity of a good at a higher price. Therefore, when the competitive market becomes monopolistic, the price will increase and the quantity produced will decrease.

51. E. The answer is E because a negative externality means the firm is producing at the expense of others. The answer is not A because it will be more efficient to produce a lower quantity. The answer is neither B nor C because these are not directly related to negative externalities. Choice D is incorrect because it is not true.

52. E. Although Bob is slower at both tasks he should not give-up because he has a comparative advantage. Bob's opportunity cost of making paper airplanes is less than Bill's. Therefore gains from trade can occur if Bill specializes in swans and Bob specializes in planes.

53. A. As income rises, the consumption of a normal or ordinary good increases. Normal goods increase in demand when individuals' incomes increase.

54. C. Advertising is not a determinant of demand. Choices A, B, D, and E are all factors that change demand or shift the demand curve.

55. C. The increase in the amount of corn supplied will shift the supply curve to the right. This increase in supply will result in a new equilibrium in which the price of corn is lower and the quantity supplied is higher than at the original equilibrium. Choices A, D, and E are incorrect because the price of corn does not increase (as is the case with A and E), or stay the same (as is the case for D). Choice B is incorrect because it assumes that the quantity supplied will decrease, but it actually increases.

56. A. A decrease in the price of a substitute will cause a decrease in the price of widgets, and a decrease in the number of firms in the industry will cause a decrease in the supply of widgets. Choice B is incorrect because an increase in the average income of consumers will cause the price of widgets to rise due to an increase in demand. Choice C is incorrect because a decrease in average income and a decrease in the price of a complement will cause only the demand curve to shift, not the supply curve. Choice D is incorrect because both changes only affect the supply curve and not the demand curve. Choice E is incorrect because an increase in the number of consumers will cause an increase in the price of widgets

57. B. If clean air is important to the town, the town should be willing to pay to have the chemical plant stop polluting. In other words, if the costs of bad air are high enough for the town, the town could pay the chemical plan to stop polluting. This turns the town's incurred cost of pollution into a monetary cost, and the monetary amount paid to the plant is the equal to the amount the chemical plant would pay to be able to pollute. This is the most efficient solution. Choices A and D are incorrect because government regulation is not economically efficient.

58. C. The definition of an inferior good is a good that a consumer buys less of when his or her income increases.

59. A. Elasticity of demand is determined by the percent change in demand divided by the percent change in price. Using this equation we have % change in demand/50% = 0.6% change in demand = 30%.

60. B. The equation for computing the elasticity of demand is the percent change in demand divided by the percent change in price. Using this equation we have 5%/10% = 0.5.

Free-Response Answers and Explanations

1. A.

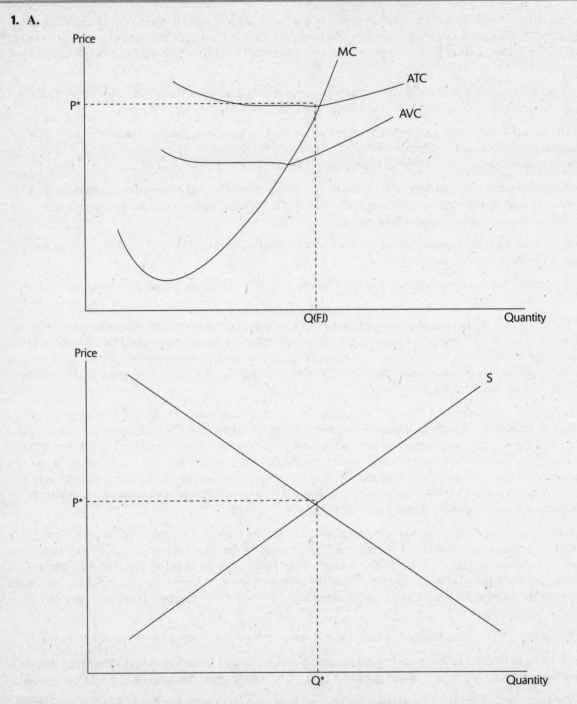

B. Farmer Joe's profit maximizing output is at quantity Q(FJ), and his profit maximizing price is price P*. The profit maximizing point for all firms is where marginal cost is equal to average total cost. For Farmer Joe this point occurs at quantity Q(FJ) and price P*. Farmer Joe's total revenue is equal to the product of the quantity of peaches he produces and the market price of peaches, or (Q(FJ))(P*)=TR.

C. A sudden decrease in the demand for peaches will cause the quantity of peaches demanded to decrease and the market price of peaches to decrease. The new market price of peaches means that Farmer Joe will have a new marginal revenue line that is below the original line of P*. The new lower price of peaches means that Farmer Joe is not producing at the profit maximizing point, and is now producing at a point lower than the profit maximizing point.

D.

    (i) Any farmer who is producing at a point below his average variable cost curve is operating with losses. In the long run these farmers will leave the peach industry and try to find an industry that has profit to be captured.

    (ii) Industry supply will decrease as a result of farmers exiting the market for peaches. This decrease in supply will increase the price of peaches slightly.

E. If Farmer Joe monopolizes the peach industry, there will be a new price and quantity supplied in the market place. The quantity supplied will decrease to the point at which marginal cost is equal to marginal revenue, and the price will be increased to either the maximum amount a consumer will pay for peaches or to the price that corresponds to the new higher price read off the demand curve for peaches.

F. In the short run, the farmers would collude and charge the monopolistic price and quantity for peaches. In the long run, the cartel would fail because of the increased incentive of each farmer to produce a little more output to capture more revenue. Because of the higher price in the peach market, each farmer has a higher incentive to produce more peaches. This extra production of peaches by each farmer will work to decrease the price of peaches because of the extra supply in the market. In the long run the cartel would collapse.

G.

    (i)

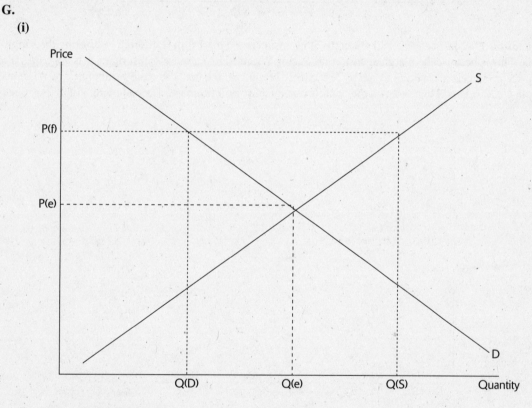

    (ii) A price floor effectively sets a price higher-than-market price; in this case equilibrium market price is at PE, and the price floor price has been set at P(f). At this new higher price for peaches, consumer demand less peaches than the equilibrium quantity (consumers now demand QD amount of peaches as opposed to the equilibrium level of QE amount of peaches). Also, at the new higher price farmers want to produce more peaches than the equilibrium quantity (producers now produce Q(S) amount of peaches as opposed to the equilibrium quantity of QE amount of peaches). In the long run, there will be a surplus of peaches in the market because of this inequity between the quantity supplied and quantity demanded.

2. A. Since we assumed that California cheese and Wisconsin cheese are substitutes and that they are the only two cheeses available in California, the tax on Wisconsin cheese would cause the demand for California cheese to shift out. The equilibrium price of California cheese would increase, and the equilibrium quantity would increase. The following graph illustrates this.

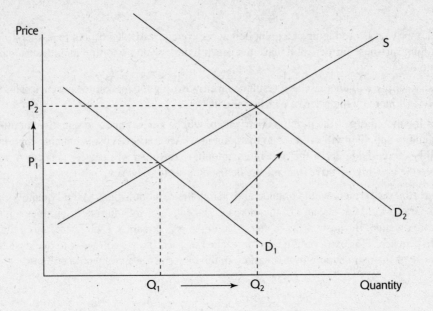

B. The tax on Wisconsin cheese will affect the Wisconsin cheese market in California by shifting the supply curve in. This is because the marginal cost of producing Wisconsin cheese for Californians has gone up. At any given price producers are willing to supply less cheese because of the tax. The equilibrium price of Wisconsin cheese in California will increase and the equilibrium quantity will decrease. The following graph illustrates this.

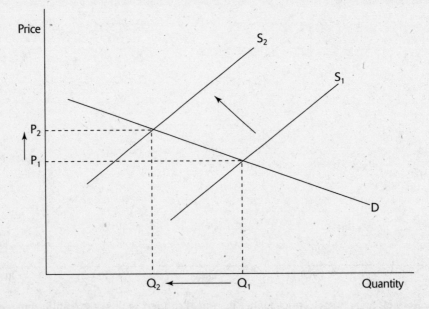

C. The demand for Wisconsin cheese is price elastic; a small increase in price will cause a large decrease in the quantity demanded. Therefore the amount of money Californians spend on Wisconsin cheese will decrease.

3. A.

    (i) The market price of pistachios will remain the same, but since production of pistachios is cheaper for Jack, he would earn economic profit. Jack has a production advantage because the cost of production is heavily dependent on the number of pistachio pickers. If Jack can decrease his number of pistachio pickers, then he can drastically decrease the cost of production.

    (ii) Since Jack owns a small farm and a pistachio tree takes 5-10 years to produce pistachios, the supply of pistachios would not change in the short run. The production per worker has increased because of the new tool. Jack will benefit if he plants pistachio trees for the long run.

B.

    (i) The overall market price of pistachios will fall significantly because the overall cost of pistachio production will decrease.

    (ii) In the short run, production will not change dramatically, but in the long run pistachio production could increase because of the lower variable costs to production.

C.

    (i) Two effects will cause the price of walnuts to fall. The substitution effect will shift the demand curve to the left, and (because labor is more abundant) the price effect will cause the supple curve to shift to the right. The cost of production will also decrease for the walnut industry because of the flow of unemployed workers from the pistachio industry to the walnut industry. The cost of hiring walnut pickers will decrease.

    (ii) The quantity of walnuts produced will increase in the long run because of the lower cost of labor.

D.

    (i) In the short run, while pistachio farmers use the new technology for picking pistachios, the supply of laborers will shift to the right. This would cause the wage rate to decrease. In the long run, the walnut industry would indirectly benefit from the new technology because of the increase in the amount of workers. In the long run the walnut industry will see the benefits of cheaper labor and will increase the number of trees for production. This will cause a significant decrease in the price of walnuts.

    (ii) In the long run equilibrium will be reached between walnut and pistachio prices. The decrease in the price of labor will be absorbed into the cost of walnut production; this will cause the cost of production to decrease. In the long run the walnut industry would benefit from the new technology indirectly.

Section I

- 60 multiple choice questions   70 minutes

Section II

- 1 long free-response question and
- 2 short free-response questions   10 minutes for planning
                                         50 minutes for writing

Total Time: 2 Hours and 10 Minutes

Microeconomics Section I: Multiple-Choice Questions

Directions: You have 70 minutes to complete the 60 multiple-choice questions in this section of the exam.

Questions 1 and 2 refer to the following graph.

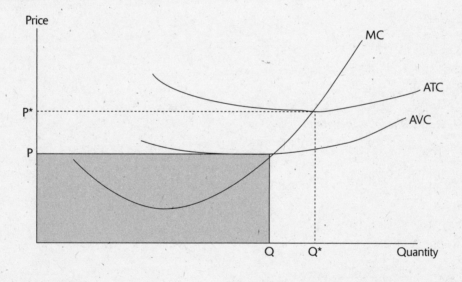

1. The area of the shaded region represents:

   A. Consumer surplus
   B. Producer surplus
   C. Total fixed costs
   D. Total variable costs
   E. Total losses

2. In the long run, the horizontal line representing price, P*, also represents:

   A. Marginal revenue
   B. Marginal cost
   C. Market price
   D. Total revenue
   E. Foregone price

3. *Question 3 refers to the following graph.*

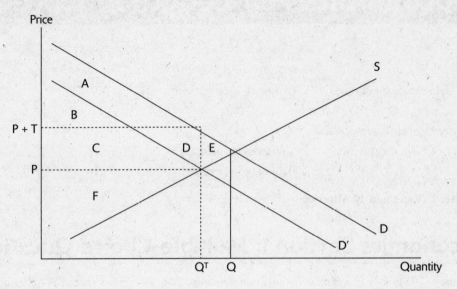

The chart above shows the supply and demand for gasoline. After a government tax is imposed the demand for gasoline falls from D to D'. What area represents consumer surplus?

A. A+B+C+D

B. B+C

C. C+D+E+F

D. A+B

E. A+B+C+D+E

4. *Question 4 refers to the following graph.*

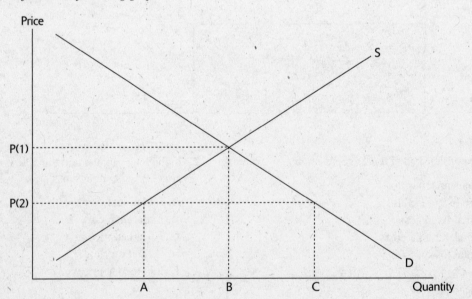

If a price ceiling is set at price P2, what will happen to quantity demanded?

A. Quantity demanded will increase to A.

B. Quantity demanded will stay the same.

C. Quantity demanded will decrease significantly.

D. Quantity demanded will decrease to A, and quantity supplied will increase to C.

E. Quantity demanded will increase to C.

5. *Question 5 refers to the following graph.*

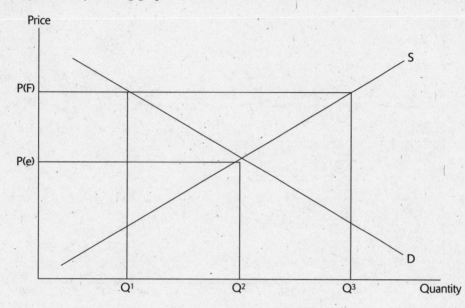

The graph above shows the supply and demand curves for the lemon market. How will a price set at P(F) affect the market for lemons?

A. There will be a surplus of Q2 – Q1 lemons.
B. There will be a surplus of Q2 – Qe lemons.
C. There will be a shortage of Q2 – Q lemons.
D. There will be a shortage of Qe – Q1 lemons.
E. There will be a surplus of Qe – Q1 lemons.

GO ON TO THE NEXT PAGE

6. *Question 6 refers to the following graph.*

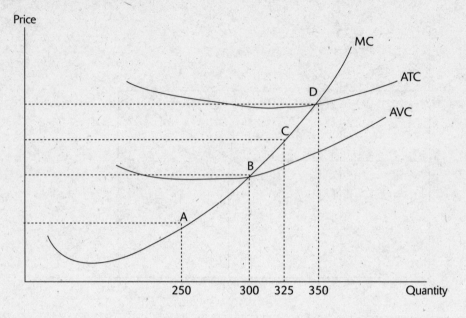

The graph above shows the cost curves of a firm in a perfectly competitive market. Which of the following statements is false?

A. The firm is earning negative economic profits when its output is 325 units.
B. The firm should shut down when its total profit is $1,250.
C. The firm's profit maximizing output is 350 units.
D. The firm's profit maximizing price is $15 a unit.
E. The firm's maximum profit is $7,000.

7. *Question 7 refers to the following graph.*

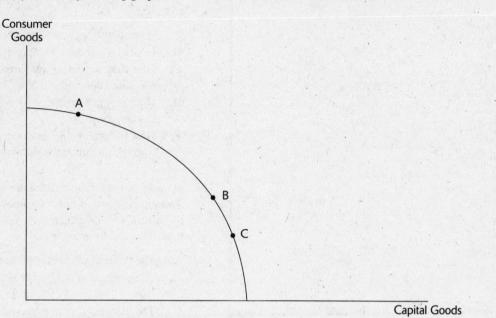

The graph above shows the production possibilities curve of a society. Which of the following statements is false?

A. If the society chooses point A, it chooses to consume more consumer goods than capital goods.

B. If the society chooses point C, it chooses more future consumption and less current consumption.

C. If the society chooses point B, it chooses more capital goods than at point A.

D. If the society chooses point A, it chooses less current consumption and more future consumption.

E. If the society chooses point C, it chooses less current consumption than at point B.

GO ON TO THE NEXT PAGE

8. *Question 8 refers to the following graph.*

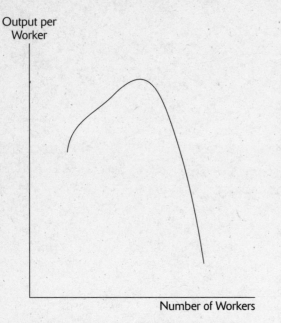

The graph above depicts the economic idea of:

A. Diminishing marginal price of labor

B. Diminishing marginal returns of labor

C. Marginal cost of labor

D. Total cost of production

E. Marginal variable cost of labor

9. What holds true for a perfectly competitive market?

A. Many firms producing many types of products.

B. Few firms producing one type of product.

C. One firm producing one product.

D. Many firms producing one type of product.

E. Few firms producing many types of products.

10. Which of the following best describes the basic economic problem that faces all countries?

A. How to utilize profits for investment

B. How to integrate our technology in production

C. How they utilize our resources to meet unlimited demands

D. How they establish quality and resource management

E. How to combine government and private firms to maximize production

11. What is the basic economic problem that faces all countries?

A. How to utilize profits for investment

B. How to integrate our technology in production

C. How they utilize our resources to meet our unlimited demands

D. How they establish quality and resource management

E. How to combine government and private firms to maximize production

12. Suppose butter and margarine are substitutes. Assume the price of milk, an input in the production of butter, increases. What will happen to the demand for margarine?

A. The demand of margarine will stay the same.

B. The demand of margarine will shift to the right.

C. The demand of margarine will shift to the left.

D. The quantity of margarine demanded will decrease.

E. The quantity of margarine demanded will stay the same.

13. Which series of shifts in the demand and supply curves will cause equilibrium price and equilibrium quantity to increase significantly?

A. A shift in the supply curve to the right and a shift in the demand curve to the left.

B. A shift in the supply curve to the right and a shift in the demand curve to the right.

C. A shift in the supply curve to the left and a shift in the demand curve to the left.

D. Only a shift in the supply curve to the right.

E. Only a shift in the demand curve to the left.

14. Which of the following is true for an ordinary good?

A. As income rises, consumption of the good decreases.

B. As the price of the good falls, consumption of the good increases.

C. As the price of the good falls, consumption of the good decreases.

D. As the price of the good falls, the demand curve shifts to the right.

E. An ordinary good violates the first law of demand.

15. All of the following will cause a shift in the demand curve *except*:

   A. Price of substitute increase

   B. Preferences change

   C. Advertising is increased

   D. Price of the good decreases

   E. Number of buyers in the market increase

Questions 16 and 17 refer to the following graph.

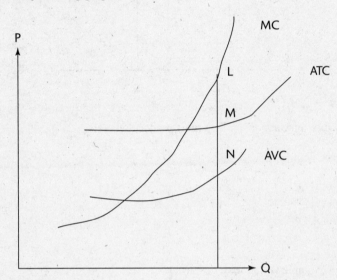

16. The graph above represents the cost curves of a firm in a competitive market. What does the distance between L and M represent?

   A. Total cost of all production

   B. Total economic profit

   C. Total profit

   D. Additional cost accrued in the long run

   E. Additional cost accrued for the short run

17. All of the following is true for a firm in a competitive market *except*?

   A. The level of production is derived from the intersection of MC and AVC.

   B. The level of production is derived from the intersection of MC and ATC.

   C. The distance between ATC and ATV, or line MN, is fixed cost.

   D. MC is the cost of producing one additional unit of output.

   E. ATC is the average fixed cost per unit plus the average variable cost per unit.

18. Which of the following is true in a perfectly competitive market?

   A. Many firms producing many products

   B. Few firms producing one type of product

   C. One firm producing one product

   D. Many firms producing one product

   E. Few firms producing many types of products

19. Assume there are positive economic profits in a competitive market. Which of the following best describes the future of this market?

   A. Firms would become efficient because they would produce more goods for the higher price.

   B. Firms would maintain their normal production levels to take advantage of the economic profits.

   C. New firms will enter the market to take advantage of the economic profits.

   D. Some firms will exit the market because there is no incentive for real profits.

   E. New firms will enter the market until the economic profit equals zero.

GO ON TO THE NEXT PAGE

20. *Question 20 refers to the following graph.*

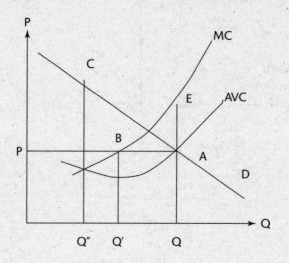

In order to increase profits, a monopolistic firm must produce where:

A. MC intersects D

B. D intersects S

C. The level of output is Q

D. The level of output is Q'

E. The level of output is Q"

21. Which of the following example is true for a giffen good?

A. Substitution effect > Income effect> Price Effect

B. Substitution effect > Price Effect > Income Effect

C. Substitution effect > Income Effect > Price Effect

D. Income Effect > Substitution Effect > Price Effect

E. Price Effect > Income Effect > Substitution Effect

22. *Question 22 refers to the following graph.*

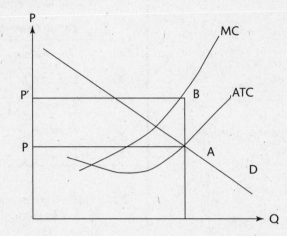

All of the following statements are true for a monopolistic firm that wants to maximize profits, *except:*

A. The monopolistic firm should produce where ATC intersects the demand curve.

B. The monopolistic firm should increase production because it is producing at an inefficient rate.

C. The distance between A and B represents the profit from each unit sold.

D. The quantity produced and sold is determined by the firm.

E. The monopolistic firm is earning economic profit.

23. Which two major factors are used to derive an individual's labor supply curve in the labor market?

A. Wage and savings

B. Income and leisure

C. Unemployment and demand for workers

D. Population and capital

E. Technology and production

24. Tornado Pizza Co. just opened for business and needs to hire workers. The wage rate for each worker is $70 per day, and the price of each pizza is $12. How many workers should Tornado Pizza Co. hire?

	Number of Workers	Number of Pizzas	Marginal Product Labor
	0	0	
	1	10	10
A.	2	18	8
B.	3	24	6
C.	4	28	4
D.	5	30	2
E.	6	31	1

25. A tire factory causes considerable air pollution in the process of making tires. Which of the following would help decrease air pollution?

A. Allow pollution based on the number of tires demanded.

B. Decrease pollution until the benefit of clean air is equal to the cost of producing less pollution.

C. Eliminate air pollution through government intervention.

D. Decrease pollution until the benefit of clean air is maximized.

E. Decrease pollution by passing regulation for cleaner air.

26. Which of the following statements best explains the opportunity cost of a firm that builds a new factory?

A. The firm will have to allocate funds from other resources.

B. Future profits are only based on current assumptions.

C. The cost of the new factory is the opportunity cost.

D. Interest that would be collected on the cash value of the building.

E. Depreciation value of the new factory.

GO ON TO THE NEXT PAGE

27. A country cannot consume more than its production capabilities when:

A. It is an open economy.
B. It is a closed economy.
C. It is a competitive market economy.
D. It is a monopolistic economy.
E. It is a oligopolistic economy.

28. Which areas in the graph represent consumer surplus and producer surplus?

A. PS = ICP, CS = PCJ
B. PS = ABC, CS = GCE
C. PS = PCJ, CS= ICP
D. PS = PCJ, CS = AT POINT Q (PL)
E. PS = ACE, CS = BCF

29. If a price ceiling is set at price P1, which of the following phenomena will occur in the market?

A. Excess demand
B. Excess supply
C. Increase of production
D. Increase of profits
E. Decrease of demand

30. Which of the following is true for a good with a price inelastic demand curve?

I. The quantity demanded is constant at any price.

II. The price is constant at all quantities demanded.

III. Producers of the good will have increased revenue if the price increases.

A. I only
B. II only
C. III only
D. I and III only
E. II and III only

31. How is the labor market for apple pickers affected by a fall in the demand for apple juice?

	Labor Demanded	Apple Pickers Hired
A.	Stays the same	Stays the same
B.	Decrease	Decrease
C.	Increase	Decrease
D.	Decrease	Increase
E.	Decrease	Stays the same

32. What is the best option for a firm if the market price of its product is $200 and market price = MC = ATC?

A. Shut down production.
B. Keep producing at the same level.
C. Produce quantity at $200.
D. Decrease production below $200.
E. Increase production above $225.

33. Why is a firm in a perfectly competitive market also known as a price taking firm?

A. Price is constant at any quantity produced.
B. The cost of their inputs is fixed.
C. Their marginal cost is constant at any quantity.
D. The price they charge is determined by the government.
E. It is impossible for them to receive economic profit.

34. Why are monopolies bad from the perspective of an economist?

A. They create negative externalities.
B. It would be better for everyone if they shut down.
C. They use price discrimination to capture consumer surplus.
D. They do not produce the optimal quantity of a good.
E. They earn a super normal profit.

35. Assume that time is the only resource required to produce a good. The following table shows the different amounts of time it takes for two individuals to make one paper airplane and one origami swan.

	Michelle	*Tom*
Plane	2 minutes	10 minutes
Swan	3 minutes	20 minutes

Which of the following statements is true according to the table above?

A. Michelle should be self-sufficient because there would be no gains from trade.

B. Tom should be self-sufficient because there would be no gains from trade.

C. There would be gains from trade if Michelle specializes in planes and Tom specializes in swans.

D. There would be gains from trade if Tom and Michelle both specialize in planes.

E. There would be gains from trade if Michelle specializes in swans and Tom specializes in planes.

36. *Question 36 refers to the following graph.*

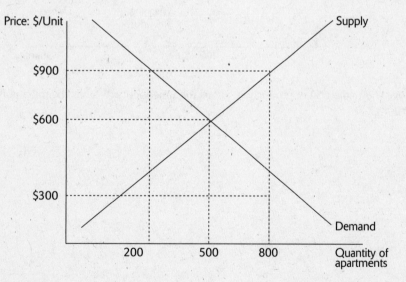

The graph above shows the supply and demand for apartments in Limsfield. If the mayor of Limsfield decides to set a price ceiling at $300 a month, what will happen in the housing market in Limsfield?

A. There will be a shortage of 200 apartments.
B. There will be a shortage of 800 apartments.
C. There will be a shortage of 600 apartments.
D. There will be a shortage of 300 apartments.
E. There will be a shortage of 500 apartments.

GO ON TO THE NEXT PAGE

37. What will happen to the supply and demand curves in the short run if the cost of production falls?

	Demand Curve	Supply Curve
A.	Shifts to the right	Stays the same
B.	Shifts to the right	Shifts to the right
C.	Shifts to the left	Stays the same
D.	Stays the same	Shifts to the right
E.	Stays the same	Stays the same

38. A firm in a perfectly competitive market has a marginal revenue of $30 per unit. Which of the following is true if the firm can produce 574 units for a total cost of $1,752 or 575 units for $1,782?

A. To sell 575 units they need to lower their price.

B. To sell 575 units they need to raise their price.

C. The firm should produce 574 units.

D. The firm should produce 575 units.

E. Unit number 575 is not worth it.

39. *Question 39 refers to the following graph.*

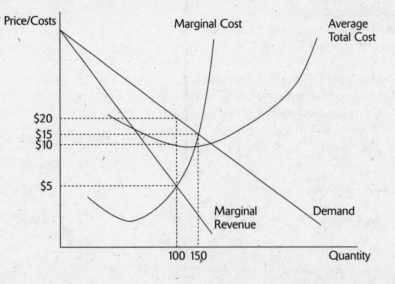

The graph above shows the cost of production curves for a monopoly. What is the monopoly's total profit when it produces 100 units?

A. $1,500

B. $500

C. $1,000

D. $2,000

E. $3,000

40. If the labor market for hotel workers is perfectly competitive, which of the following statements is true?

    A. An increase in the number of hotels will cause a decrease in the demand for hotel workers and a new higher wage.

    B. The imposition of a minimum wage will cause an increase in employment.

    C. If the demand for hotel workers falls, the wages paid to hotel workers will increase.

    D. A decrease in the supply of labor will cause the quantity of labor demanded to fall and the price of labor to increase.

    E. If the demand for hotel workers falls, there will be no change in the price of labor, only a change in the quantity demanded.

41. The reallocation of wealth in the United States is done through:

    A. Subsidizing the poor

    B. Subsidizing the rich firms

    C. Taxing income progressively

    D. Retraining unskilled workers

    E. Setting a minimum wage rate

42. *Question 42 refers to the following graph.*

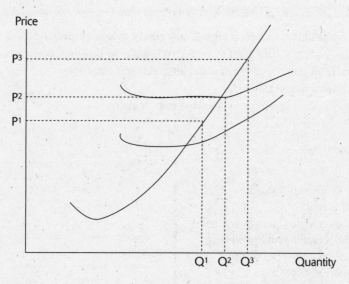

Which of the following is *not* true for a perfectly competitive firm?

    A. The marginal cost curve intersects the average total cost curve where the average total cost is at a minimum.

    B. The marginal cost curve intersects the average total cost curve where the average variable cost is at a minimum.

    C. Price is equal to marginal revenue.

    D. P^2 is the profit maximizing price.

    E. Q^1 is the profit maximizing output.

GO ON TO THE NEXT PAGE

43. *Question 43 refers to the following graph.*

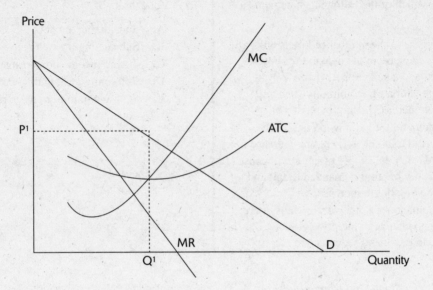

Which of the following statements is *true* for a monopolistic firm?

A. Profit maximizing quantity is where marginal cost equals marginal revenue.

B. Profit maximizing price is where average total cost is equal to marginal cost.

C. The profit maximizing point is where demand intersects marginal cost.

D. P^1 is the profit maximizing price.

E. A monopolist will make a profit no matter what price it charges.

44. Which of the following statements is *true* for a monopolistic firm?

A. A monopolistic firm always produces at an efficient level of output.

B. The price that a monopolist charges is where marginal revenue is equal to marginal cost.

C. The price that a monopolist charges is decided in the market.

D. The demand curve that a monopolist faces is industry demand.

E. A monopolist produces where average total cost is equal to demand.

45. *Question 45 refers to the following graph.*

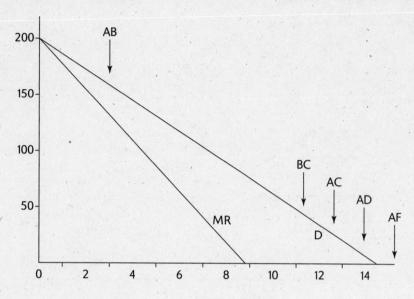

Which portion of the demand curve is elastic for this monopoly firm?

A. AB
B. BC
C. AC
D. AD
E. AF

46. *Question 46 refers to the following graph.*

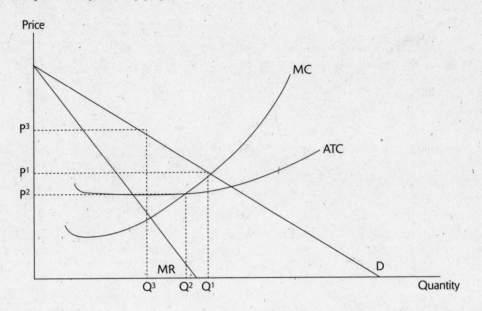

A monopolistic firm has the cost curves depicted above and operates in a monopolistic market. Which of the following statements would be true if the market becomes perfectly competitive?

A. The firm will charge price P^1.

B. The firm will charge price P^2.

C. The firm will charge price P^3.

D. The firm would produce quantity Q^1.

E. The firm will produce quantity Q^3.

47. Assume that the imported French wine market is perfectly competitive. If the government puts a tariff on imported French wines, what will be the effect on the imported wine market?

A. The price of imported French wine will decrease.

B. The price of imported French wine will stay the same.

C. The quantity of French wine produced will increase.

D. The quantity of French wine imported will stay the same.

E. The quantity of French wine imported will decrease.

48. If the price of apples decreases and as a result the quantity demanded of oranges increases, what can be said about apples and oranges?

A. The demand for oranges is elastic.

B. The demand for apples is elastic.

C. The elasticity of demand for apples is unitary.

D. Apples and oranges are complements.

E. Apples and oranges are substitutes.

49. Which of the following statements is true if a rebate is given to the consumers of domestic automobiles?

    A. Domestic automobiles are not of very good quality and need a discount in order to be sold.

    B. There will be a decrease in the quantity of foreign automobiles sold.

    C. The demand for domestic automobiles must be elastic.

    D. The price of domestic automobiles is too high.

    E. Domestic automakers will not benefit from the rebate given on the automobiles they produce.

50. *Question 50 refers to the following graph.*

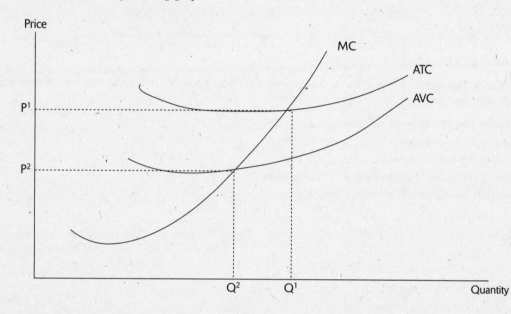

The figure above shows the cost curves of a grape producer, Farmer Jill. Farmer Jill invents a new tool which will allow her to produce more grapes and hire less labor. What will the invention of the new tool mean for Farmer Jill?

    A. Farmer Jill will produce Q^2 quantity of grapes.

    B. Farmer Jill will not be able to fully capture the benefits of the invention.

    C. Farmer Jill will be able to charge P^2 price for her grapes.

    D. Farmer Jill's cost curves will shift upward.

    E. Farmer Jill will be able to sell as many grapes as she wants to at market price.

51. Price floors are established in order to:

    A. Benefit customers

    B. Restrict entry into the market

    C. Restrict imports

    D. Ration scarce goods to the public

    E. Benefit producers

52. In general, price ceilings work to:

    A. Benefit producers

    B. Increase prices in the marketplace

    C. Cause shortages

    D. Increase production

    E. Establish a limit on production

GO ON TO THE NEXT PAGE

53. *Question 53 refers to the following graph.*

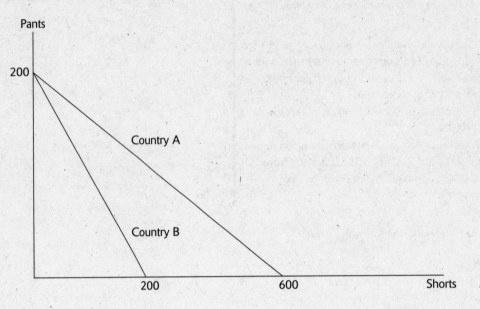

Which of the following conclusions can be drawn using the figure above if we assume that both countries have identical resources?

A.   Country A has a comparative advantage in pants.
B.   Country B has a comparative advantage in shorts.
C.   Country B has a comparative advantage in pants.
D.   Country B can produce more pants than country A.
E.   County B has no advantage over county A.

54. *Question 54 refers to the following graph.*

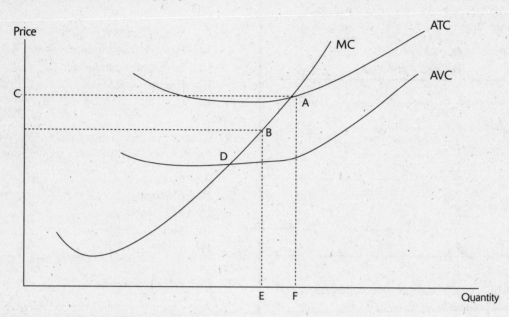

In the graph above, the marginal revenue for this perfectly competitive, profit maximizing firm is represented by the line:

A. AB
B. BE
C. AC
D. AF
E. AE

55. Suppose the government gives its citizens a $100 voucher each month which the citizens can use to purchase food. Which of the following statements is *false*?

A. A black market will form where goods other than food can be purchased with vouchers.
B. Some citizens will purchase more food than before.
C. Citizens will have more money to spend on all other goods.
D. Food producers will not benefit from the food vouchers.
E. Government spending will increase.

GO ON TO THE NEXT PAGE

56. The following table shows the production information for a profit maximizing widget producing firm.

Number of Workers	Number of Widgets Produced
0	0
1	10
2	25
3	45
4	70
5	94
6	115

With which worker does the firm maximize its marginal product?

A. 1
B. 3
C. 4
D. 5
E. 6

57. What does the term *comparative advantage* refer to?

A. When the producer requires a smaller number of inputs to produce that good.

B. The producer requires a larger number of inputs to produce that good.

C. The producer is getting all it can from the scarce resources available.

D. The producer has a lower opportunity cost when producing that good.

E. The producer is producing less than what is available to produce that good.

58. An inferior good rises in demand when an individual:

A. Has an increase in income
B. Has a decrease in income
C. Becomes unemployed
D. Becomes employed
E. Pays more for the good

59. What term refers to the economic analysis situation where all variables are held constant?

A. Fixed costs
B. Efficiency
C. Marginal costs
D. Variable costs
E. *Ceteris paribus*

60. Demand is elastic when:

A. Quantity supplied depends substantially on price.

B. Quantity demanded does not respond to price.

C. Quantity supplied does not respond to price.

D. Quantity demanded responds substantially to a price change.

E. The supply curve shifts to the right.

Microeconomics Section II: Free-Response Questions

Directions: You have one hour to answer all three free-response questions: one long and two short questions. Spend the first 10 minutes for planning, and in the remaining 50 minutes construct your responses. Explain your answers thoroughly with examples and illustrations if appropriate.

1. In the nation of Caffinia, the government regulates the coffee market by not allowing imported coffee into the country.

   A. Draw Caffinia's current supply and demand curves, as well as the supply and demand curves of the nation if imports are allowed in the market. Label the graph showing the different prices and quantities.

   B. Using the graph from Part A, describe the differences between the price and quantity in the coffee market when imports are allowed, as well as the price and quantity of coffee when imports are not allowed.

   C. Bill, a resident of Caffinia, buys coffee in an unregulated market.

   (i) Draw and label the demand and supply curves for coffee in the unregulated market.

   (ii) Using the diagram from Part B(i), label and tell what region represents Bill's consumer surplus. Why did you choose this area?

   (iii) Using the diagram from Part B(i), label and tell what region represents producer surplus. Why did you choose this area?

   D. Assume that the market for coffee is regulated and imports are not allowed into Caffinia.

   (i) Draw and label, side-by-side, the supply and demand curves for the coffee industry and the cost curves of a typical coffee producing firm. Assume the firm makes zero economic profit.

   (ii) Using the graph from Part D(i), explain in detail the changes in the market supply and demand, as well as the outcome of firms in the market in the long run if the government allows imports.

2. The fixed cost for a garden gnome firm to operate is $40. Labor is the only variable input; the firm can hire any quantity of sculptors for $5 each. The firm can sell any quantity of the garden gnomes at the market price of $2 each. The following production schedule shows the total output of each sculptor.

Quantity of Sculptors	Total Gnomes Produced
0	0
1	13
2	23
3	30
4	34
5	36
6	37

   A. Is the market for garden gnomes perfectly competitive? Explain.

   B. Is the labor market for garden gnome sculptors perfectly competitive? Explain.

   C. Perform a marginal revenue product analysis.

   (i) To maximize profits, how many sculptors should the firm hire?

   (ii) What is the profit maximizing quantity of gnomes produced?

   D. Using the profit maximizing quantities you determined in Part C:

   (i) What is the firm's total cost?

   (ii) What is the firm's total revenue?

   (iii) Is the firm earning an economic profit? Explain.

GO ON TO THE NEXT PAGE

3. Using the information provided, determine the best solution for a pizza producing firm.

■ The wage rate of each worker, working an eight hour shift, is $80.
■ The price of each pizza produced is $11.

Number Of Workers	Pizzas Produced Per Worker Per Day
1	15
2	16
3	13
4	9
5	7
6	6

A. In a short run competitive industry, how many workers should be hired in order to maximize profits?
B. What are some of the reasons that the marginal product of each additional worker decreases?
C. Justify your answer from Part A. Why do you think this many workers should be hired?
D. If the firm wanted to hire one additional worker and make 10% profit, how much should they offer the additional worker (assume the additional worker is in addition to the profit maximum amount of workers)?

Hint:

■ The marginal product of each worker is given.
■ The price of pizza remains the same.

Multiple-Choice Answers and Explanations

1. **D.** The shaded region represents total variable cost; this can be found by multiplying the quantities, or units, on the x and y axis. P is the average cost of each unit of output, and Q is the quantity of output; their product yields the total variable cost.

2. **A.** In the long run, the horizontal price line also represents the marginal revenue of a firm. Choices C and E deal with price, so they are incorrect. Choice B is incorrect because marginal cost is not perfectly elastic. Choice D is incorrect because the total revenue is the product of quantity and price, but the price line alone represents the marginal revenue.

3. **D.** Consumer surplus is the area bounded between the demand curve and the price paid by the consumers; in this figure that area is represented by A + B. Areas C and D are government tax revenues, E is dead weight loss, and F is the producer surplus.

4. **E.** A price ceiling usually causes an increase in demand; in this case, the quantity demanded increases from B to C. The price ceiling will cause an artificially low price in the market, which will increase quantity demanded.

5. **A.** Price floors have the effect of causing a surplus in the market because at a price higher than equilibrium price, consumers demand less and producers produce more. In this case, the surplus of lemons will be Q2 – Q1, the quantity supplied minus the quantity demanded.

6. **D.** Choice D is incorrect because the firm's profit maximizing price is $20 where MC is equal to ATC.

7. **D.** To clarify, capital goods ensure future consumption, and consumer goods ensure current consumption. If a society chooses to consume more consumer goods and less capital goods, as at point A, then the society will choose more current consumption and less future consumption. Choices A, B, C, and E are all correct.

8. **B.** The graph depicts the economic idea of diminishing marginal returns to labor because output per worker increases when the firm has few employees, and the output per worker decreases as the firm hires more employees.

9. **D.** Perfectly competitive firms produce many of the same or homogenous products. There are many firms in a perfectly competitive firm that produce many of the same product.

10. **C.** The problem that all countries face is how to use resources to meet unlimited wants. This problem is more commonly known as scarcity.

11. **C.** Choice A is just stating that whatever profits are made eventually is made into investment. Choice B is just a managerial problem to integrate technology. Choice D is just a managerial problem. Choice E is stating that production maximization with the help of the government.

12. **B.** Choice A is incorrect because the price rises for a substitute the demand for the substitute will increase. Choice B is correct because an increase in the price of substitute will shift the substitute demand cure to the right. Choice C is incorrect because there would be an increase in the demand of margarine if the price of the substitute increase. Choice D is incorrect because the quantity demand of margarine will increase because it is a substitute of butter. Choice E is incorrect because a change in quantity demand for a product will cause a change in the substitutes demand.

13. **B.** Choice A is incorrect because it results in a decrease in price and decrease in quantity. Choice C results in an increase in price and increase in quantity but not elastic. Choice D results in a decrease price and increase quantity. Choice E results in a decrease in price and quantity.

14. **B.** Choice A is incorrect because the income effect will cause additional consumption of ordinary good. Choice C incorrect because the first law of demand states that as price falls quantity demanded increase. Choice D is incorrect because price does not affect shifts in demand curve. Choice E is incorrect because an ordinary good does not violate the first law of demand.

15. **D.** Choice A is incorrect because substitutes are determinates of demand. Choice B is incorrect because preferences are determinates of demand. Choice C is incorrect because advertising is a determinate of demand. Choice E is incorrect because the number of buyers in the market are determinates of demand.

16. B. The distance between L and M represents economic profit. In the long run, new firms will enter the market to take advantage of the economic profits.

17. B. For a firm in a competitive market, the level of production is determined by the intersection of the MC curve and the ATC curve. ATC is the average cost of producing a unit of product. This is the sum of fixed cost per unit plus variable costs of the extra unit produced.

18. D. Choice A is incorrect. Many firms (true) many products (false). Oligopoly. Monopoly. Few firms (false) many products (true).

19. E. Choice A is incorrect because as they increase production, they would decrease economic profit. Choice B would be an incentive (extra profits) for other films to enter into the market. With Choice C, the number of firms will enter the market, but until there is no more incentive for (extra profits). With Choice D, the reverse will happen because firms would want to enter the market because of the extra profits.

20. C. A monopolist can increase profits by producing where demand, D, is equal to average variable cost, AVC, or at Q level of output.

21. D. Substitution effect: change in optimal consumption point as the price of a product changes while holding all other prices and satisfaction level constant. Income effect: the change in the optimal consumption point as the income changes while holding all prices at the new price levels. Price effect: substitution effect + Income Effect. Giffen Good = as price of product increase the amount consumed will increase. Violates the first law of demand.

22. B. All choices are explaining monopolistic firms with the exception of B. Choice B represents inefficiency for a monopolistic firm, but the firm will create more profits by producing less and selling its product for a higher price.

23. B. Choice A is incorrect because wage and savings just explains the microeconomics of wage and humane nature to save. Choice C is incorrect because unemployment and the demand for workers just explain the job markets. Choice D is incorrect because population and capital derive the production curve. Choice E is incorrect because technology and production are just variable in industry.

24. B. Formula is wage = MPN, where N is the last worker to be hired.

Number of Workers	Marginal Revenue per worker
0	0
1	120
2	96
3	72
4	48
5	24
6	12

25. B. A policy where the benefits of clean air are equal to the cost of less pollution would decrease the amount of pollution. The optimal point is where the cost of pollution to the public is equal to the benefit of pollution to the firm.

26. D. Choice A is incorrect because opportunity cost is by definition loss in profits from alternative projects. The firm still allocates funds to build the new factory but at what price. Choice B is true but is incorrect for this question because it only states that whatever we know now about the future is only a forecast. Choice C is false because it does not agree with the definition. Choice E is incorrect because depreciation has to do with the user cost of the new factory.

27. B. In a closed economy a firm can only consume whatever it produces.

28. C. ICP is the consumer surplus. Is the difference between the maximum amount the consumer is willing to pay for the quantity demanded and the actual payment of the purchase? PCJ is the producer surplus. Is the difference between the actual amount a seller receives and the minimum that a seller is willing to accept for the quantity supplied?

29. A. If a price ceiling is set at P1, the quantity supplied will be lower than the quantity demanded; this disequilibrium will cause an excess demand.

30. D. If the demand is price inelastic, then the demand curve is a vertical line, meaning that the quantity demanded is constant at any price (so I is true). Because the quantity purchased is constant, an increase in price will raise a producer's revenue (so III is true). II is not true because the demand would have to be a horizontal line, which it isn't. Since I and III are true, the correct answer is D.

31. B. The fall in the demand for apple juice will lower the market price, thus lowering the quantity of apples supplied. This would affect the labor market for apple pickers by decreasing the demand for apple pickers, thus decreasing the quantity of apple pickers hired.

32. B. When the market price goes below the AVC and does not even cover part of the fixed cost, and if subsequently the market price falls below the intersection of AVC and MC, then production should be shut down. If it is still above the intersection of the AVC and MC, it is still paying for some of the fixed cost.

33. A. The correct answer is A because a price taking firm charges the same price at all quantities. The price they charge is determined by the market, so choice D is incorrect. Choices C and E are false statements. Choice B is irrelevant.

34. D. Choice D is the correct answer because it would be better for the economy if monopolies produced more of a good at a lower cost. Choices C and E are both true of monopolies, but they aren't necessarily bad for the economy. Choices A and B are both irrelevant.

35. E. Although Tom is slower at both tasks, he has a comparative advantage. Tom's opportunity cost of making paper airplanes is less than Michelle's. Therefore gains from trade can occur if Michelle specializes in swans and Tom specializes in planes.

36. C. Choice C is the correct answer because at $300 the difference between the quantity demanded and the quantity supplied is 600 apartments. Therefore there is a shortage of 600 apartments.

37. D. Since we are dealing with the short run effects and a fall in the cost of production, only the supply curve will be affected. A fall in the cost would enable firms to produce more at the same cost; therefore, the supply curve would shift to the right.

38. D. A profit maximizing firm will produce where marginal revenue is equal to marginal cost. In this example, the marginal cost of unit 575 is $30 ($1,782 - $1,752), and the marginal revenue is $30. Therefore, the firm should produce 575 units.

39. C. A monopoly produces where marginal cost is equal to marginal revenue, and it charges a price where that quantity meets the demand. The total profit is the difference between the price charged and the average total cost, multiplied by the quantity produced. This is represented on the graph as ($20 - $10)*100units = $1,000 profit. The correct answer is C.

40. D. Using demand and supply analysis for the labor market, we can see that when the supply of labor decreases, the price of labor increases and quantity of labor demanded decreases. Choice A is incorrect because an increase in the number of hotels will cause an increase in the number of workers demanded. With Choice B, a minimum wage would likely cause more unemployment. With Choice C, if the demand for hotel workers falls, the wages paid to workers will also fall. With Choice E, if the demand for hotel workers shifts, there will be a new equilibrium in the labor market and a new wage.

41. C. The United States reallocates wealth by taxing different income levels at different rates.

42. E. A perfectly competitive firm's marginal cost curve intersects both, average variable cost and average total cost, at their minimum (Choices A and B). Also, for a profit maximizing firm, price is equal to marginal revenue, and in this figure P(2) is the profit maximizing price (Choices C and D). The only statement that is not true for a perfectly competitive firm is E.

43. A. The only statement that is true for a monopolistic firm is statement A—the profit maximizing quantity for all monopolists is where marginal cost is equal to marginal revenue.

44. D. The demand curve that a monopolist faces is the industry demand curve because it makes up the market for its product. Choice A is incorrect because monopolists do not produce the efficient level of output. The price that a monopolist charges is the price read off the demand curve corresponding to the quantity at which marginal cost is equal to marginal revenue, not the price where marginal cost equals marginal revenue (Choice B). Choice C is incorrect because the price that a monopolist charges is not decided in the marketplace, but it is actually set by the firm.

45. C. The elastic portion of the demand curve is the portion AC. This is the only portion that is elastic because it is the only portion that can be influenced by the consumer by his or her demand.

46. B. If the market in which the monopolist operates becomes perfectly competitive, the monopolistic firm would have to charge a price where marginal cost is equal to average total cost—in this case P(2).

47. E. If the government puts a tariff on imported wines, the cost to producers will go up and so will the price for consumers. This increase in price will yield a lower quantity demanded, and the quantity of French wine imported will decrease.

48. D. Because apples and oranges are complements, a decrease in the price of apples will cause an increase in the quantity demanded of apples. Since oranges are complements to apples, the increase in the demand for apples will cause an increase in the demand for oranges. Apples and oranges cannot be substitutes because if the price of apples fell, there would be a decrease in the quantity demanded of oranges (Choice E).

49. B. The rebate will make the cost of domestic automobiles lower for consumers. This lower price will attract consumers of foreign automobiles into the domestic market, and there will be fewer foreign automobiles sold.

50. E. The invention will effectively shift Farmer Jill's cost curves downward, allowing Farmer Jill to produce more grapes. Since the grape market is perfectly competitive, Farmer Jill will be able to sell as many grapes as she wants to at market price.

51. E. Price floors are established in order to benefit producers at the expense of consumers. Consumers pay a higher price for the good, and producers capture the benefits of this higher price charged in the market.

52. C. Price ceilings usually cause shortages in a market because at the lower price that is set by a price ceiling, consumers are willing to buy a large quantity, but producers are not willing to produce this quantity at such a low price.

53. C. Using the figure provided we can see that the ratio of shorts to pants for Country B is 1/1 and for Country A it is 3/1. Using this ratio we can see that Country A clearly has a comparative advantage in shorts because they can produce three shorts for every pair of pants they forego making. Also, we can see that Country B has a comparative advantage in pants because for every pair of pants they produce they forego one pair of shorts. However, Country A has to give up three pairs of shorts in order to produce one pair of pants.

54. C. The marginal revenue for perfectly competitive firms is equal to the market price of the goods they produce. In this case the best choice is line AC.

55. D. If the government gives food vouchers to its citizens, one of the beneficiaries will be the producers of food because the vouchers will increase the demand for food.

56. C. In order to answer this question we can make a table to show the marginal product of each worker:

Number of Workers	Marginal Product Per Worker
0	0
1	10
2	15
3	20
4	25
5	24
6	21

Using this table we can see that the marginal product per worker is maximized at four workers: Choice C.

57. D. The producer has a comparative advantage when production of a good consists of lower opportunity costs than another producer.

58. B. A decrease in income increases the demand for inferior goods. Demand for inferior goods increases when individuals' income's decrease.

59. E. *Ceteris paribus* is the Latin phrase that holds all variables constant when analyzing a particular economic situation.

60. D. Elastic demand refers to a situation where quantity demanded is sensitive or responsive to a price change.

Free-Response Answers

1. A.

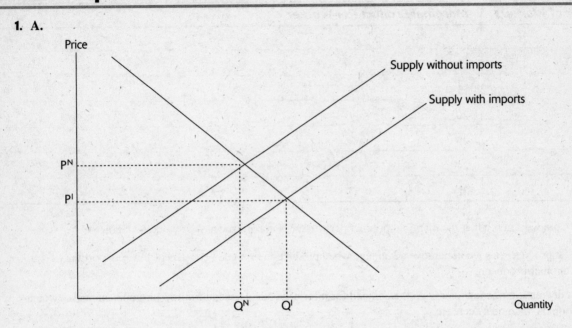

B. When imports are allowed into the coffee industry, there is going to be a larger supply of coffee; this larger supply of coffee also accounts for a lower price for the coffee in the market. These points can be seen in the graph as quantity Q^I and price P^I. When the market for coffee is regulated and imports are not allowed, there is going to be less coffee available in the market, and at this lower quantity there is going to be a higher price for coffee. These points can be seen in the graph as quantity Q^N and price P^N.

C. (i)

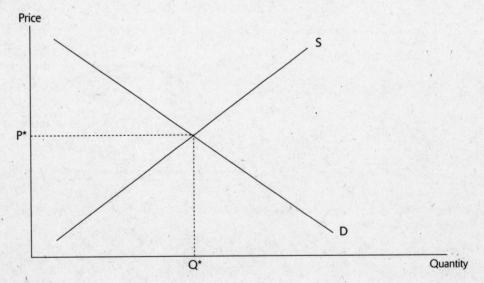

(ii)

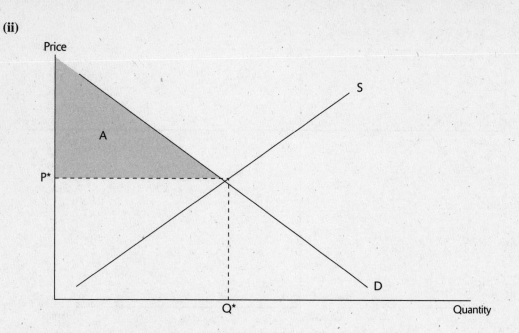

Area A in the chart above represents Bill's consumer surplus because consumer surplus is the area trapped between the demand curve, the line representing price, and the vertical axis.

(iii)

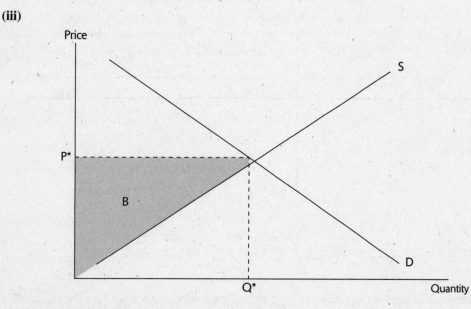

Area B in the chart above represents producer surplus because producer surplus is the area trapped between the supply curve, the line representing price, and the vertical axis.

D. (i)

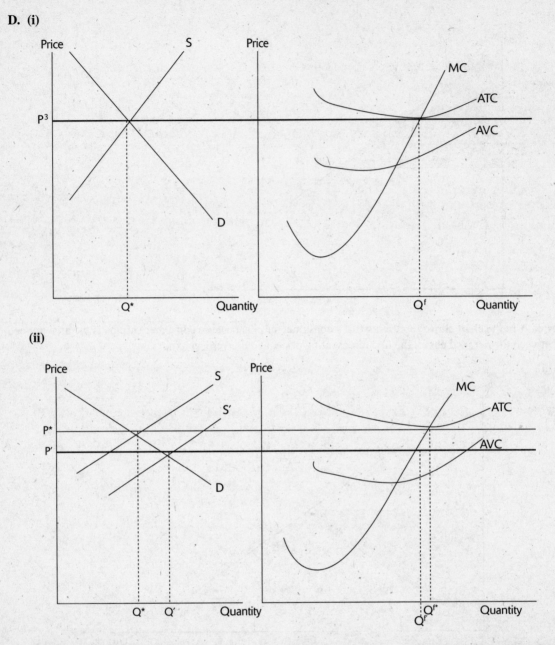

In the regulated coffee market there was a price of P* and a quantity produced of Q*. The typical firm was producing Q^f amount of coffee at price P* and was earning zero economic profits, as seen in the chart for Part D(i). When the government allows imported coffee to be sold in the market, the supply curve will shift to the right, depicting the increase in supply. The new quantity supplied in the market will be Q' at a new market price of P'. At this new price of P', the typical coffee producing firm produces less coffee than before, a quantity of Q^f. At this new price the typical firm in the industry is now operating under negative economic profits. In the long run, some coffee producing firms will leave the coffee market because they now operate with losses. This decrease in the number of firms will slightly decrease the quantity of coffee supplied in the market; also, this decrease in quantity will cause a slight increase in price. The coffee market will find a new equilibrium price and quantity. The new price will be between P* and P', and the new quantity will be between Q^{f*} and $Q^{f'}$.

2. A. Yes, the garden gnome market is perfectly competitive. This is because the firm can sell any quantity of the gnomes at the market price (the firm is a price taker).

B. Yes, the labor market for sculptors is perfectly competitive because the firm can hire any quantity at a given market price.

C.

Quantity of Sculptors	Total Gnomes Produced	Price	Marginal Revenue	Wage
0	0	-	-	-
1	13	$ 2	$ 26	$ 5
2	23	$ 2	$ 20	$ 5
3	30	$ 2	$ 14	$ 5
4	34	$ 2	$ 8	$ 5
5	36	$ 2	$ 4	$ 5
6	37	$ 2	$ 2	$ 5

(i) A profit-maximizing firm will employ a variable input until the marginal revenue is equal to the marginal cost. In this case the firm will hire sculptors until the marginal revenue is equal to the wage. Therefore, to maximize profits the firm should hire four sculptors. Although the marginal revenue is not equal to the wage, four sculptors is the best quantity because the fifth sculptor's marginal cost exceeds the marginal revenue ($ 5 > $ 4), so the profit-maximizing firm won't hire the fifth sculptor.

(ii) The profit maximizing quantity of gnomes produced is 34.

D.

(i) The total cost for the firm is the quantity of sculptors multiplied by the wage plus the fixed cost. When the firm hires four sculptors, the total cost is $60 (4 * $ 5 + $ 40).

(ii) The total revenue for the firm is the total output times the price. When the firm's total output is 34 gnomes, the total revenue is $68 (34 * $ 2).

(iii) Yes, the firm is earning an economic profit because the total revenue is greater than the total cost ($68 > $60).

3. A. The pizza parlor needs to hire enough workers to get to where marginal profit is equal to the marginal cost of one additional worker. The equation is:

(marginal product of each worker)(price of each pizza) – (wage rate of one additional worker)

The marginal revenue per worker would be:

Number Of Workers	Marginal Profit Per Worker
1	165 – 80 = 85
2	176 – 80 = 96
3	143 – 80 = 63
4	99 – 80 = 19
5	77 – 80 = -3
6	66 – 80 = -14

Since the 5th worker would actually decrease profits, the firm should stop hiring after the 4th worker.

B. Some reasons for diminishing marginal product of labor are:

- Equipment is limited in a firm because of limited resources.
- The area of each worker becomes smaller as more labor is hired.
- Employees would get in each others' way and cause a decrease in production.
- In a large firm communication is another problem of production, and suppliers cannot supply as many raw goods as needed.

C. As the marginal product of workers decreases, the firm would stop hiring at point A shown on the graph.

Production Function

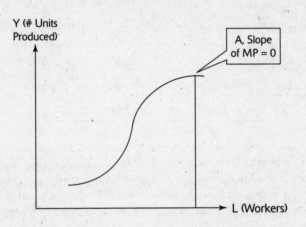

The first and the second workers are producing increasing marginal returns, but the third and fourth workers are producing with diminishing marginal returns. After the fourth worker is hired, the fifth worker would get in the way of the others, and incremental production per worker would decrease.

D. The fifth worker would agree to work at a wage where the firm makes 10-percent profit on the salary. Because the fifth worker would only make 7 pizzas, the worker brings in $77 , so we have the formula:

$$Y(1+0.1) = \$77$$

Where Y is the amount of wage the firm would pay the fifth worker. Here Y equals $70.

Glossary

A

absolute advantage: When one entity has a lower production cost (monetary) than another entity in the production of a certain good or service.

accounting profit: Total revenue minus total cost, not counting opportunity costs or the use of capital.

adaptive expectations: Expectations or ideas formed that are based on information in the recent past.

adding/added value: Creating output that is more valuable than the resources used to make the output.

aggregate demand curve: A graphic illustrating the relationship between an economy's output and the price level.

aggregate expenditures: The sum total of government, household, business, and foreign spending. Consumption, government, investment, and net exports expenditures make up aggregate expenditures.

aggregate supply curve: A graphic illustrating the relationship between the price level and output for an economy.

allocative efficiency: A condition in which firms are producing and distributing the exact amount of goods and services that consumers are willing and able to purchase.

annual return: The dividend plus any capital gained in a given year.

antitrust policy: Government policies designed to promote competition and limit monopoly control to develop efficiency.

appreciate: The increase in value of a currency, entity, or product due to the forces of supply and demand.

arbitrage: Buying in a market in which the price is low and then selling in the market in which the price is higher. The main idea is to profit from the price difference.

asset: A good or service that is owned by a business, household, or government, such as machines, education, or loans made to individuals.

automatic stabilizer: An element of fiscal policy that changes automatically as income changes.

autonomous consumption: Expenditures of households, regardless of the level of income households earn; consumption that is independent of income.

average fixed costs: Total fixed costs divided by the quantity produced.

average product: Total product divided by the quantity of a specific input.

average propensity to consume: The proportion of disposable income spent for consumption.

average propensity to save: The proportion of disposable income saved.

average revenue: Total revenue divided by output.

average total cost: Total cost divided by the total output.

average variable cost: Total variable cost divided by the quantity produced.

B

balance of payment: A record of a country's trade in goods, services, and financial assets relative to international dealings.

balance of trade: The equilibrium in the merchandise account in the United States' balance payments.

balanced budget multiplier: A measure of the impact that government spending and taxes has on a nation's equilibrium output.

barriers to entry: Any variable that prevents a firm from entering an industry, such as price control or market share.

barter: Exchanging goods and services without using money.

base year: A year that is used for relative analysis with inflation and output.

bilateral monopoly: When a monopolistic buyer of resources faces a monopoly seller of resources.

bond: A binding agreement between a borrower and a lender that allows the lender to receive interest payments as well as the repayment of the principal amount.

break-even price: A price that is equal to the minimum point of the average total cost curve.

budget deficit: The gap that results when spending exceeds revenue.

budget line: A line showing all the combinations of goods that can be purchased with a given amount of income.

budget surplus: The gap that results when spending is less than revenue.

business cycle: The normal fluctuation of GDP that includes contractions, expansions, peaks, and troughs.

business firm: A business organization controlled by management and entrepreneurs.

business sector: The part of an economy that consists of individuals who rent or purchase factors of production to create revenue by the selling of goods and services.

C

capital: Anything that is used to make another good or service. Education, machines, and building space are all considered capital.

capital account: The record in the balance of payments of the flow of financial assets into and out of the country.

capital control: Government-controlled restriction of capital into and out of the country.

capital gain: A rise in the price of capital.

capitalism: The notion of participating in an economy with supply and demand as regulating forces rather than the government.

cartel: A formal organization formed of independent entities with the intention to control price and output in a specific market.

cash transfers: Money allocated from one group, sometimes the government, to another group.

central bank: A money-monitoring organization that regulates banks in the economy and controls the nation's money supply.

centrally planned economy: An economic system in which the government owns and controls the factors of production.

ceteris paribus: Latin phrase meaning all other things held equal or constant.

circular flow diagram: An illustration that demonstrates the flow of output and income between the government, households, and firms.

classical economics: An economic perspective that states that real national income is determined by aggregate supply and that the economy is self-correcting.

closed shop: A workplace in which union membership is a condition of employment.

collective bargaining: A process of negotiation between union management and labor management to settle contract discrepancies.

commercial bank loan: A loan that comes from a bank at market interest rates.

commodity money: Money that has intrinsic value and that has more than three functions (store of value, medium of exchange, and unit of account).

comparable worth: The notion that wages should be determined by job characteristics rather than the forces of supply and demand.

comparative advantage: When one entity has a lower opportunity cost than another entity in the production of a good or service.

complementary goods: Goods that are used together (such as DVD movies and DVD players); when the price of one rises, the demand for the other shifts to the left.

constant returns to scale: Unit costs remain stable as the quantity of production is increased and all the resources are variable.

consumer price index: An index that has been created using a "market basket" of goods; its purpose is to measure the price level for consumer-bought goods and services in the economy.

consumer sovereignty: The authority consumers have by purchasing power to determine what is produced and how much it is sold for.

consumption: Expenditures by the household sector on goods and services calculated in a single year.

contraction: A period of declining GDP, usually preceded by a peak in GDP.

contractionary fiscal policy: Governmental action used to contract real GDP. Policy includes the raising of taxes and/or decreasing government spending. It is used to deal with inflation.

contractionary monetary policy: Central banking policy used to deal with inflation by decreasing the money supply.

copyright: Exclusive privilege granted by the government to reproduce, publish, and distribute with intentions of obtaining revenue.

corporation: A legal grouping or entity owned by shareholders whose liability is limited to the value of the stock they own.

cost-benefit analysis: The process of evaluating the costs and benefits of choices to arrive at a decision.

cost-of-living adjustment (COLA): An increase in wages that is designed to match increases in the price level. Its main goal is to stabilize consumer purchasing power.

cost-push inflation: Inflation caused by the increase in prices for business costs of production.

coupon: A fixed amount that a borrower agrees to pay a bondholder each year.

credit: Available savings that are lent to borrowers for consumption.

credit card: A card that can be used to buy on the margin; allows a consumer to purchase goods and services on credit and repay the amount with a rate of interest.

cross-price elasticity of demand: The percentage change in demand for one good that results from a percentage change in price from another good.

cross-subsidization: Using profits from one area to recover losses experienced in another area of operation.

crowding: Singling out a group into certain occupations.

crowding out: Occurs when the government competes in the loanable funds market, thereby driving up interest rates and decreasing the amount firms can borrow.

currency convertibility: The ease with which domestic currency can be converted into foreign currency so that foreign exchange rates can accurately depict the domestic prices of foreign prices.

currency in circulation: Coins and paper money used as media of exchange for daily activities.

currency substitution: The use of foreign money as a substitute for domestic money when the domestic money has a high rate of inflation.

current account: A list that includes the values of a nation's imports and exports.

current account deficit: Occurs when current account imports outweigh current account exports, forming a negative balance for the current account.

current account exports: The total value of all goods and services exported internationally plus the income earned from domestically owned firms internationally.

current account imports: The total value of all goods imported from other nations plus the income paid to foreigners who own domestic assets.

current account surplus: When current account exports are larger than current account imports. The balance on the current account is positive.

customs union: An organization of nations whose members have no trade barriers.

cyclical: Any variable that increases or decreases according to the level of GDP.

cyclical majority: A situation in which choices on an issue depend on the order the issue is presented in.

cyclical unemployment: Unemployment caused by fluctuations in GDP.

D

deadweight loss: The reduction of consumer surplus without a corresponding increase in monopoly profit when a perfectly competitive firm is monopolized.

debt: Money or credit that is borrowed and owed to a lender.

deficit: The point at which debits exceed credits.

deflation: A decrease in the price level.

demand: The quantities of a good or service that individuals are willing and able to buy at different prices.

demand curve: A graphical illustration of quantities of goods and services individuals are willing and able to buy at various prices.

demand deposits: Deposits that typically do not earn interest, such as checking account deposits.

demand for currency: The demand created by individuals who purchase currency that is already being traded to purchase goods and services in the international market.

demand for loanable funds: The demand firms and the government create in the loanable funds market.

demand-pull inflation: Inflation caused by an increase in aggregate demand.

demand schedule: A schedule of quantity demanded at various prices; shows an inverse relationship between price and quantity demanded.

dependent variable: A variable whose value relies on another variable's performance.

deposit expansion multiplier: The reciprocal of the reserve requirement.

depreciation: A reduction in the value of capital over a period of time.

deregulation: Reducing and or removing the presence of governmental restrictions in an industry or environment.

derived demand: The demand stemming from what a good or service can produce.

determinants of demand: Factors other than price that influence the demand for a product; these include income, taste/preference, expectations, population, price of complementary products, and price of substituted products.

determinants of supply: Factors other than the price of the good that determine the supply; these include technology, expectations of producers, number of producers, and prices of related goods and services.

devaluation: A deliberate decrease in the official value of a currency.

development: Having the process of research yield products that can be used to improve efficiency.

differentiated products: Goods and services that vary, allowing producers price leverage.

diminishing marginal utility: The principle stating that the more a good or service is consumed by an individual, the less utility it yields with each consumption.

direct relationship: A relationship of variables where the dependent variable does what the independent variable does.

discount rate: The interest rate the Federal Reserve charges to banks.

discounting: Reducing the value of something, usually to increase the quantity demanded.

discouraged worker: An individual who has given up looking for a job after searching for employment. Discouraged workers are not members of the labor force.

diseconomies of scale: Occurs when an increase in production yields a higher average production cost.

disequilibrium: A condition of imbalance between the quantities of supply and the quantities of demand (when one is not equal to the other).

disequilibrium price: The price of a good in a market that is experiencing disequilibrium.

disposable income: Household income after taxes.

dividend: The per-share profits of stock distributed to shareholders.

division of labor: Splitting up the production of a good or service into subdivisions.

double counting: An inclusion in the value of an intermediate good or service in the calculation of GDP.

double taxation: Income that is taxed twice because corporations pay taxes on income before dividends are paid and shareholders pay taxes on dividends received as a result of holding stock.

dumping: Selling goods internationally at lower prices relative to domestic prices.

durable goods: A good that is consumed at a slower rate that is capable of lasting for an extended period of time.

E

earnings: Total compensation paid for employment (wages, salaries, bonus, and commission).

economic costs: Total costs, including opportunity costs and implicit and explicit costs, of a resource for a producer.

economic efficiency: A situation in which resources are allocated and used to their maximum capabilities.

economic profit: Explicit and implicit costs subtracted from total revenue (pure profit).

economic regulation: Government regulations related to the workings of the economy.

economic rent: Earnings a resource owner obtains after opportunity costs have been calculated.

economic system: A way of allocating goods and services to society.

economics: A social science that necessitates choice because of the existence of scarcity.

economies of scale: The decrease of per-unit costs as production increases and all resources are adjustable.

efficiency: Using available resources to produce the maximum amount of goods.

elastic demand: A formula that determines the sensitivity of quantity demanded to a price change. It occurs when the percentage change in quantity demanded is greater than the percentage change in price.

elastic supply: A formula that indicates when suppliers are sensitive to a price change. It occurs when the percentage change in quantity supplied is greater than the percentage change in price.

elasticity: A measure of how responsive quantity supplied or quantity demanded is to a change in price.

entrepreneur: A risk taker who starts a business or monetary enterprise.

equation: A mathematical formula that relates two or more variables.

equation of exchange: A formula that relates the quantity of money to nominal GDP.

equilibrium: The point of balance at which quantity demanded and quantity supplied intersect at a specific price.

equilibrium price: The price that balances quantity supplied and quantity demanded.

equilibrium quantity: The quantity at which quantity supplied and quantity demanded intersect.

equity: Shares of stock or value earned.

excess capacity: The production level that is located below the average total cost. A firm can increase production in this range while decreasing production costs.

excess demand: The difference when quantity demanded exceeds quantity supplied at a specific price.

excess supply: The amount where quantity supply exceeds quantity demanded.

exchange rate: The value of one unit of currency in terms of another country's currency.

excise tax: A sales tax that is levied only on the sale of specific items.

exclusion principal: The idea that one person can keep others from benefiting from a private good.

expansion: The period of time where GDP is growing at a steady pace.

expansionary fiscal policy: Governmental policies that cause the economy to grow by increasing aggregate demand; lowering taxes and/or increasing spending help accomplish this.

expansionary monetary policy: Money supply policy with the intention of increasing the money supply to help the economy.

expenditure: The monetary amount used to buy goods and services over a period of time.

explicit costs: Monetary payments made to resources owners with the goal of operating a business.

exports: Money spent by the foreign sector on domestic goods and services in a given year.

external debt: The part of national debt that is owed to people or governments outside the Untied States.

externalities: Costs or benefits passed on outside the market transaction.

F

factor market: A market in which firms send monetary payments to households for a physical flow of land, labor, capital, and entrepreneurship.

factor of production: Any input or resource used to make goods and services (land, labor, capital, and entrepreneurial ability).

fallacy of composition: An incorrect belief or assumption that what is good for the individual is good for the group.

Federal Deposit Insurance Corporation (FDIC): The agency that insures bank deposits of individuals and businesses for up to $100,000 in the event of bank failure.

federal funds rate: The interest rate banks pay to borrow from each other on a short-term basis.

Federal Reserve System: The central monetary authority that controls the money operations in the United States.

financial intermediary: An organization that helps the flow of money from people with money to save to people who need to borrow money.

firm: A business created by an entrepreneur with the intention of creating a profit by using factors of production to make goods and services.

fiscal policy: The changing of government spending and taxes in order to control and stabilize economic activity.

fixed cost: The short-run costs a firm must pay regardless of the level of production.

fixed factor: A factor resource or source of input that cannot be changed in the short run.

fixed income: Income that is set and that does not change from year to year.

flexible exchange rates: A system in which the laws of supply and demand are allowed to dictate the prices of various international currencies.

foreign aid: The money that more advanced countries provide to help the less developed countries in their economic development.

fractional reserve banking system: A system in which banks must keep some percentage of a deposit in the form of reserves.

free enterprise: A market economy with no government regulation.

free rider: A person who benefits from a public good without sharing its costs.

frictional unemployment: Unemployment of people who are temporarily between jobs.

full employment: When between 95 and 96 percent of the labor force is employed.

functional distribution of income: The way in which income is divided by economic functions.

G

game theory: A tool for analyzing oligopoly behavior; predicts a firm's pricing decisions based on its competitors' decision to increase or decrease prices.

GDP gap: The difference between potential GDP and real GDP.

gold standard: A system in which each nation sets the value of its currency in accordance with the amount of gold it possesses.

good: An item that usually satisfies a need or want.

government budget: A listing of government's spending and income for a period of one year.

gross domestic product: The total value of all final goods and services produced on a nation's soil within a specific year.

gross national product: The total dollar value of all final goods and services produced in an economy during one year.

H

homogeneous products: Goods that have no variance from one producer to another.

horizontal merger: A combining of two companies in the same market.

household sector: The part of a nation's economy in which the consumers are the owners of the factors of production, and households provide the factors of production to businesses for a monetary payment.

human capital: Intangible skill (knowledge) individuals possess used to produce goods.

human resources: Individuals who are productive aids in creating goods and services.

I

imports: Goods and services that one country demands from another country.

incentives: Factors that aid the decision-making process when dealing with scarcity.

income: Money that is earned by households and businesses.

income distribution: The allocation of earnings in an economy between the various economic classes.

income effect: The effect of increasing or decreasing prices on the purchasing power of income.

income elasticity of demand: The percentage change in quantity divided by the percentage change in income that caused the change in demand.

independent variable: A variable that determines the value of another variable.

index numbers: The numbers used by economists to illustrate relative changes in prices, GDP, and other measures.

indirect tax: A tax that can be shifted in part to a party other than the one on whom the tax is levied.

individual choice: Decisions made by individuals who are acting separately from one another.

inefficient: The underutilization of available resources.

inelastic: An economic condition where the price of a good or service does not change as a result of supply or demand.

inferior goods: Goods for which demand decreases as income increases (the inverse relationship between income and demand).

inflation: The economic condition in which the average level of prices rise.

inflationary expectations: Being able to predict changes in the price level average.

injection: Expenditures by firms, foreign sectors, and the government on goods and services produced within an economy.

injunction: A court order mandating action or a halt to action.

inputs: Factors of production (resources) used to make goods and services.

inside lag: The amount of time it takes policymakers to agree on an economic remedy.

interdependence: The relationship between different sectors of the economy, such as firms, households, and the government.

interest: The monetary cost for the use of money.

interest rate: The percentage of total amount borrowed that is required when paying the principal back to the lender.

inverse relationship: A type of relationship that describes the opposite nature between variables.

investment: An increase in the amount of productive capital in an economy.

invisible hand: The forces of supply and demand that guide prices in the economy based on individual choices.

irregular economy: Economic activity that purposely ignores market system traits to avoid paying taxes on income and transactions.

J

job discrimination: The denial of employment to certain individuals because of their race, gender, religion, or other characteristic.

K

kinked demand curve: The demand curve that illustrates the behavior of competing oligopolistic firms; outlines a firm's expectation that its competitor will match its price.

L

labor: Human effort used to produce goods and services, including human capital.

labor union: An organization of workers formed to give workers greater bargaining power in their dealings with management.

laissez faire: No government involvement in an economic system.

land: The natural resources that come from land (soil) used to produce goods and services.

law of comparative advantage: The law that states that an entity benefits when it specializes or concentrates on goods for which it has the lowest opportunity cost producing.

law of demand: The rule that as prices rise, the quantity demanded falls, and vice versa; there is an inverse relationship between price and quantity demanded.

law of diminishing marginal returns: As more and more units of variable resources are used for production, the marginal product produced declines.

law of diminishing marginal utility: As more and more units of a good are consumed, the less total satisfaction that good yields.

law of increasing opportunity costs: As more units are produced, the opportunity cost of producing those units increases.

law of supply: The idea that as prices increase, producers can increase their quantity supplied; there is a positive relationship between prices and quantity supplied.

limited liability: The concept that owners of a corporation are responsible for its debts only up to the amount they invest in the firm.

limited resources: The idea that scarcity will always exist.

loanable funds market: The area of exchange where the suppliers and consumers of loanable funds exchange money and loan contracts.

lobbying: The act of communicating with government representatives with the objective of swaying their votes in a favorable manner.

long run: The period in which all inputs used for production can be changed.

long-run average cost curve: The curve that illustrates the average cost for a firm for the period of time where all factors that are used to produce are interchangeable.

long-run average total cost: The average total cost when all factors can be changed.

long-run supply curve: The supply curve that illustrates price and quantity supplied at a point where all factors of production can be changed.

loose monetary policy: A policy of the Federal Reserve that causes the money supply to rise.

Lorenz curve: A graphic illustration showing the amount of income inequality that exists in society at any point in time.

M

macroeconomics: The branch of economics that examines the behavior of the whole economy at once.

marginal cost: The additional cost experienced when one more unit is produced.

marginal cost curve: The curve that illustrates the marginal cost of each unit produced.

marginal private benefit: The added benefit that individuals directly involved in an activity pay to increase the activity by one unit.

marginal private cost: The added cost individuals directly involved in an activity pay to increase the activity by one unit.

marginal product: The amount that the total product increases or decreases if one more unit of an input is used.

marginal revenue: The additional revenue realized when one more unit is produced.

marginal social benefit: The added benefit that society gets from increasing an activity by one unit.

marginal social cost: The added cost society pays to increase an activity by one unit.

marginal utility: The added productivity or use that one additional unit yields.

market: An exchange between a buyer and a seller.

market demand: The quantities of a product or service that the total of all consumers are willing and able to purchase at various prices.

market economy: An economy in which economic questions are decided mostly by individuals in the marketplace.

market organization: The way participants in markets are organized and the number of participants.

market supply: The quantities that are supplied by producers at various prices in a particular industry or market.

mean: The average in which the total value of the items in a distribution is divided by the number of items in the distribution.

median: The middle number in a distribution.

merger: The combining of one firm with another firm it purchases.

microeconomics: The branch of economics that examines the choices and interactions of individuals producing and consuming one product, in one firm or industry.

minimum wage law: A law that sets the lowest wage that can be paid for certain kinds of work.

model: A simplified form of reality, which shows the relationship between different factors.

monetary policy: The changing amount of money in the economy in order to reduce employment, keep prices stable. and promote economic growth.

monopolistic competition: A market organization in which many firms produce products that are different but similar enough to be substitutes.

monopoly: A form of market organization in which there is only one seller of a product.

multiplier effect: The concept that any change in fiscal policy affects total demand and total income by an amount larger than the amount of the change in policy.

mutual savings banks: Banks that were first formed for the same reason as savings and loans associations and that promote thrift by their members.

N

national debt: The amount of money that the federal government owes; it is owned by the American public.

natural monopoly: A single firm that has complete control over pricing and output in a market where it is impractical to have competition.

natural resources: The total raw materials supplied by nature.

negative externality: The result when costs are shifted to people who are not directly involved with the production or consumption of a good.

negative income tax: Poverty programs in which a person or family below some income level receives a payment from the government rather than paying some amount of tax to the government.

nominal: The face value of a good or service measured in current currency values.

nondurable goods: Goods that do not last for a long time.

normal goods: Goods for which demand increases as income increases.

O

objectivity: Ruling out the aspects of a problem that might be influenced by personal attitudes or opinions.

oligopoly: A form of market organization in which there are relatively few firms.

open-market operations: The buying and selling of U.S. government securities by the Federal Reserve.

opportunity benefit: The portion gained from making a choice.

opportunity cost: The value of the next best alternative in a decision-making process.

outside lag: The time it takes for the effects of a policy change to be completely felt in the economy once the policy has been determined.

P

parity price: A price that changes as prices of other goods change so that the income of producers can purchase the same amount of these goods as in any given base year.

partnership: A type of business organization in which two or more people form a business.

patent: A legal protection for the inventor of a product or process that gives that person or company the sole rights to produce the product or use the process for an specified period of time.

payment: Any monetary form of retribution for a good or service.

per capita income: The average income that is calculated on a per-person basis.

percentage: A ratio converted to a base using 100 equal parts.

perfect competition: A market organization in which a great many small firms produce a homogeneous product with no individual price control.

personal distribution of income: The way that income is shared among people in a particular economic system.

personal income tax: A tax on the income of individuals.

population: The amount of individuals in a particular economic system.

positive externality: The result when benefits are shifted to people who are not directly involved with the production or consumption of a good.

poverty: The condition in which people do not have enough income to provide for their basic needs, such as food, water, shelter, and clothing.

price ceiling: A maximum price set by government that is below the market equilibrium price.

price elasticity of demand: The ratio or percentage change in quantity demanded relative to the change in price that caused the change in quantity demanded.

price elasticity of supply: The ratio of the percentage change in the quantity supplied to the percentage change in the product price.

price floor: A minimum price set by the government that is above the market equilibrium price.

price index: A number that compares prices in one year with some earlier base year.

price setter: A firm that has some control over the price at which its product sells.

price support program: A government program designed to keep prices from falling below some level the government decides is fair.

price taker: A firm that takes a price determined by forces outside the firm's control.

prime rate: The interest rate that banks charge their best corporate customers.

private enterprise: A system in which private individuals take the risk of producing goods or services to make a profit.

private goods: Goods that are privately owned to benefit only their owners.

private sector: The part of an economy that is owned by private individuals and operated for their personal benefit.

product differentiation: The concept that the product of one firm can be distinguished from the products of other firms.

production possibilities curve: A graphic illustration of the combination of output an economy can produce if all of its resources are utilized efficiently, given the state of technology.

profit: Total revenue minus total costs.

progressive rights: The rights that define who owns what rights to property and how individuals or groups may use their property.

progressive tax: A tax that takes a larger percentage of higher incomes and a smaller percentage of lower incomes.

property tax: A tax levied on real estate, such as a home, land, and buildings.

proportional tax: A tax that takes the same percentage of income from all taxpayers.

proprietorship: A form of business in which one individual owns the entire business.

protectionism: The idea that we should limit trade to protect our own self-interest.

psychic income: The nonmonetary reward we get from taking some action.

public goods: Goods and services available to the whole society.

public goods rationale: The argument that some public goods can be produced more efficiently by social choice.

public institutions: Publicly owned organizations established by government to serve the wants and needs of a whole society.

public sector: The part of an economy that is owned by and operated for the benefit of the whole society.

pure oligopoly: An oligopoly in which the products are the same for all firms.

Q

quota: A limit on the amount of imports or exports.

R

range: The largest number in a distribution minus the smallest number.

rate of growth: The percentage change in the level of economic activity from one year to the next.

rates: An indication of how quickly absolute numbers are changing.

ratio: A way of showing the proportion between numbers.

real GNP: The value of the gross national product after eliminating the effect of price changes.

real GNP per person: The real value of the total output of goods and services divided by the number of people in the economy.

real value: A nominal value that has been adjusted for changes in prices.

recession: The condition in which unemployment is high and GNP falls for two or more quarters.

redistributing income: In an effort to provide equity, the public sector gives to people who do not work money collected from taxing the incomes of those who do work.

regressive tax: A tax that takes a larger percentage of lower incomes and a smaller percentage of higher incomes.

research and development (R&D): The activities undertaken to find new and more efficient methods of production.

reserve ratio: The fraction of deposits that the Federal Reserve determines banks must keep on reserve.

reserve requirement: The dollar amount banks must keep on reserve.

restrictive fiscal policies: Fiscal policies that cause the economy to run more slowly by reducing aggregate demand.

returns to scale: The relationship between changes in scale of production and changes in output.

S

sales tax: A tax on goods that are purchased.

savings and loan association: A financial intermediary that mainly provides a place for people to save money and then lends that money to people to purchase houses or other things.

scale of production: The overall level of use of all factors of production.

scarcity: The condition that occurs because people's wants and needs are unlimited, and the resources needed to produce goods and services to meet these wants and needs are limited,

seasonal unemployment: Unemployment of people who are out of work because of factors that vary with the time of the year.

set-aside program: A government program that reduces the supply of farm products by keeping land out of production.

share draft account: An account with a credit union from which withdrawals can be easily made using a draft.

shortage: The condition in which demand is greater than supply at a certain price.

short run: Any period during which the usable amount of at least one input is fixed, whereas the usable amount of at least one other input can change.

slope: The description of a graphical curve; the amount of change (in what is being measured) on the vertical axis divided by the amount of change on the horizontal axis; "the rise over the run."

social benefits: The benefits received by a society from a social choice or some other action.

social choice: Decision making by government in the interest of society.

social cost: The cost to a society of a social choice or some other action.

social economy: An economy in which the major economic questions are determined by the government representing the interest of the entire society.

social goals: The goals of an entire society.

socialism: An economic system in which most of the basic industries are government owned and operated.

social security tax: A tax that provides disability and retirement benefits for most working people.

special interest group: An organized subgroup of society bound together by a common cause.

specialization: In producing goods and services, an economic entity produces only those products, which it can produce with some advantage.

stock: Shares of ownership in a cooperation.

structural unemployment: Unemployment resulting from skills that do not match what employers require or from being geographically separated from job opportunities.

subsidy: A payment made by government to encourage some activity.

substitute products: Products whose uses are similar enough that one can replace the other.

substitution effect: The effect of increasing or decreasing relative process on the mix of goods purchased.

supply: The quantities of a product or service that a firm is willing and able to make available for sale at different prices.

supply curve: A graphic representation of the quantities that would be supplied at each price.

supply of labor: The amount of labor that would be available at each wage rate.

supply schedule: A table showing quantities that would be supplied at each price.

surplus: The condition in which supply is greater than demand at a certain price.

T

table: A simplified way of showing numbers.

tariff: A tax on imports.

technology: The body of knowledge that is used for the production of goods and services.

theory: A simplified description of reality.

tight monetary policy: A policy of the Federal Reserve that causes the money supply to decrease.

total product: All the units of a product produced in a given period of time, such as one year.

total revenue: The amount of money a company receives from sale of a product.

trade barriers: Methods of restricting trade between countries.

trade deficit: The result when a country imports more than it exports.

trade-offs: Decisions among alternatives in allocating economic resources.

trade surplus: The result when a country exports more than it imports.

traditional economy: An economy in which the three economic questions are decided mainly by social customs.

transaction demand for money: The demand for money to make exchanges.

transfer payments: Public expenditures made for reasons other than paying for goods and services.

U

unemployment: The condition of those who are willing and able to work and are actively seeking work, yet who are not currently working.

unemployment rate: The percentage of the civilian labor force that is considered unemployed.

union shop: A business that requires workers to join a union shortly after taking the job.

unlimited liability: The concept that an owner's personal assets can be used to pay bills of the proprietorship or partnership.

unlimited wants and needs: The human characteristic of never feeling that all wants and needs have been satisfied.

util: The unit of measure for utility.

utility: The satisfaction one receives from the consumption, use, or ownership of a good or service.

V

vertical merger: A merger of two companies that are at different stages in the same production process.

W

wage and price controls: Government controls on the levels of wages and prices.

wage rate: The price paid for each unit of labor.

World Bank: A source of aid to less-developed countries.